Early praise for The Healthy Programmer

Joe Kutner offers practical, readable, and well-researched advice for those who sit at a keyboard. I've incorporated his health-and-fitness regimen into my writing routine.

➤ **Dr. Steve Overman**
   Professor of Physical Education (retired), Jackson State University

Health and programming should go together like a horse and carriage. You can't have one without the other. In our sedentary office work, we often forget that an absence of health is as bad as a lack of programming skills. Joe points out a dozen areas where you and I can do better. Every office worker should read this book and self-reflect on health improvements.

➤ **Staffan Nöteberg**
   Author of *Pomodoro Technique Illustrated*

This book introduced me to the term *conditioned hypereating*. It felt life-changing. Being aware of this has made it easier to experiment with smaller, less-ambitious changes that actually have a chance at succeeding. I'm very curious to see where this puts me a year from now.

➤ **Katrina Owen**
   Developer, Jumpstart Lab

The Healthy Programmer is excellent. In many ways it's a spiritual continuation of *The Hacker's Diet*.

➤ **Stephen Ball**
   Senior Rails programmer, PhishMe, Inc.

The Healthy Programmer

Get Fit, Feel Better, and Keep Coding

Joe Kutner

The Pragmatic Bookshelf

Dallas, Texas • Raleigh, North Carolina

Many of the designations used by manufacturers and sellers to distinguish their products are claimed as trademarks. Where those designations appear in this book, and The Pragmatic Programmers, LLC was aware of a trademark claim, the designations have been printed in initial capital letters or in all capitals. The Pragmatic Starter Kit, The Pragmatic Programmer, Pragmatic Programming, Pragmatic Bookshelf, PragProg and the linking *g* device are trademarks of The Pragmatic Programmers, LLC.

Every precaution was taken in the preparation of this book. However, the publisher assumes no responsibility for errors or omissions, or for damages that may result from the use of information (including program listings) contained herein.

Our Pragmatic courses, workshops, and other products can help you and your team create better software and have more fun. For more information, as well as the latest Pragmatic titles, please visit us at *http://pragprog.com*.

The team that produced this book includes:

Brian P. Hogan (editor)
Potomac Indexing, LLC (indexer)
Candace Cunningham (copyeditor)
David J Kelly (typesetter)
Janet Furlow (producer)
Juliet Benda (rights)
Ellie Callahan (support)

Copyright © 2013 The Pragmatic Programmers, LLC.
All rights reserved.

No part of this publication may be reproduced, stored in a retrieval system, or transmitted, in any form, or by any means, electronic, mechanical, photocopying, recording, or otherwise, without the prior consent of the publisher.

Printed in the United States of America.
ISBN-13: 978-1-937785-31-4
Printed on acid-free paper.
Book version: P1.0—June 2013

Disclaimer

This book is intended only as an informative guide for those wishing to know more about health issues. In no way is this book intended to replace, countermand, or conflict with the advice given to you by your own healthcare provider, including physician, nurse practitioner, physician assistant, registered dietician, and other licensed professionals.

Keep in mind that results vary from person to person. This book is not intended as a substitute for medical or nutritional advice from a healthcare provider or dietician. Some people have a medical history, condition, and/or nutritional requirements that warrant individualized recommendations and, in some cases, medications and healthcare surveillance.

Do not start, stop, or change medications or dietary practices without advice from a professional healthcare provider and/or registered dietician. A healthcare provider should be consulted if you are on medication or if you have any symptoms that may require diagnosis or medical attention. Do not change your diet if you are ill or on medication, except under the supervision of a healthcare provider. Neither this nor any other book or discussion forum is intended to take the place of personalized medical care and treatment provided by your healthcare provider.

This book was current as of June, 2013, and as new information becomes available through research, experience, or changes to product contents, some of the data in this book may become invalid. You should seek the most up-to-date information on your medical care and treatment from your healthcare professional. The ultimate decision concerning care should be made by you and your healthcare provider.

Information in this book is general and is offered with no guarantees on the part of the author, editors, or The Pragmatic Programmers, LLC. The author, editors, and publisher disclaim all liability in connection with the use of this book.

Contents

Foreword

Ask a nondoctor about the likely afflictions of young patients, and he or she will most likely mention ankle sprains, tendonitis, and a few types of unpalatable infections.

However, the truth is rather less exciting, and certainly less related to sports. Our list instead includes back pain, headaches, irritable bowel syndrome, upper-limb syndromes, and low mood—a list of maladies that is almost without exception due to a lifestyle filled with time spent stationary indoors, excess typing and repetitive wrist movements from mouse to keyboard, and inappropriate dietary intake.

Interestingly and, may I say, without coincidence, these themes mirror the contents of this book, with chapters related to topics such as the right chair, preventing eye strain, agile dieting, and the fascinating topic of vitamin D deficiency, which is only just being adequately explored in the scientific and medical literature.

It's a cliché often used in the medical field, but "prevention is better than cure" is both relevant and highly correct. As doctors we so often find that by the time a patient presents with wrist or back pain, it will remain no matter what we do. Yes, we try everything that we have: analgesics, antispasmodics, physiotherapy, and even alternative therapies such as acupuncture and chiropracty. However, they tend not to work. There are often two factors at play. The first is that our patients, due to the pressure of their work, are incapable of improving the factors that drive their illnesses; the second is that good advice is hard to find and evaluate. For example, a simple Internet search for back-pain remedies will yield thousands of non-evidence-based diagnoses, cures, and quackeries. Is it a surprise that doctors, researchers, and even IT professionals have difficulty evaluating and recommending specific interventions?

In this book the author manages to take the most recent scientific literature, dissect it, analyze it, and apply it to a group of professionals whose needs are very specific. Of particular importance here is the focus not only on the immediate physical complications that can result from working as a software developer, but also on long-term cardiovascular health. It is now well recognized that those who spend their work lives sitting at computers, taking few total steps per day, are significantly more likely to suffer from hypertension (high blood pressure) and type-2 diabetes, both of which can have serious long-term consequences and increase the risk of heart attacks and strokes.

For a software developer who made the leap from looking after patients to looking after code (and myself!), it is refreshing and enlightening to see so many of the problems that I reflected upon for myself being given the proper exposure to a much wider audience. This is a text that both new and veteran developers should, and I might even say *must*, read.

Dr. Ed Wallitt
Physician and software developer

Acknowledgments

I could not have written this book without the support of a large and diverse group of friends. I've consulted with more health experts and software professionals than I can count. I will try to properly thank them all here, but my words cannot truly express my gratitude.

Thank you to Chad Fowler, Xavier Shay, Staffan Notéberg, Andy Smith, Jessica Allen, Hiro Asari, and Mark McGraw who helped me brainstorm, research and find my direction with this book. I could not have done this without you.

I would also like to thank the many doctors, scientists, nutritionists, physical therapists, physical educators and other health experts who provided the clinical research that made this book possible. Of particular importance are those who took the time to review my analysis and ensure my facts were correct. Thank you to Ethan Kind, Dr. Steve Overman, Dr. Ed Wallitt, Dr. Peter Katzmarzyk, Dr. John Ratey, Dr. Anand Viswanathan, and Dr. Satu Suuronen. These people not only helped guide my research, but also provided moral support for this great effort.

I give an extra special thanks to the programmers who posed as models for the exercise figures in the book. Thank you to Michael Stephenson, Johnathon Powell, and Erin Spiceland. Your generosity is humbling.

A big thank you goes to the reviewers who provided incredible insight and advice that helped shape the content of this book. I was yet again shocked by the attention to detail and wise feedback they provided in making my book a finished product. Thank you to Bryan Powell, Matt Blackmon, Kevin Gisi, Chris Warren, Jeff Holland, Jeremy Walker, Ian Dees, Mark Anderson, Jan Nonnen, Jared Richardson, Karoline Klever, Mike Riley, Stephen Orr, Matt Smith, Trevor Burnham, Katrina Owen, and Stephen Ball.

Thank you to the staff at the Pragmatic Bookshelf: Brian P. Hogan, Susannah Pfalzer, Dave Thomas, Andy Hunt, David Kelly, and probably a whole bunch of other people I didn't know were helping me. This publisher put full support behind a book that some might consider odd. I thank them for taking this important topic seriously.

Finally, I would like to thank my family. In particular my mother, a life-long gymnastics coach and physical educator who raised me to appreciate the value of good health. Thank you to my wife, who went to sleep without me on many nights because I was either writing or doing research. And thank you to my son, who often accompanied me to the library and wondered "why does daddy work all the time?" I could not have completed this project without your love and support.

Preface

Holmes County, Ohio, may be one of the healthiest communities in the United States. A study done from 1996 to 2003 on more than half of the residents in that county found that the cancer rate was an amazing 72 percent lower than the national average.[1] Another study found that a similar group had almost no cases of heart problems or diabetes and practically no obesity-related issues.[2] But the population used for these studies was not random—all of the participants were Amish.

Amish communities are known for their embrace of a rural lifestyle, manual labor, and a reluctance to adopt modern technology. It's a far cry from the world of programmers, where we have to remind ourselves to get outside and walk around every now and then.

Programming requires intense concentration that often causes us to neglect other aspects of our lives—the most common of which is our health. Our bodies haven't evolved to accommodate a lifestyle of sitting, and there are many negative health effects from it.

The predominant occupation for Amish families is farming, which requires a great deal of physical labor. The average Amish man spends fifty-three hours a week doing vigorous-to-moderate activities and walks nine miles every day except Sunday. Fortunately, the rest of us don't need quite that much activity to stay healthy. In fact, very small interventions can have profound effects on your wellness.

Your job shouldn't hurt you, and with the right tools it won't. The health effects of being a sedentary programmer are treatable, and in most cases reversible. This book will help guide you in that transformation.

---

1. *Low cancer incidence rates in Ohio Amish [WFKM10]*
2. *Health Risk Factors among the Amish: Results of a Survey [FLSM90]*

Why Should I Read This Book?

The number-one reason you should read this book is that your life depends on it. But the second most important reason is that your career depends on it. If you want to continue doing the job you love for years to come, this book is for you.

I've met programmers whose backs are in so much pain that they cannot sit at a desk. I've also met programmers whose wrists have been injured by their repetitive use of a keyboard and mouse. These injuries can make your job unpleasant at best, and impossible at worst.

Beyond minor ailments, a life of programming can lead to an early death. That claim may sound extreme, but the leading cause of death in the United States is heart disease.[3] Furthermore, conditions like type-2 diabetes and obesity are on the rise. The programming lifestyle contributes to these problems, but in most cases they can be prevented through exercise and nutrition. We'll discuss causes of these and other health problems in the book. Then we'll lay out a plan for overcoming them.

Who Should Read This Book?

Although this book should appeal to a wide range of programmers, it's primarily directed at those that are sedentary. The less you are doing for your health right now, the more you'll get out of this book.

But even if you are a generally active programmer or even an athlete, you'll likely find this book useful. It may help you justify an existing health plan, or it may help to correct things you're doing that are problematic. You'll also learn how to stay healthy in your office by creating a workstation that prevents pain and helps you avoid injury when it comes time to exercise.

There are no prerequisites for reading this book. If you have an existing health condition, then you'll need to consult a doctor before acting on any advice it provides. But even if the most exercise you've done in the last year is walking from your desk to the bathroom, you'll be able to use this book.

What's in This Book?

This book will guide you in a transformation from an achy, unhealthy, and possibly grumpy hacker to a happy and productive programmer. We aren't going to set unreasonable goals like having six-pack abs, buns of steel, or Michelle Obama arms, but if you follow the plan in this book, you'll be able

---

3.   http://www.cdc.gov/nchs/fastats/lcod.htm

to adjust your weight, get stronger, and have more endurance. These are not your goals, however. Being healthy is your goal.

We'll begin with a discussion of habits in Chapter 1, *Making Changes*, on page 1. We aren't born unhealthy—we become unhealthy through a combination of bad habits and environmental pressures. In this chapter we'll discuss how your brain develops habits and what you can do to change them. We'll also meet Chad Fowler, whose story of weight loss and transformation is a testament to the power you have within yourself.

Once we understand how to change habits, we can start applying this to our health. In Chapter 2, *Bootstrapping Your Health*, on page 13, we'll discuss how a simple walk can have a profound impact on your well-being. But it can also improve your ability to think. We'll discuss what science tells us about the effect exercise has on the brain. We'll also lay out a very simple daily walking plan that is proven to bootstrap your health.

One of the best things about walking is that it gets you up and out of your chair. In Chapter 3, *A Farewell to Chairs?*, on page 29, we'll discuss why sitting is so dangerous and what you can do about it. You might be surprised to learn that standing up isn't always the best solution. But with the right workstation, you'll be able to improve your health right from the comfort of your office.

In Chapter 4, *Agile Dieting*, on page 47, we'll start to discuss health from a different angle. Programmers are not known for having good diets, and that's probably a result of the environmental pressures that come with a high-stress, startup-like job. Combating those pressures can be an iterative and incremental process just like everything else in the software industry. You'll learn how to experiment with your meals until you find a diet that works for you.

Being healthy isn't just about heart disease and obesity, though—it's also about living pain-free. In Chapter 5, *Preventing Headaches and Eye Strain*, on page 65, Chapter 6, *Preventing Back Pain*, on page 79, and Chapter 7, *Preventing Wrist Pain*, on page 103, we'll discuss the most common sources of pain for programmers: back aches, wrist strain, and headaches. You'll learn how to prevent these conditions and what to do when they occur.

However, the activities and best practices in this book won't be any good if they interfere with your job. That's why we'll discuss an exercise plan in Chapter 8, *Making Exercise Pragmatic*, on page 121, that dovetails with your career goals and routines. You'll learn how to structure your workouts in a way that actually enhances your ability to write code.

In Chapter 9, *Thinking Outside the Cube*, on page 135, we'll explore why it's important to get outside every now and again. This will replenish your vitamin D levels, which may boost your immune system. We'll also discuss how to prevent and treat the common cold.

Then we'll take your fitness to the next level. In Chapter 10, *Refactoring Your Fitness*, on page 147, we'll discuss how to improve our aerobic capacity and muscular endurance while following the daily plan defined in the previous chapters. You'll have to push your limits, but maintaining a higher level of fitness can improve mood and productivity in the workplace.

In the penultimate chapter, Chapter 11, *Teaming Up*, on page 173, you'll learn how your coworkers and your employer affect your health. You'll also learn how you can improve the health of those around you and why it's good for all parties involved. You'll learn some activities you can do with your coworkers and how to best motivate them to join you in being a healthy programmer.

Finally, we'll discuss where to take your health goals after finishing this book. In Chapter 12, *Onward, Healthy Programmer*, on page 187, you'll learn some tricks that will help you move your health forward every day.

In each chapter, we'll define goals that you should strive to meet, and set forth a daily checklist of activities that will help you get there. To follow along with these, you can download the Healthy Programmer iPhone app, shown in Figure 1, *The Healthy Programmer iPhone app*, on page xix, or visit http://healthyprog.com.

You Can't Fool Nature

Unless otherwise stated, every point made in this book is backed up by scientific research. The recommendations and claims I will make are directly supported by evidence. But I haven't accepted just any kind of evidence—nearly every study I used met two criteria: it was published in a peer-reviewed journal and the results agreed with the existing body of scientific evidence. The few that do not meet these criteria are explicitly called out as such, and they are used only to provide discussion on topics where a scientific consensus has not yet emerged.

When studies are referenced in this book, be sure to pay close attention to the language that is used. Terms such as *linked*, *associated with*, and *correlated with* imply that two variables move in sync with each other. But they do not imply that one *causes* the other. For example, sitting and cancer are correlated. It's possible that sitting causes cancer, but it's also possible that

This application will help you follow the goals and activities presented in the book.

Figure 1—The Healthy Programmer iPhone app

cancer causes more sitting. Furthermore, it could be that some overarching condition causes an increase in both sitting and cancer risk. We just don't know yet—we know only that the two variables follow similar trends.

To avoid having the book read like a Ph.D. thesis, I have not included a citation for every paper and book that I used to support my research. However, you can find a complete list of references and suggestions for further reading in Appendix 3, *Further Reading*, on page 197.

Most of these publications relate to medicine and biology, but a surprising number relate to psychology, sports, anthropology, music, business, and even computer science. I believe this illustrates one of the most important points you can take away from this book: your mind and body are not independent entities. They are intimately coupled, and for one to perform at its best, both must be healthy.

You're going to see the word *healthy* a lot in this book. Before we get started, it's important that you understand exactly what it implies.

What Does It Mean to Be Healthy?

The title of this book may seem self-evident, but it was not easy to include a word that nearly every person has preconceptions about. As Mark Twain once said, "The only way to keep your health is to eat what you don't want, drink what you don't like, and do what you'd rather not."

Twain's quote rings true because the volume of information we are confronted with when learning about our health is enormous (in Twain's time it was probably just erroneous). We receive conflicting information and are often forced to conclude that everything we enjoy is now off limits. The discussion around health in popular media has essentially devolved into a "he said, she said" game. In truth, healthy choices are a personal decision. What's right for you may not be right for someone else.

Health is a nebulous thing that involves many aspects of life. Thus, it's important to clearly define it for the purpose of this book. A healthy person is at low risk for developing lifestyle-induced diseases. Furthermore, a healthy person should be relatively pain-free. These two criteria may not provide a universal definition of health, but they will provide a good basis for our discussion. Fortunately, achieving this kind of health is not nearly as hard a Twain envisioned—in fact, it requires only small changes.

This book does not expect you to give up any part of your life to improve it (with the exception of long periods of sitting and an overindulgence in desserts). The goals and activities you'll learn about can all fit into your existing schedule and still make you healthy.

Let's refactor your health.

CHAPTER 1

Making Changes

"I guess I was somewhere close to 300 pounds (136 kg)," Chad Fowler says of his weight in 2009. "It's hard to say because at a certain point you stop weighing yourself." Today Chad weighs a little over 200 pounds (90 kg), which is just about right for a guy who's 6 feet, 2 inches tall (1.8 m). He's a runner; he's completed two half marathons and he's preparing for his first full marathon. But in 2009 he was just a programmer making excuses for his poor health.

Chad's career in software began as it does for most programmers: writing code and hacking on open source projects. Eventually he wrote some books, organized some conferences, and started a company, and he's now enjoying a great deal of success. He's the chief technology officer at a fast-growing software startup and he's one of the most respected people in the industry. But for nearly a decade, Chad used his success with software as a justification for his unhealthy lifestyle.

The turning point for Chad came during a trip to Tokyo, Japan. He was visiting the Harajuku fashion district when he made a comment about his own physical appearance to a friend. "I said something like, 'It doesn't matter what I wear, anyways. I'm not gonna look good.'" Chad recalls. "I thought to myself—literally at that moment—that was lame. It's lame and embarrassing because it's so counter to everything I say."

Chad has a passion for teaching and he tries to inspire new programmers to be motivated, uplifted, and driven in their careers. At the same time, he was being complacent by accepting his own unhealthy lifestyle. "I sounded like someone I would criticize in any other domain," he laments. As soon as he returned to the United States, Chad began to make changes despite his busy schedule.

Chad and his wife started going to the gym. "We'd go at eleven o'clock every night," he recalls. More importantly, Chad was becoming conscious of his health, which is precisely how we'll begin this book.

Find a scale right now and weigh yourself. Knowing and understanding your body is the first step in making changes. On the other hand, ignoring your body is a surefire way to make things worse. You might not be 100 pounds (45 kg) overweight like Chad was—you might not even be overweight at all. But that doesn't necessarily mean you're healthy. You should think of a scale as a diagnostic tool for monitoring your health just as you might monitor the consumed memory on a server. Like memory, weight is only one of the factors you need to watch.

In fact, many people who consider themselves to be very healthy are overlooking important factors that dramatically increase their risk of disease and even a premature death. Many recent studies have revealed that the lifestyle habits associated with being a programmer can actually counteract the benefits of regular exercise and good nutrition. Sitting for prolonged periods can increase your chance of developing heart disease even if you go to the gym every day. Staying indoors all day can weaken your immune system and deplete your body's level of vitamin D, which affects many aspects of your health. Even if you're already doing a lot to stay healthy, there are many habits you probably need to break.

This book is about more than staying healthy, though. It's also about how to do your job better. Exercise can increase your creativity, attention span, and ability to remember new concepts. Furthermore, reducing pain can help you focus and concentrate better. Many of the experts and programmers you'll meet in this book have dealt with these issues, and they've developed revolutionary techniques for staying healthy. They'll teach us how to subdue many common programming-related ailments like back ache and wrist pain.

Let's begin by doing a high-level assessment of your health.

1.1 Unit-Testing Your Health

You wouldn't refactor some misbehaving code without running a few unit tests first, and you shouldn't try to refactor your health without testing, either. In the coming chapters we'll use very specific exercises and activities to test different aspects of your body. But we'll begin with some simple yes-or-no questions that can provide a good overview of your current condition. Write your answers on a piece of paper or in the margin—you may want to revisit these questions later in the book.

- Do you lose your breath after climbing a single flight of stairs?

- Do you regularly sit for more than one hour without getting up?

- In the last year, have you experienced back, neck, shoulder, or wrist pain that interfered with your ability to do your job?

- In the last week, have your eyes become dry, red, irritated, or difficult to focus after looking at your computer screen?

- Have you eaten until you were uncomfortably full more than once in the last month?

- Have you been exposed to direct sunlight for less than 10 minutes today?

- Have you noticed an increase in the number of cavities you've developed in the last five years?

- Is it uncomfortable for you to bend over and tie your shoes?

- Has your pants size increased significantly in the last five years?

If you answered yes to any of these questions, there is a good chance your well-being is in danger—even if you think you're in pretty good shape. That's because each of these questions is related to risk factors associated with several diseases and health conditions. Fortunately, mitigating these dangers isn't complicated. In the coming chapters, you'll learn exactly what you need to do to prevent them.

Living longer and feeling better are great reasons to be healthy, but many people are not sufficiently motivated by these factors because they take a long time to pay off. That's why the discussion in this book will also emphasize the immediate benefits that physical health bring to the brain. There is a deeply rooted connection between your mind and body that can be enhanced through exercise and nutrition.

1.2   The Mind-Body Connection

The last decade of science has revealed remarkable insights about the relationship between the brain and other parts of the body. We've learned that exercise stimulates the production of proteins that strengthen neurochemical connections in our brain tissue. It also increases the brain's oxygen and glucose levels, which can improve our cognitive abilities.

Individual laboratory experiments have shown that subjects learn vocabulary words 20 percent faster,[1] memorize strings of letters more accurately,[2] and shift their thinking between two different concepts more rapidly after a single bout of exercise.[3] Other studies have shown that regular exercise can improve problem-solving skills, fluid intelligence, cognitive flexibility, and memory.

The evidence supporting the mind-body connection has become so convincing that it's actually changing our understanding of how human beings evolved. Anthropologists have found that animal species with higher endurance capacities—such as rats, dogs, and humans—also have larger brain volumes compared to their body sizes.[4] This research, coupled with the evidence that shows exercise promotes the growth of brain tissue, has led to a very recent hypothesis that the human brain "evolved due to selection acting on features unrelated to cognitive performance."[5] In other words, running after prey may be responsible for our superior brains.

In the coming chapters, we'll discuss many of these studies and how they relate to a programmer's duties. It's possible that the right dose of healthy living can help improve your job skills. But too often, our jobs block us from being healthy. That's why the plan in this book is designed to fit into your workday without even requiring a trip to the gym. That may sound unconventional, but there are many things you can do in and around your office to improve your health. In fact, the simplest activities are the ones that have the most significant impact on your well-being. Most of them are not difficult, but they will require that you make some changes.

Change is hard, and changing successfully requires a plan.

1.3 An Iterative Approach to Health

Chad's moment in Harajuku is an inspiring story, but it's the least important part of his transformation. The year of dedication and determination that followed his epiphany was far more critical to his health. In that year, he learned what it takes to be successful.

"The magic is having a system," Chad says. Chad realized that his success hinged on his ability to stick to a schedule and trust in the scientific data

---

1. *Exercising during learning improves vocabulary acquisition: behavioral and ERP evidence [SKGR10]*
2. *The Effect of Acute Aerobic and Resistance Exercise on Working Memory [PHFT09]*
3. *The effect of a single aerobic training session on cognitive flexibility in late middle-aged adults [NTAA07]*
4. *Relationship between exercise capacity and brain size in mammals [RG11]*
5. *Linking brains and brawn: exercise and the evolution of human neurobiology [RP13]*

that backs it up. He began to view healthy food as medicine that could eventually save his life. "Pretty quickly, it got kind of easy," he remembers.

Having a system or a process is crucial to getting things done. In software, we often use an agile method to guide our development efforts. Agile processes are characterized by an iterative and incremental approach to development, which allows us to adapt to changing requirements. The method you use to stay healthy shouldn't be any different.

In this book you'll learn how to define a system of time-boxed iterations that will improve your health. We'll start with two-week intervals, but like with any agile method, you'll be allowed to change that as needed. At the end of each iteration you'll do a retrospective to assess your progress.

Measuring the progress of your health can be tricky when done ad hoc, and that's why this book includes a set of goals that you can strive to achieve. Each chapter will define new goals, and in each retrospective you'll review your progress against this list. The first goal, Goal 1, *Change one habit*, on page 11, appears in this chapter—it's a simple one to help you get started. The goals will get progressively more difficult and eventually we'll build a complete list, which you can find in Appendix 1, *Goals*, on page 193. You can also view the list at http://healthyprog.com or track your progress with the Healthy Programmer iPhone app, as shown in Figure 2, *Goals on the companion iPhone app*, on page 6.

To achieve these goals you'll need some kind of structure within your iterations. For that, we'll use a checklist of action items that you'll be asked to carry out every day (see Figure 3, *Checklist of daily action items*, on page 6). You'll learn about each item in the coming chapters, but the complete list is shown in the following figure. Try to put aside any preconceived notions you have about the activities described in the list—just practice the ones you've read about and gradually introduce the others as you read their associated chapters.

Let's begin with the first one: the Healthy Stand-Up. Every morning, just as with Scrum or some agile process, you'll have a quick planning meeting with yourself (or with some friends if you can). During this stand-up meeting, you'll ask yourself three questions:

- What did I do yesterday to improve my health?
- What will I do today to improve my health?
- Is there anything blocking me from staying healthy?

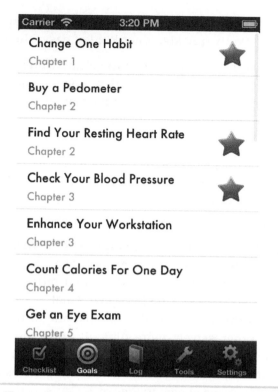

Figure 2—Goals on the companion iPhone app

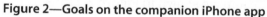

DAILY CHECKLIST

☒ PLAN: Healthy stand-up
☐ WALK: 10,000 steps/day with 20 mins. brisk
☐ MOVE: 5 mins./hr. Change position every 20 mins.
☐ EAT: 5 servings of fruits or vegetables
☐ BUILD: 5 bodyweight exercises

Figure 3—Checklist of daily action items

These questions may be difficult to answer at first, but as you work your way through the book you'll find activities and exercises that you can use to plan your day. Most of these will become a part of your daily checklist.

The following figure shows the big picture. You can think of the outer loop being driven by goals and the inner loop being driven by the daily checklist.

Figure 4—The iterative model for health

You can even do your first stand-up today! The answer to "What will I do today to improve my health?" should be "Read more of this book."

As you continue reading, you'll be asked to try new activities and learn new techniques. But more importantly, you'll be asked to break bad habits. Habits are tough to change, but by understanding how the brain works you can make intelligent decisions that will help you overcome them more easily. Chad sums up his transformation as a process of creating new patterns, and the latest science is beginning to explain why he's right.

1.4 The Science Behind Habits

The Massachusetts Institute of Technology (MIT) is known for its advances in the field of computer science, but researchers at MIT are doing a lot more than building robots and improving cryptography. They're also studying the human brain.

In fact, the best place to go if you want to learn how the brain remembers patterns is the McGovern Institute for Brain Research at MIT. In 2005, researchers at the institute published a study that revealed the complex nature of how the brain creates habits. As with many experiments in cognitive science, this one involved rats in a maze.[6] What made this experiment unique was that the rats had sensors surgically placed deep within their brains (almost at the center).

The procedure used a *T*-shaped maze with chocolate on the left side of the crossbar, as shown in the following figure. The rats were placed at the bottom behind a partition. The experiment began with an audible *click*, which was followed by the raising of the partition.

Figure 5—*T*-shaped maze from the MIT experiment

---

6. *Activity of striatal neurons reflects dynamic encoding and recoding of procedural memories* [BKHJ05]

Once the partition was up, the rats could smell the chocolate and their brains worked ferociously as they moved through the maze looking for it. The rats were sniffing the air, looking at the walls, and generally studying this new environment. When they reached the top of the maze, some rats would turn left and others would turn right, but eventually they all found the chocolate.

The same rats repeated the procedure hundreds of times. After a while the sensors started to detect a change in those tiny little brains. The rats developed a habit.

When the rats were initially placed behind the partition, their brain activity was normal. But as soon as the *click* was played, the rats that were already familiar with the experiment had a sharp decrease in overall brain activity. As they followed the maze directly to the chocolate (always turning left now), their brains seemed to be fairly idle—except for one part, deep within the center of the brain, called the basal ganglia. This is an area of the brain that scientists originally thought was related only to movement and so-called muscle memory.

When the experiment was new to the rats, their entire brains worked to process the environment. After repeating the procedure dozens of times, the rats stored this routine in the basal ganglia and thus reduced the amount of work the brain had to do the next time it went through the maze.

In some ways, the rats' brains were functioning like a computer's CPU, which might store the result of some repeated computation in its cache. The cache mechanism saves clock cycles, just as the basal ganglia reduces brain activity.

The MIT experiment shed a great deal of light on the structure of the brain, but it also revealed something new about the structure of habits. For the rats to make this activity a habit, it needed to follow a certain format. It's now accepted among psychologists that every habit has at least these three components:

- A cue
- A routine
- A reward

The cue for the rats was the *click* sound. It signaled their brains to fetch the routine from the basal ganglia. The routine was the path through the maze that led to the chocolate on the left. The chocolate, of course, was the reward.

The science behind these elements is new, but advertising agencies have known about them for a century. McDonald's uses its golden arches as a cue, the drive-thru for routine, and a big greasy hamburger as a reward. Other examples include toothpaste, air fresheners, and soft drinks, which all achieved marketing success because these three elements created habits in consumers.

That's not to say habits are a bad thing. There are good habits and bad habits, just like anything else. Imagine a Vim user thinking through the details of every command while editing a shell script. The absence of habits would make programming tasks a lot harder and we would need a lot more coffee to do our jobs. But for most programmers, bad habits go beyond the keyboard. Sometimes, they extend to food and exercise.

1.5 Reprogramming Your Habits

Creating new habits works much the same way for us as it did for the rats in the MIT experiment—we develop new cues, routines, and rewards. But changing existing habits is different. That's important to understand because the challenge when it comes to staying healthy is often to overcome bad habits that have existed for years.

The key to changing habits is to keep the same cues and rewards while replacing the routine with something new. The best example of this is smoking cessation. Smoking is much more than a habit—it's a chemical addiction. But the habits that surround cigarette smokers make overcoming the dependence on nicotine even harder. Routines like smoke breaks, lighting up, and even buying cigarettes all have to be changed for a smoker to quit.

Despite how hard it is to quit, smoking rates have plummeted in the United States in the last decade.[7] One reason for the sharp decline is that we better understand how cues trigger smoking habits. That's why the American Cancer Society recommends replacing smoking with tea, coffee, exercise, or something that gives you the same reward.[8]

> The key to changing habits is to keep the same cues and rewards while replacing the routine with something new.

For Chad, having the same reward is exactly the reason his new habits started to stick. He felt good after eating a healthy meal in the same way he used to feel good after eating an unhealthy meal. In fact, the unhealthy meals started to make Chad feel bad. "I do a cheat day or binge day every Saturday," Chad says. "It makes me sick every time and I look forward to it less and less."

---

7. http://www.cdc.gov/nchs/fastats/smoking.htm
8. http://www.cancer.org/Healthy/StayAwayfromTobacco/GuidetoQuittingSmoking/guide-to-quitting-smoking-how-to-quit

The rewards of being healthy come in many different forms. You may get extra energy, be able to concentrate longer, reduce pain, or just do your job better. In this book, you'll learn how to create a system of change that helps you realize these rewards. Then you'll have the tools you need to achieve the goals defined throughout the book. Let's get started. Your first goal is to change a small habit in your life.

Goal 1

Change one habit

Pick a simple habit of yours and change it. A good example might be walking to the vending machine at work to buy a candy bar every afternoon. If you want to change a habit like this, you'll need to do three things:

Identify the Cue   Sometimes cues are obvious. Your morning routine is probably cued by an alarm clock. The habit of putting on your seat belt is cued by sound of starting a car. Other cues are subtle. However, they all fall into one of five categories: location, time, emotion, social setting, or action. To identify your cue, try answering each of the following questions as soon as you feel the urge to indulge your habit:

- Where are you?
- What time is it?
- How are you feeling?
- Who is with you?
- What action preceded the urge?

After a few times, you'll probably see a pattern. Is it always the same time of day? Are you with the same people? Are you always bored when the urge strikes?

Identify the Reward   The reward for a habit like buying a candy bar may seem obvious, but it's not always what you think. The reward could be the walk to the vending machine. Getting your blood flowing can reward your brain just as much as candy. The reward could also be social. Maybe there is a group of people you like to talk to near the vending machine. The best way to identify a habit's reward is to experiment. Try going for a walk without going to the vending machine. Trying socializing without buying the candy. You may find that you get the same reward.

Plan Your New Routine   Once you've identified the cue and the reward, you'll need a new routine. The best way to make sure you follow up on that routine is to write it down. It can even look like something out of behavior-driven development:

```
When CUE
I will ROUTINE
In order to get REWARD
```

Put this on a sticky note and keep it near your desk as a constant reminder. Eventually, the new routine will become a habit.

1.6   Retrospective

Making changes takes time. It requires active intervention and experimentation over several iterations. That's why you should use an agile approach as you work your way though this book. Applying these principles to your life will facilitate your ability to change.

As with building software, we'll construct your healthy routines and habits in small doses. You won't be bombarded with exercises and activities right away. Instead, we'll spend the first few chapters introducing some very simple, but essential, components of a healthy lifestyle. Don't think that they are too simple, though. These are the activities that will have the biggest effect on your life.

If you're anything like Chad was in 2009, then you probably don't want to jump into a marathon or even a 5k right away. You'll only hurt yourself. The system in this book is designed to be incremental. For that reason, we'll start slowly—at a walking pace.

Act On It

- Weigh yourself, but don't become obsessed with the scale. Your health has many facets, and focusing on only one of them won't give you an accurate picture.

- Write down your answers to the list of questions at the beginning of the chapter. Review them from time to time and see if you are improving.

- Download the companion iPhone application for this book and start tracking your progress against the goals.

- Start slowly. You can't make noticeable changes to your health in a single day. If all you've done so far is read this chapter, then you're off to a great start.

CHAPTER 2

Bootstrapping Your Health

One of the greatest mathematical puzzles to ever be solved was Fermat's last theorem. More than 300 years ago, Pierre de Fermat conjectured that there were no solutions to the following equation where n is greater than 2:

$$x^n + y^n = z^n$$

It was not until 1995 that Andrew Wiles succeeded in proving this conjecture, and the solution did not come easily. Wiles retreated to his attic and secretly struggled with problem after problem for eight years. The secrecy was necessary because of the popularity of the theorem. If word got out that Wiles was working on it, the distractions would never end.

When Wiles released his proof to the public, it re-energized the field of number theory. But the question most people wanted to ask him was not about mathematics. They wanted to know how he was able to remain creative and generate new ideas while working alone for such a long period of time. His answer was surprising.

"I would go for a walk," Wiles told Simon Singh in *Fermat's Enigma: The Epic Quest to Solve the World's Greatest Mathematical Problem [Sin98]*. "When I'm walking I find I can concentrate my mind on one very particular aspect of a problem, focusing on it completely. I'd always have a paper and pen ready, so if I had an idea I could sit down at a bench and start scribbling away."

Walking is a powerful activity. It can stimulate creative thinking and it's the best way to bootstrap your health. In fact, a few brisk strolls might be better for you than a single cardio session at the gym. In this chapter, you'll learn how walking periodically throughout the day can have a dramatic effect on your risk of developing many diseases and even on your mortality. We'll discuss how much to walk, how fast to walk, how often to walk, and even how to walk. Ultimately, you'll learn why this simple form of exercise is one of the most important things you can do in your life. It certainly was for Andrew Wiles.

Wiles's effort during those eight years was monumental and his genius is unparalleled, but much of his thought process during that time was similar to the way in which programmers find solutions to problems in software. Both tasks require intense concentration and creativity. As it turns out, walking is a great way to promote this kind of brain function. Let's begin by discussing why this happens and how you can leverage it to become a more productive programmer.

2.1 Thinking on Your Feet

Go for a walk right now. Put this book down, walk around, and get your blood flowing. After five or ten minutes, come back and pick up where you left off. Your ability to think, remember, and concentrate will be enhanced as blood returns to your brain. In fact, a number of scientific studies have shown that this kind of exercise has a direct impact on your ability to learn new things.

Few people better understand the link between exercise and learning than John Ratey, MD. His book, *Spark: The Revolutionary New Science of Exercise and the Brain [Rat08]*, begins with the story of Naperville Central High School in Illinois. At this school, a revolutionary approach to gym class has transformed the student body of 2,947 into perhaps the fittest in the nation. The students have access to climbing walls, video game–based aerobic machines, heart-rate monitors, and weight machines. The results have been remarkable. In one class of sophomores only three percent were overweight versus the national average of thirty percent.

Even more remarkable, this high school's students are also some of the smartest in the nation. Naperville's graduating class of 2012 had an average ACT score that was 4.9 points higher than the rest of the state's.[1] And when the school's students took a test called the Trends in International Mathematics and Science Study (TIMSS), they finished sixth in the world in math and first in science. This is the test that *New York Times* columnist Thomas Friedman refers to when he laments that children in Asia are "eating our lunch."

Naperville isn't your run-of-the-mill town, though. It's an affluent suburb of Chicago, and its proximity to Fermilab (a particle-physics laboratory) makes it home to a very well-educated population. In terms of environment and

---

1. http://schools.chicagotribune.com/school/naperville-central-high-school_naperville

genetics, the kids in Naperville have a distinguished pedigree. But that doesn't mean the correlation found at this school is an anomaly.

The California Department of Education (CDE) has found that students with higher fitness scores also have higher test scores.[2] The CDE factors in socioeconomic status when aggregating its results, which makes the numbers less biased. Results like this, along with the findings of many other studies, are beginning to reveal a profound link between physical fitness and academic achievement.[3,4]

That's all well and good for school children, but what does it mean to we programmers? To begin with, programmers are perpetual students. In a field like technology, where change is constant, learning new concepts is a part of the job. A programmer's ability to absorb new technology is essential to staying relevant. Unfortunately, this often leads to a sedentary lifestyle as we hack on code late into the night or read the latest tech books. In some cases, it leads to consumption of too much caffeine.

But as we've started to learn from the kids in Naperville, one of the best ways to enhance your ability to learn is to get some exercise. There's also a lot of laboratory evidence showing that our brains work better when our bodies are active. In particular, they become better at remembering new concepts, ideas, and patterns.

Here's a simple example. Try to memorize the following string of letters:

```
I N T S M L I F H
```

Okay, you've got it. But how will you remember it tomorrow? The basic memory mechanism in your brain works by recruiting nerve cells, called neurons, which build new pathways that transmit electrochemical signals. To oversimplify things, the strength of these pathways determines how well you remember something. Over time, these pathways weaken and eventually fade away—especially if you don't make them strong in the first place. However, studies have shown that the walk you took a few minutes ago helped to strengthen the connections you made when memorizing those letters.

In one experiment, which was published in the journal *Medicine and Science in Sports and Exercise*, participants were asked to memorize some letters just like you did a moment ago. They were then asked to either sit quietly or run.

---

2. *Physical Fitness and Academic Achievement [Gri05]*

3. *Physical Fitness and Academic Achievement in Third- and Fifth-Grade Students [CHBE07]*

4. *Is there a relationship between physical fitness and academic achievement? Positive results from public school children in the northeastern United States [CSMM09]*

The participants who ran were quicker and more accurate when they were tested than subjects who sat.[5]

The link between memory and exercise can most likely be explained by a class of protein called brain-derived neurotrophic factor (BDNF). This protein is responsible for strengthening the connections between neurons. As it turns out, exercise increases the production of BDNF. Shortly after the link between BDNF and memory was discovered (and a Nobel Prize was awarded), a researcher at the University of California, Irvine, devised an experiment to show that more BDNF is produced in the brains of mice that run on an exercise wheel than those that sit around.[6]

When you went for a walk earlier, you were encouraging your brain to produce BDNF. Now that you've returned to reading, those proteins are being put to work as your brain creates new neurons and synapses. The result is that you have a better chance of remembering things you learn shortly after exercising. This applies to programming as well as reading.

Try it out the next time you're working on something new. Go for a walk before you start researching the distributed-data-clustering software you've been wondering about. Or maybe stroll around the block after you've exhaustively debugged some tough legacy code. When it comes time to refactor it, you'll probably be quicker at remembering how it works.

> **Tip 1** Studies show that doing exercise before or after learning something new can help you remember it.

Can you still remember that string of letters? You probably can.

Unfortunately, most programmers' lifestyles tend to favor the activity levels of the sedentary mice in the study from UC Irvine, which means their brains are lacking BDNF and may not be reaching their learning potential. Programmers who make regular trips to the gym aren't doing much better if they sit idle for the remaining ten to fifteen hours each day. In either case, taking a few daily walking breaks can make a big difference. It can boost your brain power, but it's also the best way to stay healthy.

---

5. *The Effect of Acute Aerobic and Resistance Exercise on Working Memory [PHFT09]*
6. *Exercise: a behavioral intervention to enhance brain health and plasticity [CB02]*

2.2   Walking Your Way to Better Health

It's common to say that humans were born to run, but it's more likely that we were born to walk. The ratio of distance covered to energy expenditure when we walk is much higher than it is when we run. You can test this out right now. Find a hallway and walk down it, wait a few minutes, and then run down it. Which one left you more tired?

The chances are that you didn't even start breathing heavily when you walked down the hall, but you may have broken a sweat when you ran. That doesn't mean the walking wasn't good for your health, though. The initial difference between walking and not walking provides the biggest impact on improving your overall health.

In a recent study done at the Shinshu University School of Medicine in Japan, researchers enrolled hundreds of sedentary Japanese citizens in a five-month-long program of brisk walking. The results showed that the physical fitness of the participants (as measured by aerobic power and thigh muscle strength) increased by twenty percent.[7] They also had a significant drop in blood pressure, and reduced their lifestyle-related diseases, like heart disease and type-2 diabetes, by another twenty percent. All of these improvements came just from walking—nothing else.

The Shinshu study is a testament to the importance of walking, but it's not the first of its kind by any means. One of the oldest studies was done in 1949, when a British physician named Jeremy Morris began tracking the health of postal workers in England. He found that mail carriers who walked their delivery routes were significantly less likely to develop or die from heart disease than the postal clerks and telephone operators who sat in the office all day.[8]

Despite the undeniable value of walking, most software programmers don't do it enough. In fact, the average IT professional takes a mere 4,300 steps per day (a little less than two miles).[9] That's below the national average in the United States, and less than half the number of steps taken by the average Australian, who walks more than anyone in the world, with 9,700 steps per day.

---

7. *Effects of high-intensity interval walking training on physical fitness and blood pressure in middle-aged and older people [NGMO07]*
8. *Coronary heart disease and physical activity of work [MC58]*
9. *How Many Steps/Day Are Enough?: Preliminary Pedometer Indices for Public Health [TB04]*

The amount of walking that programmers do is especially low in comparison to professionals with more-active careers. Restaurant servers take an average of 14,000 steps per day, which is still shy of the mark set by the average Amish man, who takes about 18,500 steps per day (or roughly nine miles), as you can see in the following figure. The Amish lifestyle is one of hard labor, which is probably more akin to the lifestyle of our ancient ancestors who had to hunt for their food. We're all glad that we don't have to work so hard to eat, but that doesn't mean we have to be unhealthy.

The average IT professional takes a mere 4,300 steps per day.

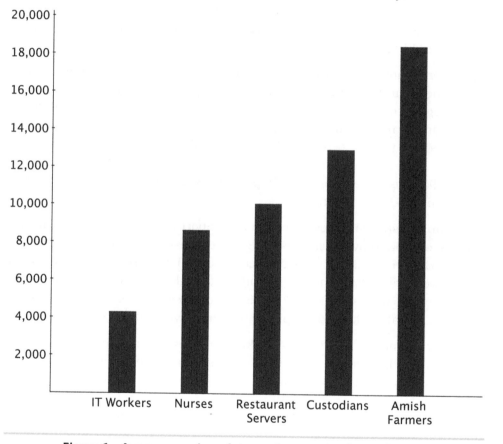

Figure 6—Average number of steps taken per day, by profession

How many steps do you take each day? There's a good chance you don't know the answer. Go back to the hallway you ran down a moment ago, and walk down it again. This time, count the number of steps you take. Depending on its length, you probably took somewhere between twenty and fifty steps. If that's the case, it means the average Amish man does the equivalent of walking down it close to 1,000 times per day.

Counting steps is hard, though. A better way to find out how many steps you take each day is to get a pedometer, which is one of your goals for this chapter. Use it for a few days and get a feeling for how much (or how little) you're actually moving. Keep a log of your daily step count, and check your average over time. If you're using a pedometer on your smartphone, it might even take care of this for you.

You'll probably discover that you take fewer than 5,000 steps per day, which means you'll need to find ways of increasing your step count if you want to be healthy. Fortunately, simple changes like taking the stairs instead of the elevator can have profound effects on these numbers and on your health.

Many groups, such as the Centers for Disease Control and Prevention (CDC), have long recommended that people take 10,000 steps per day (about five miles of walking). But research in the last few years has shown that steps per day alone is not a sufficient measurement because it doesn't capture intensity.[10] Instead, the CDC is now recommending that your daily total come from spurts of 3,000 steps in thirty minutes or 1,000 steps in ten minutes to ensure that some of your walking is done briskly. It doesn't matter how you break up these walking sessions, but you should get at least twenty minutes in total each day. That's because twenty minutes turns out to be a very important amount of time.

Goal 2

Buy a pedometer

This is the easiest goal in the book, but possibly one of the most useful. In fact, many studies show that simply wearing a pedometer is correlated to taking more steps.[11,12] If you're into high-tech gadgets, try picking up a Fitbit or Nike FuelBand.[13]

---

10. *How Many Steps/Day Are Enough?: Preliminary Pedometer Indices for Public Health* *[TB04]*
11. *A Preliminary Study on the Impact of a Pedometer-based Intervention on Daily Steps* *[Cro04]*
12. *Physical Activity Assessment Using a Pedometer and Its Comparison with a Questionnaire in a Large Population Survey [SRWT95]*
13. http://www.fitbit.com/ and http://www.nike.com/FuelBand

2.3   The Time of Your Life

The absolute best thing you can do for your health is to be active for at least twenty minutes per day. Why twenty minutes? It's because the best science we have shows that a person's risk of dying prematurely from any cause drops by nearly twenty percent with at least twenty minutes of exercise each day.[14] More specifically, a study from the Biostatistics Center at George Washington University found that a lifestyle intervention including moderate physical activity for at least twenty minutes per day was more effective than the medication metformin alone in reducing the incidence of diabetes.[15] That kind of research is exactly why the CDC recommends a minimum of 150 minutes of moderate-intensity aerobic activity each week.[16]

Walking is a great way to fill those minutes, but any exercise will do. Examples include dancing, basketball, and playing a Wii game. The important thing is to ensure the intensity level is sufficient by getting your heart rate up.

> **Tip 2**   Twenty minutes of exercise each day can reduce your risk of dying prematurely by twenty percent.

The Shinshu study referenced earlier provides a good baseline for determining the best intensity level for walking or any other activity. It required its participants to walk at an intensity that was fifty percent of their *maximal oxygen uptake* ($VO2_{max}$). Converting this to heart rate is tricky—especially since it needs to be done on a person-by-person basis—but it's roughly sixty percent of your *maximum heart rate* (HR_{max}).[17] Your HR_{max} can be estimated by subtracting your age from 220. Thus, the average thirty-year-old's heart rate needs to come up to about 114 beats per minute (BPM) to make any particular exercise effective. This also aligns well with the CDC's generic recommendation to "walk fast."

The easiest way to check your heart rate is to feel for your pulse on either your neck or your wrist; the following figure shows the latter. Count the number of beats during a ten-second period and multiply it by six.

---

14. *The First 20 Minutes: Surprising Science Reveals How We Can: Exercise Better, Train Smarter, Live Longer* [Rey12]
15. *Reduction in the incidence of type 2 diabetes with lifestyle intervention or metformin* [KBFH02]
16. http://www.cdc.gov/physicalactivity/everyone/guidelines/adults.html
17. *Prediction of energy expenditure from heart rate monitoring during submaximal exercise* [Key05]

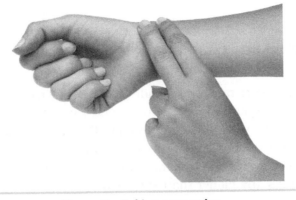

Figure 7—Taking your pulse

Take your pulse right now. If you've been sitting and reading this book for a few minutes, then you are probably close to your resting heart rate. This is basically the lower bound of your pulse. Go find some stairs and walk up and down them a few times. When you come back, take your pulse again. This time your heart rate is probably more in line with the sixty-percent number you calculated earlier.

No matter what activity you choose to fill your twenty minutes per day, be sure to check your heart rate during and after the exercise to ensure that you're reaching your target.

You've already gone for a few walks in this chapter, which means you've probably come close to your twenty-minute-per-day goal without even realizing it! That's because it's okay to break your walks into shorter spurts. It's actually what the CDC recommends, and the Shinshu study reinforced it.

In fact, the researchers in the Shinshu study included a group in their experiment that walked at higher intensity for short intervals. This group had better results than the group that walked continuously, which reinforces the claim that you can split your workouts into two ten-minute sessions, four five-minute sessions, or whatever you'd like. Just make sure that as you shorten the interval you also increase the intensity.

As you begin to walk more and walk faster, your health will improve. But you'll also increase your risk of injury—so you need to make sure you're doing it right. After we discuss your next goal, you'll learn some tips for walking well.

Goal 3

Find your resting heart rate

If you took you heart rate while reading this book, then you have a pretty good estimate of its lower bound. But the best way to get your true resting heart rate is to take your pulse first thing in the morning before even getting out of bed. Set a reminder on your phone and do it tomorrow morning. A normal range is between sixty and ninety beats per minute (BPM)—you should see a doctor if it's any higher than 100 BPM.

Resting heart rate can tell you a lot about your body. In 2011, researchers in Norway and Sweden published the results of a ten-year study that tracked the resting heart rates of 29,000 people.[18] The participants whose resting heart rate was under seventy BPM at the start of the study and rose to over eighty-five BPM by the end of the study were ninety percent more likely to have died in those ten years. The results suggest that lowering your heart rate over time may be beneficial to your mortality, but the researchers could not say that for certain.

There are many ways to lower your resting heart rate; including losing weight, quitting smoking, and reducing stress. But the factor we'll focus on is exercise. If you follow the suggestions in this book and get twenty minutes of moderate activity every day, it will help to lower your resting heart rate.

2.4 Learning How to Walk

You have to learn how to walk before you can run, but you also have to learn how to walk before you can walk. Most people don't think much about the form they use while walking because they do it so often. But using the proper walking technique can reduce injuries, provide a better workout, and make the activity more enjoyable.

The image in the following figure provides a good overview of how you should look while walking. Try the tips presented next to achieve the best technique.

Bend Your Arms You wouldn't run with your arms straight and you shouldn't walk with them straight, either. When walking, your arms should be slightly bent and you should hold this position as your arms move—don't

---

18. *Temporal Changes in Resting Heart Rate and Deaths From Ischemic Heart Disease [NJVW11]*

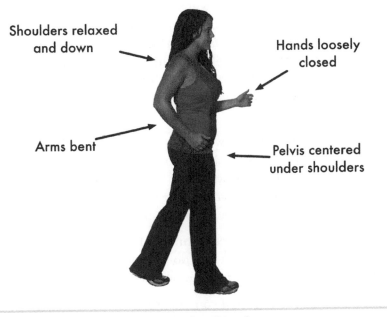

Shoulders relaxed and down

Hands loosely closed

Arms bent

Pelvis centered under shoulders

Figure 8—Good walking form

extend them as they swing back. You should also refrain from swinging your arms across your body. Instead, imagine that you are holding a flashlight and you want to keep it pointing forward as your walk.

Roll from Heel to Toe Landing on your heel and rolling to your toes should come naturally. But as you walk faster to increase the intensity, you'll need to concentrate more on this motion to ensure that it happens correctly. When your foot comes forward, you'll want your heel to hit the ground first. As this happens, lift your toes toward your shins. This will increase your range of motion.

You can try this right now while sitting in a chair. Lift your foot off the ground and bring it back down again as though you are walking. Touch your heel first and pull your toes up as it lands. Then roll through to your toes and push off with the ball of your foot.

Take Short, Quick Steps Taking longer steps is a common mistake when trying to increase walking speed and intensity. This increases your pace, but it also increases the impact on your forward foot, which can lead to injury. The best way to increase your pace is to take quicker, shorter steps. This will reduce the impact on your legs and increase your heart rate more effectively.

Breathe with Your Belly   If you watch a professional cycling race like the Tour de France closely, you might notice that a lot of the riders appear to have a beer belly. That's far from the case with those elite athletes, though. Instead, they are belly-breathing to maximize the volume of air they intake. Without belly-breathing, it's impossible to fully expel air from your lungs, which means you can't fill them with fresh air when you breathe in.

Try to belly-breathe right now. As you breathe in, push your belly button out as far as you can. As you breath out, pull your belly button in toward your spine. If you find it awkward at first, try doing it while lying flat on your back. This technique will ensure that you get the most out of each breath and it will likely prevent you from getting winded.

Learning to walk with the correct technique is just like learning to program with the correct paradigms. You can do both in many different ways, but if you want to be successful you need to practice.

Walking won't do you any good if you only read about it, though. As with any new habit, you must actively intervene if you want it to stick.

2.5   Getting Out the Door

The hardest part of any walk is the first step. Our minds play tricks on us as we lead up to any kind of exercise, and we often find excuses for not following through. But once we have a foot out the door, there is almost no turning back. The following tips will help you win at those mind games.

Prepare   Do every thing you can to prepare for your walk hours in advance. This will reduce the number of barriers your mind can erect when creating excuses. If you like walking in the morning, try laying out your clothes the night before. Put a reminder on your calendar. Plan the route you'll take when you walk. The fewer obstacles you have leading up to exercise, the more likely you are to follow through with it.

Do it right now. Go get your walking clothes and lay them out—even if you won't walk again until tomorrow. You'll have one fewer obstacle in your way.

Make It a Date   Having a walking partner is the best way to ensure that you'll go for walks. A partner not only provides a form of peer pressure, but also makes the time you spend walking more enjoyable. Don't wait—do it now. Get out your phone or computer and send an email inviting a friend to join you for a walk.

Explore   Make your walks exciting by exploring new territory. Try new routes and new locations every chance you get. If you're traveling for work, explore your new surroundings instead of using the trip as an excuse for not walking.

Don't Fear the Weather   Cold temperatures shouldn't stop you from walking if you have the right clothes. If Sir Edmund Hillary climbed Mount Everest without Gore-Tex, then you can probably make a trip around the block in rainy or cold weather. If you embrace the elements, they'll eventually cease to be a factor. However, there are two kinds of weather you should be wary of: extreme heat and lightning. If these conditions are present and you don't have access to a treadmill, try substituting your walks with other forms of exercise. You can play motion-based video games, ride a stationary bike, or do some bodyweight exercises like push-ups and squats. These activities will get your heart rate up, and provide many of the same benefits as walking.

Don't Fear the Night   The darkness shouldn't be an excuse for skipping a walk if you have a good strobe light or flashlight. This is especially true in the winter months, when daylight is scarce. Walking in the dark is a great way to shrug off the melancholy that comes with cabin fever. Of course, you may need to take extra precautions if you are in an unsafe or unfamiliar area.

After a while, you won't need to worry about these tricks anymore. Walking will be a habit. Instead of fighting with yourself to get out the door, you'll be able to enjoy the rewards of walking—many of which affect your brain.

It's possible that the walking Andrew Wiles did during his eight-year battle with Fermat's theorem did more than help him concentrate. It may have made him smarter. But regardless of what it did for Wiles, you'll probably find that some amount of physical activity is valuable to your mind as well as your body.

2.6   Retrospective

When your next iteration ends, you'll have some more interesting things to think about. But first, can you still remember that string of letters you memorized earlier in the chapter? The two walks you took during this chapter make it very likely that you can.

Let's put what you've learned into action. You can start by walking every day: 10,000 steps. In addition, you should do some of those steps briskly (achieving roughly sixty percent of your maximum heart rate) for at least twenty minutes—that's the next item on your daily checklist. You can split that twenty minutes up any way you'd like, but make sure you're doing it at the right intensity level. You can substitute other activities as long as the intensity is the same.

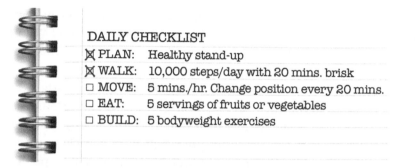

DAILY CHECKLIST
- ☒ PLAN: Healthy stand-up
- ☒ WALK: 10,000 steps/day with 20 mins. brisk
- ☐ MOVE: 5 mins./hr. Change position every 20 mins.
- ☐ EAT: 5 servings of fruits or vegetables
- ☐ BUILD: 5 bodyweight exercises

It's okay if you miss a day every now and again, but try to make up for it the following day so you still come close to or even surpass the CDC's recommended 150 minutes for the week. There is a surprising number of ways to get to this point without even setting aside time. Try walking down the hall to talk to a coworker instead of sending an email. Try taking the stairs instead of the elevator—in fact, try never taking an elevator again.

With all of this walking, you're going to need some feedback. That's why we've added two new goals in this chapter. The first is to buy a pedometer—but you also need to wear it! This little tool will not only shed light on your current activity level, but also help you keep track of your improvement. The second goal is to find your resting heart rate. This is an important indicator of your health that you can use to test your progress.

Goals
+ Buy a pedometer
+ Find your resting heart rate

Write these goals down. Put them on a whiteboard, a sticky note, the back of your hand, or anything else that will remind you to achieve them. You can even keep track of them with this book's companion iPhone app. If you put them on the back burner, they simply won't get done.

All of this talk about walking has probably been exhausting. Let's move on and discuss something less strenuous: sitting.

Act On It

- Take a walk if you're having trouble solving a tough problem.
- Take a walk after learning something new.
- Park your car at the back of the parking lot to encourage a longer walk to the office.
- Take the stairs instead of the elevator.
- Play video games that require movement instead of using a controller.
- Check your resting heart rate every couple of weeks.
- Keep a log of your daily step count, and try to set personal goals for yourself.
- Practice your walking technique and try to correct mistakes in your form. This should help you to increase your speed without becoming injured or excessively fatigued.

CHAPTER 3

A Farewell to Chairs?

Ernest Hemingway was not a healthy person. He suffered from severe headaches, high blood pressure, weight problems, and eventually diabetes. Hemingway was also a notoriously heavy drinker, which probably contributed to his liver disease. If there is a model of health that you should not follow, it's Hemingway's life.

Yet Hemingway worked from a standing desk for most of his career. He discovered the concept while visiting his editor at Charles Scribner's Sons and fashioned his own desk from a bookcase in his bedroom. Hemingway had a traditional desk, but it served more as storage than anything else.

No one is certain why Ernest Hemingway preferred to stand, but it's highly unlikely that he was doing it for his health. Instead, he probably stood while working because it helped him stay focused and be more productive. According to the latest scientific research, he would have been correct in that belief. Standing up can increase your alertness and concentration, but the health effects of a standing desk may not be what you expect.

The reality is (you may need to sit down for this), standing desks can have unhealthy consequences. In fact, standing all day is downright dangerous. Even standing for just a few hours at a time can put you at risk for many health problems—some of which are life-threatening.

Despite these drawbacks, a standing desk can be healthy if you use it correctly. In this chapter, you'll learn how to balance the dangers of standing against its potential benefits. In the end, you'll be able to create a workspace that's both healthy and productive. But it's important to remember that standing—by itself—is not a solution to your health problems. If that were the case, Hemingway would have been a lot better off.

Surprisingly, the best reason to use a standing desk actually has nothing to do with being on your feet. Instead, the number-one advantage of standing is that it's the opposite of sitting. That's important because sitting is not the metabolic equivalent of breaking even—it's far worse.

3.1 Sitting Is Considered Harmful

Stand up right now. You can keep reading this book, but get out of your chair and stay up for the next few minutes. Congratulations; you've just extended your life. That may sound glib, but there's a lot of science that links sitting to decreased life expectancy.

In 2009, researchers at the Pennington Biomedical Research Center in Louisiana published a study suggesting that the amount of time a person sits is directly associated with mortality from all causes.[1] The study examined 17,013 Canadians over a period of twelve years. The researchers measured each participant's time spent sitting over those years and adjusted for factors like smoking, alcohol consumption, and physical activity. In the end, they found that the participants who sat the most were fifty percent more likely to die prematurely.

Importantly, this study was controlled for physical-activity levels, which means that exercise was not a contributing factor in the results. In fact, many of the higher-risk participants were actually getting a sufficient amount of exercise but were also sitting for prolonged periods during the day. Thus, the correlation between sitting and dying was independent of physical activity.

The results from the Pennington study are by no means an anomaly. Dr. Christine Friedenreich, an epidemiologist at the Southern Alberta Cancer Research Institute in Canada, has been researching the link between cancer and inactivity for the better part of a decade. Her most recent research shows that prolonged inactivity is associated with as many as 49,000 cases of breast cancer and 43,000 cases of colon cancer a year in the United States.[2] A study from Australia found that each hour of daily television-viewing is associated with an eleven percent increase in mortality risk from all causes, regardless of age, sex, waist circumference, and physical-activity level.[3] This study was titled "Television Viewing Time and Mortality," in case there were any doubts about its results.

------

1. *Sitting time and mortality from all causes, cardiovascular disease, and cancer [KCCB09]*
2. *Effect of Physical Activity on Women at Increased Risk of Breast Cancer: Results from the E3N Cohort Study [TFO06]*
3. *Television Viewing Time and Mortality [Dun10]*

> Each hour of daily television-viewing is associated with an eleven percent increase in the risk of death.

Before jumping to conclusions about these studies, it's important to understand the nature of their results. These studies do not find that sitting causes any diseases—only that it is associated with them. However, other studies have shown why the link could, in fact, be one of causation. The explanation may be that gene activity in our muscles changes when the muscles don't contract for long periods of time. In one experiment, researchers at the University of Massachusetts asked a group of healthy young men to walk around using crutches such that the muscles in their left legs never contracted. After only two days of inactivity, the scientists biopsied muscles in both legs. In the left leg, the DNA repair mechanism had been disrupted, insulin response was dropping, oxidative stress was rising, and metabolic activity within individual muscle cells was slowing.[4]

For programmers this may sound like a death sentence. Sitting in front of a computer is our passion and our career. But the good news is that avoiding the consequences of sitting all day requires a very small intervention. In fact, a recent research survey in the *British Journal of Sports Medicine* suggested that just five minutes of activity per hour is enough to counteract most of the negative effects of sitting.[5] In many cases, a break as simple as walking to the bathroom was sufficient to improve metabolic health.

> **Tip 3** Five minutes of activity every hour can reduce your risk of developing many life-threatening diseases.

But sometimes you simply can't get away from your chair. When that happens, you can make sitting less dangerous by forcing your muscles to contract without even getting up. The following are a few calisthenics you can do right in your office. They won't cause you to break a sweat, and probably won't bring your heart rate up as much as walking. But they will force your muscles to contract and prevent you from stiffening up, which could otherwise lead to injuries during your walks. Have a seat and try these right now.

Leg Circles Sit toward the edge of your chair with your knees bent and your feet on the floor. Then lift your left foot slightly off the ground and rotate counterclockwise from the knee such that you are drawing circles in the air with your heel. Do this for thirty seconds, and then rotate it clockwise for another thirty seconds. Finally, do the same exercise with your right

---

4. *Forty-eight hours of unloading and 24 h of reloading lead to changes in global gene expression patterns related to ubiquittination and oxidative stress in humans [RCTH10]*
5. *Too much sitting: a novel and important predictor of chronic disease risk? [OBB09]*

leg. If you get tired of drawing circles, you can mix things up by drawing each letter of the alphabet.

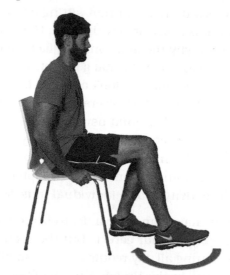

Lower-Leg Lift   Sit toward the edge of your chair again, with your knees bent. Then lift your left foot toward the ceiling such that your toes are pointing up and your leg is straight and parallel with the ground. You should feel a stretch in your hamstring (the muscle on the back of your thigh). Return your foot to the ground and repeat the exercise for a total of five repetitions. Then do the same with the right leg.

Knee Lift   This time, sit slightly back in your chair and lean against the backrest. Then bring your left leg up toward your chest while keeping your knee bent. Do this five times for each leg.

Overhead Clap   Sit in the middle of your chair with your back straight. Put your arms out to your side such that you are forming the letter *t* with the upper half of your body. Then bring your hands together above your head while keeping your arms straight—like the top half of a jumping jack. Do this twenty to thirty times.

These calisthenics are what we'll call *mobility* exercises. They are intended to move your joints through a range of motion, but not necessarily build strength. Later in the book, you'll learn many more activities like these that can help break up long periods of sitting. We'll also discuss process models that can make getting out of your chair a pleasurable and productive habit. In all cases, these will be activities that come naturally to programmers.

For now, try to fill five minutes of every hour with some standing, walking, or the exercises just discussed—those five minutes can have profound effects on your health. But if you're going to use standing as part of these breaks, you have to make sure it's safe.

3.2 Standing Up for the Truth

Standing desks have grown in popularity in the last few years, but it's certainly not their first appearance in offices. They were used by clerks, draftsmen, and bankers as far back as the nineteenth century. Some schools at the time even provided them for students.[6]

Many standing-desk-users of old were standing for reasons that we now know to be invalid. They were often concerned about crushing their abdominal organs or developing kyphosis (a hunchback). None of these concerns were based on scientific evidence. Yet most programmers are making the same mistake by not considering the real impact of standing while working.

According to the research of Dr. Alan Hedge, the benefits of standing must be balanced against its potential dangers.[7] Dr. Hedge is a professor of design and environmental analysis at Cornell University and a leading researcher of workplace ergonomics as it affects people's health. Despite doing numerous field studies with standing workstations, he hasn't found any significant evidence to support the widespread benefits to office workers.

To make things worse, Dr. Hedge claims that standing can dramatically increase a person's risk of developing carotid atherosclerosis (constriction of the carotid artery) because of the additional load on the circulatory system. Standing also increases the risk of developing varicose veins and blood clots—the latter of which can be deadly. In fact, if you fall into any of the categories in the following list, then you should avoid standing desks altogether because of the increased risk of developing a blood clot.

- You have high blood pressure
- You have high cholesterol
- You have diabetes

---

6. *School Hygiene [WK12]*
7. *Sitting or Standing for Computer Work — Does a Negative-Tilt Keyboard Tray Make a Difference? [HJAR05]*

- You use tobacco products
- You're pregnant
- You have a family history of blood clots
- You have hypercoagulability

Dr. Hedge has also found that the performance of many fine motor skills decrease when people are standing. You can test this right now, but you'll need someone to help you.

Once you've found a partner, face each other and stand about one arm's length apart. Then hold your hands up against the other person's hands such that each of your fingers is touching one of your partner's fingers (your left hand to the other person's right hand and visa versa). Have your partner randomly apply pressure to one finger and see how quickly you can press back. Now repeat the test while sitting instead of standing—you'll probably react more quickly this time.

Dr. Hedge's studies have shown that the decrease in dexterity while standing can even lead to pain. That's because most people tend to become tired and lean to one side or the other after standing for an extended period of time. This compromises posture, which increases the pressure on many joints, including the hips, ankles, and even wrists.

That's the bad news. But standing isn't all doom and gloom.

Despite Dr. Hedge's disconcerting findings, many researchers still advocate the use of standing desks. That's because there are studies that show promising signs of the potential benefits of standing. For example, the average person burns an extra fifty calories per hour when standing instead of sitting—that's not a lot, but it's more than inconsequential. In fact, the energy used while standing is considered nonexercise activity thermogenesis (NEAT), which plays a significant role in how our bodies regulate weight gain.

Are you fidgeting while reading this book? Maybe you're bouncing your knee. If so, then you're burning NEAT calories. NEAT is the energy our bodies expend during everyday life (that is, anything that is not exercise or sleep). Some seemingly trivial activities, such as cleaning the house, can increase a person's metabolic rate substantially. An increase in NEAT is unlikely to make a noticeable different on its own, but there is evidence to suggest that it plays a role in how we maintain our bodyweight or develop obesity.[8]

---

8.   *Non-exercise activity thermogenesis (NEAT) [Lev02]*

Will standing give you six-pack abs? No, but it might help you regulate your bodyweight after reaching a diet goal.

Another advantage of standing is that it's not sitting. This simple fact means that standing can reduce your risk for many of the diseases we discussed in the previous section. To be specific, standing forces the muscles in your legs and abdomen to contract more often than when you sit. This is important because when those muscles don't contract, your body suppresses the production of an enzyme in the skeletal muscle called lipoprotein lipase (LPL).[9] LPL plays an important role in transporting fats and breaking down fat-carrying molecules in the bloodstream. When the enzyme is not available, fatty materials can build up on the walls of your arteries.

As with everything in life, there are two sides to this coin. Standing has good and bad consequences. Thus, your goal when using a standing desk is to take advantage of the benefits while mitigating the factors that Dr. Hedge warns of. Here are a few guidelines you can follow:

Change Often Dr. Hedge recommends sitting for no longer than twenty minutes, but you shouldn't stand for longer than twenty minutes at a time, either. The key is to keep your body moving—adjust your position often and take many breaks.

Change If It Hurts If you've been standing for a few minutes and your legs or feet are starting to hurt, then sit down. Likewise, if you've been sitting and your back or shoulders start to hurt, then stand up. Neither of these positions should be painful, so the best position is the one in which you are able to hold good posture.

Walk When You Can If at all possible, walk instead of stand. This will eliminate most of the risks associated with standing and burn even more calories (about 100 per hour). In general, the risks associated with standing are related to immobility. If you can find ways of moving while standing, you'll be better off. An excellent time to try this is during phone calls.

Use the Right Footwear Most people will want a sturdy shoe with a solid sole (that is, not flip-flops). This will prevent the arches of your feet from collapsing and inducing pain after standing for a while. You'll also want a soft floor surface. This is often achieved by placing a large gel mat under the standing area of your desk.

---

9. *Lipoprotein particle distribution and skeletal muscle lipoprotein lipase acitivty after acute exercise [HMZG12]*

Those are great guidelines, but you need to make sure it's feasible to follow them. If it's difficult to switch between sitting and standing then you probably won't do it. After we've discussed your next goal, we'll build a better desk.

Goal 4

Check your blood pressure

If you have high blood pressure, then it is not recommended that you use a standing desk. For that reason, you should get your blood pressure checked before trying one out, but it's not the only reason you should get it checked. Your blood pressure can be an early indicator of many health problems.

Blood pressure is the force of blood against the arteries created by the heart as it pumps blood through the circulatory system. Like all muscles, the heart alternates between contracting and relaxing, and blood pressure varies between these two states. That's why we measure it with two numbers: systolic blood pressure (the pressure when the heart contracts), and diastolic blood pressure (the pressure when the heart relaxes). Overall blood pressure is expressed as systolic over diastolic (for example, 120/85).

Most pharmacies are equipped with machines that allow customers to measure their own blood pressure. This is probably the quickest way to get a reading. You can also buy a device that hooks up to you iPhone if you like tech gadgets.[10] But a trained professional, such as the nurse at your family doctor's office, will usually give you the most reliable reading.

The following table provides an overview of how blood pressure corresponds to risk levels.

Sys.	Dia.	Stage	Health Risk
210	120	Hypertension stage 4	Very severe
180	110	Hypertension stage 3	Severe
160	100	Hypertension stage 2	Moderate
140	90	Hypertension stage 1	Mild
130	90	Normal	Low
120	85	Normal	Low

---

10. http://www.withings.com/en/bloodpressuremonitor

Sys.	Dia.	Stage	Health Risk
110	75	Low	Low
90	60	Low	Moderate
60	40	Hypotension	Severe
50	33	Hypotension	Very severe

Get your blood pressure checked as soon as you can. It's also a good idea to recheck it every now and again. This will alert you to any possible health issues.

3.3 Enhancing Your Workstation

To answer the question posed in this chapter's title, we should not bid adieu to our chairs. Instead, we should be aware of the health risks they present and learn how to account for them. Unfortunately, there's a good chance your current workstation is preventing you from doing this.

How many different positions does your desk allow you to work in? Probably only one or two at the most. But a good workstation should allow for at least three positions. You might expect a desk like that to cost a fortune (they certainly exist), but you can achieve the same result with a few simple enhancements to your existing desk. It will take a little do-it-yourself (DIY) initiative, but you can create a standing desk that is versatile enough to keep you healthy.

> **Tip 4** A good workstation should allow you to work from at least three different positions.

Standing desks come in many shapes and sizes, but there are a few guidelines you should follow whether you're enhancing a existing desk, building a new standing desk of your own design, or just buying a prefabricated desk.

Rule 1: Make It Adjustable According to Dr. Hedge's research, fixed-height desks are most likely to cause discomfort. They've also been shown to reduce productivity. Ideally, your desk should be electronically height-adjustable so that you can vary the height throughout the day. At the least, try to get one that can be adjusted easily.

The preferred height for a standing desk is elbow level. This will allow your arms to bend at a ninety-degree angle when typing and prevent your wrists from flexing. But be sure to elevate your monitor above the desk.

It will need to sit higher than the tabletop to prevent your neck from flexing.

Rule 2: Allow for Movement Make sure that your desk allows room for you to move. There should be space below the desk for your legs to swing, and room to your sides so that you can move laterally. Because of the dangers that standing desks create, it's critical that you move as much as possible when using them.

An even better solution is to have a walking desk. If you can integrate a treadmill into your workstation you'll avoid most of the dangers we've discussed. However, treadmill desks have been shown to further reduce fine motor skills, which means you might struggle with productivity.[11] Cycling desks are also available (but swimming desks haven't hit the market yet).

Jessica Allen, a graphic designer at Engine Yard, has built several standing desks for herself and her coworkers. She even presented the results of her work at a software conference in 2012.[12] Jessica recommends three basic models of DIY desk:

Free Standing Desk That's *free* as in *free beer*. You might be able to convert an existing desk by putting cinder blocks under it. Or you can build a new desk from found objects—use a door as a tabletop, or bookshelves as legs. The disadvantage of the free desk is that it's not usually very configurable or adjustable, so it's not recommended.

Ikea-Hack Standing Desk A slightly more expensive (but still cheap) option is to buy the basic components of a desk from a furniture store like Ikea. Many of these stores sell adjustable-height legs that can be fixed to the bottom of tabletops, TV stands, or anything else you find for sale. The following figure shows Jessica's version.

Industrial-Strength Standing Desk Jessica's most robust standing desk used industrial-strength materials. The legs were cut from steel piping and the tabletop was solid oak. She also elevated the monitor with an additional piece of wood, which gave the desk a nice aesthetic. Unfortunately, this desk was not adjustable. However, other DIYers have experimented with using automotive scissor jacks to add an adjustable element to their desks. This fits well with the industrial appeal of Jessica's model.

---

11. *Productivity of transcriptionists using a treadmill desk [TL11]*
12. http://www.confreaks.com/videos/1075-cascadiaruby2012-diy-standing-desk-make-a-custom-rad-looking-standing-desk

On Jessica's blog, you can read more about her desks and how she built them.[13]

Figure 9—Jessica Allen working from her Ikea-hack desk

It's difficult to design a DIY desk that is height-adjustable—especially one that's easy to adjust. But there are other ways to achieve the variable positioning that a height-adjustable desk allows for—you just have to change your perch.

For example, you don't have to switch desks when you sit down. Try using a stool, drafting chair, or other high chair with your standing-height desk. This will make it faster for you to stand up and make it easier to sit down when you're done. It will also make it easier for you to take walks.

Another way to keep moving while standing is to use a balance board like the one shown in the following figure. These simple devices require that you balance your weight evenly on both feet to keep the board level. Using one of these at your standing desk will create more muscle contractions and potentially reduce the health risks associated with standing.

---

13. http://spacekat.github.com/blog/2012/07/26/diy-standing-desk/

Figure 10—Wobble board (a variant of the balance board)

No studies have been done specifically on the use of balance boards at computer workstations, but they have proven to be effective training tools for athletes who want to prevent certain injuries. They've also been used to improve cognitive function in adults.[14] The most interesting claim, although still unproven, is that balance boards boost creativity. It's been suggested that this is due to the enhanced use of both sides of the brain, which results from using both sides of the body to balance. While the connection to creativity is unproven, it has been shown that balance boards enhance the use of both sides of the brain, and that's why they're often used to rehabilitate stroke patients.[15]

But even with a balance board, you have to sit down sometimes. When you do, consider using an exercise ball like the one in the following figure. These large, inflatable, bouncy spheres have become popular chairs in the last few years. A number of studies have revealed minor benefits of sitting on an exercise ball, but there are warnings to consider, as well.

---

14. *Relationship between Improvement in Cognitive Function by Balance Board Training and Postural Control Adaptability in the Elderly [FSM05]*
15. *Effectiveness of a Wii balance board-based system (eBaViR) for balance rehabilitation: a pilot randomized clinical trial in patients with acquired brain injury [Gil11]*

The weights in this image provide a size reference. Swiss balls range in diameter from 14 to 34 inches (35 to 85 cm), but the larger end of the spectrum is best for sitting.

Figure 11—Swiss ball (aka exercise ball)

In 2008 a group of researchers in Amsterdam reported that women who sat on an exercise ball for ten minutes while performing typing activities experienced as much as seventy-eight percent more muscle activation than subjects who sat in office chairs. They also found that arm flexion was reduced, which could help avoid shoulder and neck pain. The researchers concluded that the advantages of sitting on an exercise ball outweighed the disadvantages.

However, not all research has been as positive. In 2006, a group at the University of Waterloo in Canada had subjects sit on a ball and work for one hour. They found that participants had increased muscle activation in the trunk and lumbar spine, but the changes were very small compared to subjects who sat in office chairs. They also reported that most subjects complained of back pain by the end of the study.

Unfortunately, most of the research done with exercise balls has been short-term. It's likely that the initial discomfort the subjects reported would subside after using the ball for a while. It's also unclear if the typing tasks the subjects performed were comparable to programming. The participants probably did far more typing than the average programmer, who spends a disproportionate amount of time thinking.

The takeaway from these experiments is that using an exercise ball as a chair can be healthy, but only when it's used for short periods. In fact, you probably want to use it for only ten to twenty minutes at a time. That's a common theme in this chapter. No single position is perfect. The healthiest workstation is one where you can sit, stand, balance, and bounce a little bit every day.

Your next goal for this chapter is to enhance your workstation so that changing your position is possible.

Goal 5

Enhance your workstation

The best desk position is the one you aren't in right now—movement is key to being healthy. If your workstation doesn't allow for you to change position, then it's an obstacle. Use the advice in this chapter to enhance your workstation so that it facilitates at least three different positions.

3.4 Retrospective

In your next retrospective, you'll need to look closely at health-blockers—your workstation may be one of them, and your corresponding goal is to fix it. You'll also need to get your blood pressure checked to make sure a standing desk is safe for you to use. As before, write down these goals (see Figure 12, *Goals for standing*, on page 44).

In addition to setting some new goals, you've learned about another item on your daily checklist. You need to move your body as much as possible throughout the day. In general, you should aim to get at least five minutes of movement every hour. If you can't get away from your desk, try doing some of the sitting calisthenics presented earlier. You should also change positions every twenty minutes. If you've been sitting, then stand up. If you've been standing, then sit down.

Figure 12—Goals for standing

DAILY CHECKLIST
☒ PLAN: Healthy stand-up
☒ WALK: 10,000 steps/day with 20 mins. brisk
☒ MOVE: 5 mins./hr. Change position every 20 mins.
☐ EAT: 5 servings of fruits or vegetables
☐ BUILD: 5 bodyweight exercises

Later in the book you'll learn about more exercises that can add some variety to this action item, but it's important to remember that doing these exercises and improving your workstation are only part of your healthy lifestyle. A standing desk is not a substitute for aerobic activity and it isn't going to help you lose weight. You'll need to refactor your diet for that.

Even if losing weight is not one of your goals, an unhealthy diet can kill you. In the next chapter, we'll discuss how food can affect risk factors for many of the same diseases that exercise helps prevent. If you're serious about getting healthy, you'll need a holistic plan that includes good nutrition.

Act On It

- Take a five-minute break every hour.

- Work from at least three different positions every day.

- Don't stay in any one position for longer than twenty minutes.

- Do some mobility exercises from your desk while you work.

- Regularly check your blood pressure. Learn what kind of measurement you should expect, and watch for significant changes over time.

- Keep more than one kind of chair in your office—a regular office chair, an exercise ball, a drafting stool, or even a cycling desk.

CHAPTER 4

Agile Dieting

As a high-school wrestler, I had some unusual eating habits. I weighed my food, ate raw potatoes, and kept my portions very small. But things got really strange in my senior year when I lost a spot on the varsity team to a talented young sophomore. To stay on the squad, I had to cut 25 pounds (11 kg) and compete in the 135-pound (61 kg) weight division. Within a month I had shed more than fifteen percent of my body mass.

I did well at first and even won an important match against a state finalist from the previous year. But 135 pounds was not a natural weight for me and I struggled to maintain it. I would usually skip breakfast, have no more than a bag of dry Cheerios for lunch, and eat just enough dinner to keep my parents from being suspicious. Eventually, the lack of nutrition caught up with me and I finished the season with an abysmal record.

My mistake in high school was letting my ambition cloud my judgment. I was driven to extremes by goals that seemed important at the time. I didn't realize that I was wreaking havoc on my health.

As programmers, we drive ourselves to unhealthy extremes for the sake of different but equally powerful goals. We might rush to the drive-thru on our way home from work, eat at restaurants every day with our coworkers, or grab candy in the office because we don't have time for lunch. In all cases, we're developing bad habits. If you want to correct those habits, you must become aware of them.

In this chapter you'll learn how to change your eating routines to combat the external pressures you face in the software industry. You'll learn the real causes of weight gain and you'll learn about solutions that are proven to work. We'll take a close look at your dietary habits and use the latest science to create an eating plan that's personalized for you.

Customizing your diet is important because every person's needs are different. There is no one-size-fits-all diet. Some people like grapefruit and some don't. Some people want to lose weight and some people need to gain weight. As a result, finding the best diet requires experimentation and iteration—a so-called agile diet.

The agile diet isn't itself really a diet plan. Instead, it's a way of creating a diet that suits your particular health needs. That's why this chapter will focus less on losing weight than on correcting the unhealthy aspects of your diet. Remember as you read this chapter that there two kinds of diets: the one that helps you lose weight, and the one you follow for the rest of your life. They don't have to be the same, and it's especially important that the latter be enjoyable.

In some cases, the issues driving an unhealthy diet are the result of psychological or emotional trauma, which requires treatment prescribed by a doctor. But most of the time, bad habits are to blame for the unhealthiness. To change those habits, you'll need to learn how to eat consciously.

4.1 An Iterative Approach to Dieting

If you're already using a diet that you enjoy and it's working, then keep with it. But you may be disappointed to learn that most fad diets work by tricking you into eating fewer calories because that's the only proven way to lose weight. Usually this is the result of forcing you to eliminate a particular kind of food. But a successful diet must also provide a structured system of eating, which is almost as important as cutting calories.

So here's your next action item: start a diet and don't stick with it. You read that correctly. Pick a popular diet plan, use it for about two weeks and then try a different diet. Many people enjoy systems like the raw-food, slow-carb, Paleolithic (aka paleo), and vegan diets. These plans can be healthy if you keep them balanced, and in the next section we'll discuss how to do that.

For now, don't even cut back on calories—just restrict what you eat to the system defined by your chosen diet. You *will* need to make sure you get the right nutrients, which we'll discuss in Section 4.2, *Balanced Nutrition Over Idiosyncratic Diets*, on page 50, and eat enough calories, which we'll talk about in Section 4.4, *Counting Calories Over Following Trends*, on page 55. But the important thing is that you'll be using a system and learning how to eat consciously.

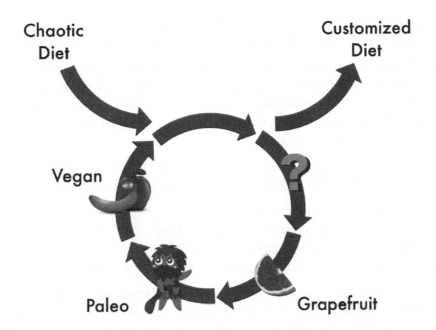

Start right now. Don't be afraid of failing—you'll have a chance to reassess and adapt in two weeks. After a few iterations you'll figure out what works and what doesn't. Eventually, you may even want to cherry-pick aspects from each diet to create something sustainable. Mixing up your diet this way will keep things interesting and help you learn what works best. That's what Chad Fowler does.

"I'm on a slow-carb/paleo diet," says Chad. "It's a hybrid. When I lost all my weight initially, I did a standard 'eat five balanced small things a day.' But it wasn't sustainable." Chad has been managing his weight for several years, and in that time he's learned enough about his body and his metabolism that he's been able to design a diet plan that's customized for his needs. Some things work for him and others don't. "A low-carb diet makes my brain stop working. It makes me feel bad and sluggish," he explains. "But these slow-carb diets don't." Getting to this point required Chad to play around a lot.

"I decided I would experiment and do exactly the slow-carb diet for all of January 2011," Chad recounts. "The next month I switched to paleo. They're both different from low-carb diets because you actually get to eat carbs, but they're not fast-processing carbs. With slow carbs, the primary staple is beans and you don't eat any fruits. With paleo, you eat fruits but you don't eat beans. What I've done now is combine them." If you want to learn more about the diets Chad is using, check out two books he recommends: *The 4-Hour Body: An Uncommon Guide to Rapid Fat-Loss, Incredible Sex, and Becoming*

Superhuman [Fer10] and *The Primal Blueprint: Reprogram your genes for effortless weight loss, vibrant health, and boundless energy [Sis12]*.

Chad's success is probably due more to the structure that his diets provide than the science behind them. That would explain why switching between diets has provided just as much success for him as sticking to any one particular plan. Chad acknowledges this power, too. "It goes back to having a system," he says.

As with software, your system should be agile. If there were a manifesto for the agile diet, it would incorporate the following principles:

- Individual tastes over predefined menus
- Balanced nutrition over idiosyncratic diets
- Counting calories over following trends
- Responding to your environment over sticking to a diet plan

That is, while there may be some value in the items on the right, we value the items on the left more. As we work our way through this chapter, we'll discuss the differences between each of these and how you can use them to structure a personalized diet. Testing out fad diets is a good way to start, but you have to ensure that what you are eating is nutritious.

4.2 Balanced Nutrition Over Idiosyncratic Diets

Paleolithic humans were not necessarily healthy. In fact, they were probably malnourished,[1] which contributed to their very short lifespans. Why, then, would you try to follow a diet that was similar to theirs?

If a Paleolithic diet helps you control your weight, makes you happy, and keeps you satisfied, then by all means do it. But you have to make sure you're getting the right nutrients—scurvy won't make you happy (although you're more likely to end up with heart disease than scurvy from the paleo diet[2]). The paleo diet isn't the only diet that you have to watch out for—most fashionable diet trends tend to be idiosyncratic and unbalanced.

Creating a nutritious diet is actually pretty simple. Most health organizations (including the CDC, the World Health Organization, the U.S. Department of Health and Human Services, the U.S. Department of Agriculture, and the National Health Service of the UK[3]) recommend that a healthy daily diet have roughly the following composition:

---

1. *Hunter-gatherer diets - a different perspective [Mil00]*
2. http://health.usnews.com/best-diet/paleo-diet
3. http://www.nhs.uk/Livewell/Goodfood/Pages/eatwell-plate.aspx

- 30% fruits and vegetables
- 30% grains and starches
- 16% lean protein (meat, fish, eggs, and beans)
- 16% milk and dairy
- 8% fatty and sugary foods

Almost every fad diet violates one of these categories, and that's exactly why it's a good idea to rotate through them. Our bodies are very good at dealing with nutritional deficiencies over short periods of time (which is why most fad diets work only in the short term), but in the long term we need to ensure that our diets are well-rounded. Otherwise you'll end up like I did at the end of my wrestling season.

One good way to ensure a healthy balance without over-analyzing every meal is the five-a-day plan, which all of the organizations mentioned previously as well as many other groups around the world recommend.[4] The five-a-day plan suggests that you get five servings of fruits or vegetables every day—for example, half of a grapefruit with breakfast, a fruit smoothie with lunch (this counts as two servings if it's 150ml and made with 100 percent fruit or vegetable), an apple as a snack, and two spears of broccoli with dinner. Most fad diets will allow for this in one way or another, which makes it a good daily heuristic for balancing the nutritional composition of your meals. We'll add this to your daily checklist at the end of the chapter.

> **Tip 5** Eat five servings of fruits or vegetables each day to ensure your diet is balanced.

You can find a list of fruit and vegetable serving examples in Section A2.1, *Examples of Fruit/Vegetable Servings*, on page 195. But even with this guide, getting your five a day can be difficult—especially when those fruits and vegetables are not available. If that's the case, try replacing the candy bowl in your office with fresh apples, or swap the soft drinks for smoothies. If you don't like certain vegetables, try dipping them in a little ranch dressing. The key is to make them available.

There will come a time when you want to gorge yourself on candy. But the agile diet will help you overcome these cravings by teaching you how to eat consciously. That's important because the only thing preventing you from eating healthily is your brain.

---

4.   http://www.who.int/mediacentre/news/notes/2004/np17/en/, http://www.nhs.uk/LiveWell/5ADAY/Pages/5ADAY-home.aspx

Meatless Monday

One approach to dieting that has gained a lot of attention (for both weight loss and general health) is the whole-foods, plant-based diet promoted by Doctors Caldwell Esselstyn, T. Colin Campbell, and Joel Fuhrman in *Forks Over Knives: The Plant-Based Way to Health* [S E11] and *Eat to Live: The Amazing Nutrient-Rich Program for Fast and Sustained Weight Loss, Revised Edition [Fuh12]*. They essentially advocate for a vegan diet and provide a great number of clinical studies that suggest eating meat isn't good for your health. Dr. Fuhrman summarizes his plan with the following equation:

$$Health = Nutrients\,/\,Calories$$

That is, your diet should favor the foods with the highest nutrient-to-calorie ratio. Fruits and vegetables are at the top of his list (especially leafy greens like kale and spinach), whereas animal products measure very low.

These doctors do have their critics, though. Most health organizations recommend at least some dairy in a person's diet, and even Dr. Fuhrman acknowledges that the only way to get sufficient levels of calcium and vitamin D on his plan is to take a dietary supplement.

I have tried to follow a vegetarian and even a vegan diet many times. But I usually fall victim to some combination of cheese and sausage (I'm originally from Wisconsin). I've learned from these attempts that you can take cheese away from me when you pry it from my cold dead hands—but I don't need a lot of it to be happy. As a result, I've reduced my consumption of animal products to less than ten percent of my diet. That satisfies me, makes me happy, and actually aligns well with most of the studies cited by these doctors.

Meatless Monday is a great way to test a diet like mine.[a] This program recommends going meat-free for just one day a week to reduce your consumption of animal products by fifteen percent. Many meat-loving celebrity chefs, including Giada De Laurentiis and Mario Batali, have signed on.

Simple rules, like a Meatless Monday, can make your diet plan much easier to follow.

---

a.   http://www.meatlessmonday.com/

4.3   Eating Your Brains Out

Here's an activity you can try at home or in your office. Buy a food item you consider to be a dessert, like a candy bar or a cookie. Put the food right behind your keyboard while you work (if you haven't eaten it yet). Now try to get something important done. There's a good chance you'll be distracted.

Don't feel bad. You are wired to behave this way. It's called *attentional bias*, and many studies have shown that this mechanism allows food to distract us from other "neutral stimulus" activities.[5,6] It affects all people, regardless of their weight.

If you are able to overcome those first bouts of desire, you might find that it gets easier. That's because you are probably busy writing code, which activates the same reward system in your brain. It's been shown that the creative problem-solving process produces dopamine, which is the same chemical that rewards your brain when you eat.[7]

The next time you get the urge to grab a snack, trying solving a puzzle instead. There's a good chance the craving will subside (unless you are truly in need of food, in which case you should eat). When it happens again, try going for a walk or playing a game. The important thing is that you'll be interrupting your food cravings, which will allow you to ask yourself, *Was I really hungry or was it just a bad habit?*

Let's try to answer this question right now. Grab a pen and paper and write down everything you ate today. Look at each item and ask yourself, *Did I eat this because I was hungry, or did I eat it because it was there?* Too often we eat because food is readily available or social norms make it convenient. The best way to overcome these challenges is to be prepared. Try using the flowchart like the one in Figure 13, *A flowchart for eating consciously eatingflowchart eatingconsciously*, on page 54 each time you get the urge to eat. By systematically confronting your cravings, you'll learn to eat consciously. This is important whether you're trying to lose weight or gain weight, but it's especially important when trying to combat overeating.

Overeating, however, is not necessarily characterized by weight gain. Instead, scientists are starting to recognize a behavior that can best be described as a loss of control for the sake of food. Dr. David Kessler, the former commissioner of the Food and Drug Administration (FDA), calls this *conditioned hypereating*. It's "conditioned" because it's an automatic response to food cues, and "hyper" because the eating is excessive. The most surprising thing about conditioned hypereaters is that not all of them are obese or even overweight.[8]

---

5. *Selective attention to food-related stimuli in hunger: are attentional biases specific to emotional and psychopathological states, or are they also found in normal drive states? [MBHL98]*

6. *Eating Disorders and Attentional Bias: A Review [Fau02]*

7. *Frontotemporal And Dopaminergic Control Of Idea Generation And Creative Drive [Fla05]*

8. *The End of Overeating: Taking Control of the Insatiable American Appetite [Kes09]*

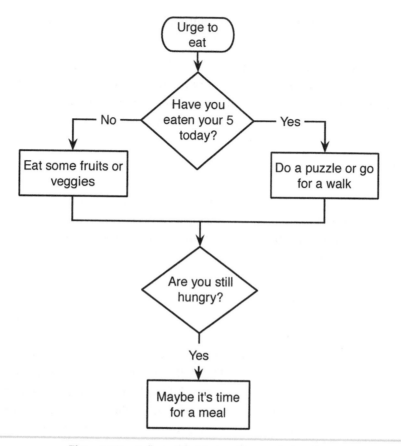

Figure 13—A flowchart for eating consciously

But in the worst cases, eating is more than a habit—it's an addiction. A lot of research is being done in this area and as many as twenty-eight papers on food addiction were published in 2011 (according to the National Library of Medicine database).[9] Despite this, undiagnosed eating disorders have become frighteningly common—especially for men.[10] Anorexia is far more prevalent among women, but binge eating affects men and women almost equally.[11]

The most surprising thing about conditioned hypereaters is that not all of them are obese or even overweight.

---

9. http://www.ncbi.nlm.nih.gov/pubmed/
10. http://well.blogs.nytimes.com/2012/08/13/binge-eating-among-men-steps-out-of-the-shadows
11. *Why men should be included in research on binge eating: results from a comparison of psychosocial impairment in men and women [SBWS11]*

The biggest difficulty, especially for men, is that binging is not usually seen as a problem. When a male college student eats an entire pizza and downs it with a two-liter bottle of Coke, the psychological aspect of why he's doing it is not usually considered. Even worse, binge eating is glamorized in popular media. Entire TV shows are dedicated to people who travel around the country and binge. There is even a televised hot-dog-eating competition each 4th of July on what should be a *sports* channel.

How much food does your body really need? It's an important question because the answer can have a dramatic effect on your life.

4.4 Counting Calories Over Following Trends

In 1987, John Walker was struggling with the same internal conflict Chad Fowler faced in Tokyo. John is a brilliant programmer and the founder of Autodesk, a multinational corporation that sells design software such as AutoCAD, but he couldn't seem to manage his own weight.

John had been a self-described "fat person" since grade school. He'd lost some weight in the 1970s, but put it back on within a year. Eventually John realized he'd been approaching the whole thing from the wrong angle. He is an engineer, so the best way to think of weight loss was as an engineering problem.

John believes that the human body is like a rubber bag. Calories go in as food while calories come out as exercise, metabolism, and various other stuff. If the number of calories that go in is greater than the number of calories that come out, you'll put on weight. But if you put fewer calories into the rubber bag, you'll lose weight.

This concept may seem painfully obvious, but for many years it was not well understood. Scientists struggled to accept that the human body's homeostatic feedback loop, which is really good at regulating body temperature and blood pressure, seems to be broken when it comes to weight management. They suspected instead that obesity was due to genetics, the way we eat (time of day and speed), diet composition, metabolic defects, or maybe lack of physical activity. But in recent years, studies have shown unequivocally that the leading cause of obesity is caloric intake.

John's plan, which he wrote about extensively in his book *The Hacker's Diet* [Wal05], was to engineer what he ate so that he consumed fewer calories than he used. As it turns out, very small changes—such as cutting 100 calories per day (about the same as a can of soda)—can have very profound effects. At the other end of the spectrum, research shows that adding 400 calories to your daily diet is enough to add two pounds (1 kg) of bodyweight every three weeks.[12]

Let's see how your rubber bag is doing. The first step is to figure out how many calories your body uses each day. In scientific terms, this is your *basal metabolic rate* (BMR). The most accurate way to measure BMR is with the Mifflin-St Jeor equation.[13] The equation, as defined for men, is shown here in Imperial and metric units, respectively:

$$BMR = (4.5 * mass(lb.)) + (16 * height(in.)) - (5 * age) + 5$$
$$BMR = (10 * mass(kg)) + (6.25 * height(cm)) - (5 * age) + 5$$

For women, the equations are as follows:

$$BMR = (4.5 * mass(lb.)) + (16 * height(in.)) - (5 * age) - 161$$
$$BMR = (10 * mass(kg)) + (6.25 * height(cm)) - (5 * age) - 161$$

Thus, a 30-year-old woman who weighs 125 pounds (57 kg) and is 65 inches (165 cm) tall would have a BMR of 1,591 calories per day.

But this number accounts for only the calories you burn sitting in your office chair all day. You'll have to incorporate any calories burned during physical activity. If you've been following along with recommendations in the previous chapters, you can add the following numbers to your BMR to get a more-accurate estimate of the calories you use each day:

- 200 calories for every 20 minutes of walking

- 50 calories for every hour spent standing instead of sitting

Calculate your number and write it down—write it big and bright on your whiteboard. Memorize it. This number can make you healthier and happier and can extend your life if you use it wisely. For most people, this means keeping the number of calories you eat within some Gaussian distribution around your BMR after adjusting for calories burned during exercise. But if you have a goal of losing weight, you'll actually have to eat less than this number.

Regardless, you need to know how many calories you eat on a typical day, and that's why your goal for this chapter is Goal 6, *Count your calories for one day*, on page 57. That's right, just one day. If that day is typical of most days, you'll have a good benchmark from which to derive your diet plan. Once you've done this, the real work can begin.

---

12. *The End of Overeating: Taking Control of the Insatiable American Appetite [Kes09]*
13. *A new predictive equation for resting energy expenditure in healthy individuals [MJHS90]*

Goal 6

Count your calories for one day

You can start by writing down calorie numbers next to each item on the list you created earlier. But there's a good chance you'll get it wrong. Studies have shown that most people are very inaccurate when counting calories. They don't include snacks, they feel ashamed, and ultimately they underestimate.

In one case, two neuroscientists at Kennesaw State University in Georgia had people photograph their food before they recorded it in a diary.[14] They found that the majority of participants had substantially underestimated their food intake—sometimes by an entire meal. Other studies have found that subjects underestimated their consumption by an average of thirteen percent.[15]

These findings can probably be explained by the same thing that causes us to overeat in the first place: we eat subconsciously. Eating is driven by cues, which are followed by routines that reward us. Those rewards turn out to be very powerful and drive us to do some unusual things. For that reason, you should start to change your eating habits before trying to count your calories. This will help you become aware of exactly how much food you are eating.

If you've already started your agile diet and you've begun to stick with a particular plan, then you are well on your way. Once you know how to interrupt your food cravings and plan your meals, you'll be ready to count. You may find it helpful to use a smartphone app or a diary. Several tools like this are listed at http://healthyprog.com.

Because you'll be counting calories for only one day, try to make it representative of your typical daily consumption. Then you can use the result as a baseline for the rest of your diet.

4.5 Adjusting Your Caloric Intake

After you know the difference between the number of calories you eat in a day and the number of calories you use in a day, you can start to make adjustments. If the net result is positive, then you'll need to cut calories from your diet. If you're overweight you'll actually need to go below the number of

---

14. *Food intake and meal patterns of weight-stable and weight-gaining persons [Pea02]*
15. *Evaluation of long-term dietary intakes of adults consuming self-selected diets [KKJM84]*

calories you use. Unfortunately, this is an uphill battle according to the research of Dr. Rudy Leibel, a molecular geneticist at Columbia University.

Dr. Leibel, who you may have seen in the HBO documentary series *The Weight of the Nation*, believes that obesity is the result of very small differences in the balance of energy intake and energy expenditure that are extrapolated over long periods of time—like years.[16] Dr. Leibel asserts that this is precisely the reason most diets fail.

In one study, Dr. Leibel and his colleagues measured the energy expenditure of obese subjects who lost ten percent of their bodyweight.[17] They found that these individuals, regardless of their sex, experienced metabolic alterations that made it difficult to maintain the lower weight. On average, the subjects used fifteen percent less energy than a person whose normal weight and body composition were the same as theirs. This meant that for the subjects to hold their weight at ten percent below their normal weight, they actually had to continually decrease their caloric intake. Even worse, the patients developed a sense of hunger or dysphoria that promoted an increase in food consumption, further widening the gap between energy output and intake.

For that reason, you should cut calories slowly. The recommendation of Dr. Judith Salerno, the author of *The Weight of the Nation: Surprising Lessons About Diets, Food, and Fat from the Extraordinary Series from HBO Documentary Films [HSM12]*, is to cut just 100 calories per day, which can be as simple as cutting out soda or any of the other examples shown in Figure 14, *Examples of 100-calorie servings serving sizes100-calorie examples*, on page 59. But you don't necessarily have to give anything up. You can replace whole milk or two-percent milk with skim or one-percent milk. If you have a bagel in the morning, try replacing it with oatmeal. At dinner, replace your twelve-ounce (340 g) steak with a ten-ounce (283 g) steak. Be creative, and you'll probably find that you don't even miss the calories.

After two weeks of adjusting to 100 fewer calories per day, try cutting another 100 calories. Do this until you've reached your target caloric intake. Reducing calories in small incremental steps is another important aspect of agile dieting. Your body needs time to acclimate to changes.

> Reducing calories in small incremental steps is an important aspect of agile dieting.

Sooner or later you're going to get hungry and want to eat more then you're supposed to for the day. It's the one thing you can count

---

16. *The Weight of the Nation: Surprising Lessons About Diets, Food, and Fat from the Extraordinary Series from HBO Documentary Films [HSM12]*
17. *Changes in Energy Expenditure Resulting from Altered Body Weight [LRH95]*

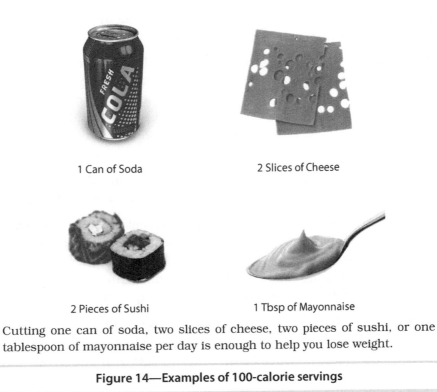

1 Can of Soda

2 Slices of Cheese

2 Pieces of Sushi

1 Tbsp of Mayonnaise

Cutting one can of soda, two slices of cheese, two pieces of sushi, or one tablespoon of mayonnaise per day is enough to help you lose weight.

Figure 14—Examples of 100-calorie servings

on as you're trying to change your eating habits. When that time comes, it's important to remember that fighting the urge to overeat is a biological challenge and not an absence of willpower. Regardless, you'll need to be prepared—you'll need to plan ahead.

4.6 Individual Tastes Over Predefined Menus

The best way to guarantee that a diet plan fails is to eat foods you don't like. A healthy diet isn't a short-term fix to an overeating problem—it's what you eat everyday for the rest of your life. It needs to be pleasant.

If you've been rotating through the fad diets listed earlier in the chapter, then you're off to a good start. But after a while, you'll probably want to settle into something on a long-term basis. The fad diets should have given you a good sense of what works, what's enjoyable, and what's sustainable, but they probably don't amount to something you want to do forever. Instead, you can use what you've learned from those diets to create your own set of rules.

Rules prevent us from eating chaotically. When there are no rules, we have little reason to avoid foods that are bad or that bust our calorie budget. Rules provide structure and a sort of top-down processing approach to our diet, which allows us to work our way down to the food from the rules.

As with getting started, the best way to add rules to your diet is through experimentation and iteration. For example, try eating only half of your next meal and then pay attention to how hungry you are thirty minutes later and ninety minutes later. If you are feeling real hunger, then make adjustments to the next meal. Iterate like this until you're able to create rules about the optimal portion size.

After you've experimented a little, you'll be able to plan a diet that is healthy and doesn't leave you hungry. A few tips that you can use are listed next.

Eat Foods That Satisfy You   The best way to prevent overeating is to prevent hunger, and the best way to prevent hunger is to eat foods that satisfy you. The problem with fatty, greasy, salty, and sugary foods is that they leave you hungry again after just a short while. Thus, it's important that you plan your diet around foods that fill you up and keep you satisfied.

Some studies have shown that protein is the most satisfying nutrient. Protein is digested at a rate of about four calories per minute, which is much slower than foods like sugar, which digests at rate of ten calories per minute. Whole grains are another source of satiating calories. Because these foods retain the tissue that is part of their architecture, they tend to digest more slowly, which keeps you from getting hungry again. Beware of fatty calories, though. They digest at about two calories per minute, but the body processes those signals very slowly, which causes us to keep eating high-fat foods. They are also very high in calories per gram.[18]

All that said, the most satiating foods are whole grains and lean protein. Try to eat brown rice instead of white rice, apples instead of applesauce, and chicken instead of processed foods built around meat fillers. When you've eaten foods that are satisfying, you'll be able to predict your hunger, which leads us to the next tip.

Schedule Your Eating   A meal that is the proper portion should keep most people satisfied for about four hours. A good snack should keep you satisfied for about two hours, but a sugary snack will satisfy you for only about an hour. As you plan your diet, schedule your meals and snacks so that you don't go hungry for long periods. Then, don't eat if it's not time to eat. When your schedule is black and white like this, it becomes

---

18. *The End of Overeating: Taking Control of the Insatiable American Appetite [Kes09]*

easier to avoid foods that are not a part of your plan. That kind of structure is a big factor in the next tip, too.

Make a List of Off-Limit Foods   Make a list of foods that you simply will not eat or drink (please put sugar-sweetened soda on this list). When you encounter these foods, don't eat them. You'll probably find that having clear rules like this makes the process of changing your habits much easier.

However, it's important that you tailor this list to your personal needs. If you absolutely love ice cream, then don't put ice cream on the list. That doesn't mean you can eat ice cream as a meal, but you shouldn't have to eliminate it because some fad diet told you to. If you eat foods like ice cream in moderation, your diet will make you happy.

Rehearse Your Diet   The habits that drive overeating begin with a cue. By now you've probably started to think about what those cues are. Maybe when you walk past the soda machine on your way to a meeting you instinctively feed it a dollar. Or maybe an invitation to lunch with coworkers leads to a double serving of fajitas.

Whatever those cues are, they aren't going to disappear. They'll still be there even after you've change your diet and routines. That's why mental rehearsal is so important.

Try rehearsing these cues in your mind. Think about what it feels like to encounter them, and imagine what you will do to avoid the bad routines that inevitably follow. This will make it much easier to resist those temptations when they actually happen.

Overeating is a biological challenge. It's not something that can be cured. Most people will have to constantly manage overeating for the rest of their lives, and that's why it's so important to have a plan for dealing with the cues that lead to bad habits—because those cues are not going away.

4.7   Retrospective

Eight million Americans struggle with a binge-eating disorder,[19] and as many as fifty-nine percent of Americans overeat.[20] If you fall into either of these two groups or you're consuming more calories than you use, then your health is in danger.

---

19. http://bedaonline.com/aboutBED.html
20. http://pewresearch.org/pubs/?ChartID=85

The best way to correct these unhealthy habits is to make incremental changes over several iterations—an agile approach to dieting. In this chapter you've learned how to recognize your eating habits, count your calories, and then cut back appropriately. That gives you a new goal for the next retrospective, Goal 6, *Count your calories for one day*, on page 57.

Once you've achieved your new goal, you'll have the information you need to set your target caloric intake. In addition to eating an appropriate number of calories, you'll need to ensure that your diet is balanced. The best way to do this is to eat five servings of fruits or vegetables a day, which is one of your daily checklist items.

DAILY CHECKLIST
- ☒ PLAN: Healthy stand-up
- ☒ WALK: 10,000 steps/day with 20 mins. brisk
- ☒ MOVE: 5 mins./hr. Change position every 20 mins.
- ☒ EAT: 5 servings of fruits or vegetables
- ☐ BUILD: 5 bodyweight exercises

You'll also want to ensure that you're not busting your caloric budget—but this has to be done on a case-by-case basis. Eating more than your BMR really depends on your personal needs. If you are maintaining weight, then you'll need to factor in exercise and eat an equivalent number of calories. But if you're trying to lose weight, you'll need to reduce calories.

Getting to your caloric target should be an incremental process of cutting 100 calories per day per iteration. If you're trying to lose weight, you'll actually need to eat fewer calories than you use, but you'll be able to come back up to your caloric target after you reach your goal weight. Be careful not to go too low, or you'll end up like I did at the end of my wrestling season. An appropriate target is to maintain a caloric intake no lower than 400 calories below your caloric output. If you're walking at least twenty minutes per day and getting out of your chair as much as possible, then this shouldn't be lower than your BMR.

Overeating and underexercising are the most common dangers you'll face as a programmer, but being healthy means more than watching your weight—it also means being pain-free. In the next three chapters, we'll discuss the most common physical ailments that programmers experience: headaches, back pain, and wrist pain.

Act On It

- Try a few different diets. Don't worry about failing; just give it a shot.

- Replace the candy bowl and soft drinks in your office with fruits, veggies, and smoothies.

- Make vegetables more desirable by dipping them in dressing or cheese.

- Try going meatless on Mondays.

- Calculate your BMR. Add in any calories burned from exercise. Become intimate with how many calories your body uses each day.

- Make some rules about your diet. You can exclude certain items, but you're more likely to succeed if your rules are inclusive. For example, try to eat five servings of fruits and vegetables each day.

- Don't count every calorie every day—you're unlikely to get it right. Instead, diligently count your calories for one day, and then estimate from that baseline by developing a point system or some other heuristic that works for you.

- Partition your customized diet plan: the diet you use to lose weight and the diet you practice for the rest of your life. Both should be pleasant.

- Iterate on your diet. Count calories slowly. Experiment with different portion sizes. Respond to your environment. Be agile.

CHAPTER 5

Preventing Headaches and Eye Strain

The peculiar imagery in the novel *Alice's Adventures in Wonderland* is often attributed to drug hallucinations, but it's more likely that the author, Lewis Carroll, was trying to capture the unusual visual experience associated with severe migraine headaches.[1] Carroll's unique depiction, however, may have been driven by more than just a desire to capture these images—the headaches may have been responsible for his creativity.

Many people claim that certain types of headaches can stimulate the imagination and inspire a creative process that leads to unique and revolutionary art. That's why Dr. Klaus Podoll, a physician at the Rheinisch-Westfaelische Technische Hochschule Aachen University in Germany, compiled a collection of illustrations and paintings created by migraine sufferers in his book *Migraine Art: The Migraine Experience from Within [PR09]*. It doesn't work for everyone, though.

Programming involves a lot of creativity, but not many software developers claim headaches improve their ability to write code. Instead, headaches are one of the leading productivity-killers for programmers—even when we're not hallucinating.

The visions Carroll experienced were the result of a change in perception as opposed to a malfunction of the eyes themselves, but many other kinds of headaches are directly related to conditions of the eyes. The most common for programmers is *Computer Vision Syndrome* (CVS), which affects roughly ninety percent of the people who spend three hours or more per day in front of a computer.[2]

---

1. *The Neurology of 'Alice' [Lar05]*
2. *Visual ergonomics in the workplace [Ans07]*

In this chapter we'll examine the conditions that lead to CVS, as well as many other kinds of headache triggers. We'll also discuss the general health of your eyes, which is relevant not only to headaches and eye strain but also to your overall health as a programmer. Many daily practices and even your computer's configuration might be damaging your eyes. Let's take a closer look.

5.1 Unit-Testing Your Vision

There is no substitute for a professional eye exam by an optometrist or ophthalmologist, and getting one is your goal for this chapter. In fact, you should get one every year or two because many eye diseases are asymptomatic, which means they could become dangerous before you realize they exist. But even in the absence of a professional examiner, you can still run some basic eye tests using an application on your phone or computer.

Most apps will test visual acuity (via reading an eye chart from a distance), retinal function (via detection of visual disturbances caused by changes in the retina) and color-blindness. Go find one right now and try it out—some good apps are listed at http://healthyprog.com. Using them takes only a few minutes, and they might reveal something surprising about your eyes: if you haven't had an exam recently, there's a good chance you'll need a new prescription for glasses.

Having the correct prescription lenses is important because without them your eyes will have to work harder to focus. This fatigues the muscles around the eyes, which can lead to headaches and even more problems with your vision.

Many factors, including your glasses, can lead to headaches, but some of the factors aren't actually deficiencies of your vision as much as deficiencies of your office. That's why we're going to run some more tests that don't involve the receiving end of your vision (your eyes). Instead, they'll test the producing end (your computer). Some of these tests are directly related to headaches and others are related to your general eye health, but they are all important if you want to be a healthy programmer.

Go sit in front of your desk or workstation right now. Set things up as though you're working—adjust the room lighting, screen brightness, chair position, and such. Now answer the following questions.

How far is your face from the computer screen? Your monitor should be no further away than 40 inches (101 cm) and no closer than 20 inches (51 cm).[3] This is roughly the length of your arm, so you can test this by reaching out toward your monitor. If you can give your screen a high-five, you're too close. If you can't touch your screen, you might want to move closer.

Viewing distances that are too long force your eyes to strain when reading small text. Viewing distances that are too short can cause eye fatigue because the muscles around the eye have to work harder to focus. This can even lead to convergence disorders, which are characterized by an inability of the eyes to turn toward each other or sustain convergence.

Is the monitor brighter than the rest of the room? Brightness may sound difficult to judge, but it's not. Take this book (or some other printed book if you're reading this onscreen) and hold it up against the screen. If it becomes illuminated as you bring it closer to the display, then your monitor is too bright (or your room is too dark).

A high disparity between the room's brightness and the monitor's brightness will quickly fatigue your eyes. It may also force you to squint at your monitor if your pupils have dilated while looking away from it. If your office has natural lighting, you may need to adjust your display's brightness throughout the day.

Is there excessive glare on the monitor? You can test this by relaxing your vision—focus your eyes as though you are looking at something behind the monitor. What do you see? If you see the window behind you, then there is excessive glare. Glare affects your eyes in the same way as a monitor that's too bright.

Are you seeing reds or blues? Generally speaking, red-hued light is safer for your eyes than blue-hued light. In fact, studies have shown that blue light can be toxic to cellular structures.[4,5] This has to do with the shorter wavelength of blue light (400 to 470 nanometers), which is very close to the more infamous ultraviolet (UV) light. UV light is somewhat filtered by the lens and cornea, which are illustrated in the following figure, but blue light passes through more easily and can still damage your retina.

---

3. ANSI/HFES [2007]. Human Factors Engineering of Computer Workstations (ANSI/HFES 100-2007). Santa Monica, CA: Human Factors and Ergonomics Society.
4. *Action spectra for the photoconsumption of oxygen by human ocular lipofuscin and lipofuscin extracts [PRZL02]*
5. *Blue light-induced reactivity of retinal age pigment. In vitro generation of oxygen-reactive species [RJKB95]*

You can mitigate your exposure to blue hues by reducing your display's color temperature. This will reduce the amount of blue light the screen emits, but it will affect your perception of any graphics or visual media you might be working on. If you can't change the color temperature, you can simply favor red tints for your desktop background, IDE color scheme, and anything else that you look at a lot.

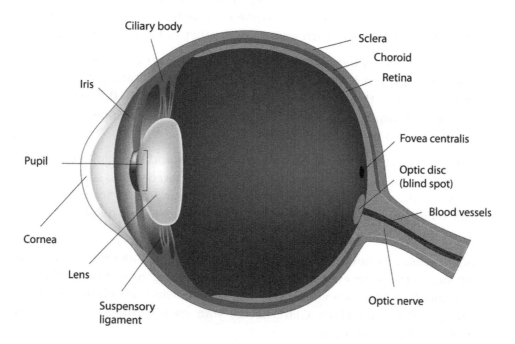

The lens and cornea, at the front of the eye, can filter ultraviolet light. But blue light passes through more easily and can still damage your retina, the light-sensitive tissue lining the inner surface of the eye.

Figure 15—Basic anatomy of the human eye

Based on your answers to these questions, you may want to make some adjustments to your workstation. The right distance, brightness, and color can reduce eye strain and headaches. But there's no way to avoid the problem entirely—you have to look at your screen for eight hours each day. With the right technique, however, you can make this experience more pleasant and avoid Computer Vision Syndrome.

Goal 7

Get an eye exam

A comprehensive eye examination is a series of tests that check your vision and eye health. It should be performed by a professional licensed optometrist or ophthalmologist. The exam includes tests for visual acuity, three-dimensional vision, peripheral vision, pupil function, and color-blindness, among other things.

According to the National Institutes of Health (NIH), adults between the ages of twenty and thirty-nine should complete a full exam every five to ten years, with regular checkups as needed. Adults who wear contacts should have an examination every year. Adults over the age of forty should have an exam every one to three years.[6]

5.2 Avoiding Computer Vision Syndrome

In 1779 Benjamin Franklin was on a diplomatic mission to France when he received a letter from an optician in Paris—his new glasses had been delayed. The optician explained that the delay was caused by the lens having broken three times during cutting, which suggested that Franklin was ordering something unusual. Indeed, most historians agree that this correspondence is the earliest evidence of a famous Franklin invention: bifocals.

In Franklin's time—and up until recently—bifocals solved the essential problem of sight: our eyes focus differently when looking near and far. But in the last century we've developed a new problem: middle-sightedness. The ideal distance for computer viewing is 20 to 40 inches (51 to 101 cm), as we discussed in the previous section, but this range is not covered by the standards optometrists use to measure vision—they primarily emphasize myopia (nearsightedness) or presbyopia (the difficulty focusing on near objects that comes with age). As a result, some prescriptions can be wildly off when applied to computer-viewing. Some researchers believe that this is a contributing factor to Computer Vision Syndrome.[7]

CVS is a temporary condition that results from prolonged focusing of the eyes on a computer screen. Its symptoms include headaches, dry eyes, irritated eyes,

---

6. http://www.nlm.nih.gov/medlineplus/ency/article/003434.htm
7. *Visual ergonomics in the workplace [Ans07]*

redness in the eyes, blurred vision, neck pain, fatigue, double vision, and difficulty refocusing the eyes. Thus, CVS is what most programmers refer to as *life*.

All of the factors we examined in our unit tests can exacerbate CVS, and that's why it's important to resolve them. But in addition to changing your workstation, you can change the way you use your workstation. Following these guidelines below will reduce your susceptibility to CVS:

Blink Often   Blinking moistens your eyes and replenishes the protective film that coats the cornea. When working at a computer, you tend to blink less often—about five times less than normal. This causes your eyes to dry out more rapidly. As a result, you need to force yourself to blink—ideally every twenty minutes. Close your eyes slowly, as though you are falling asleep, and repeat ten times.

Exercise Your Eyes   The primary reason that eyes become tired or fatigued is that they are focusing at a single depth for a long period of time. Think of holding a heavy object—after a while you need to shift it around. That's exactly why it's good to exercise your eyes. Rely on the 20-20-20 rule. That is, look away from your computer every 20 minutes, focus on an object that is 20 feet (6 meters) away, and look at it for 20 seconds.

Take Breaks Often   You're probably getting tired of being told to take breaks. But here's one more reason: according to the National Institute for Occupational Safety and Health, discomfort and eye strain were significantly reduced when computer-workers took four additional five-minute "mini-breaks" throughout the work day.[8]

Take Off Your Prescription Glasses   Many people with myopia (nearsightedness) don't actually need their glasses when using a computer. Try taking them off—you may find that you can see just fine. In fact, most optometrists recommend taking off your glasses whenever it's possible.

Wear Filtering Lenses (Maybe)   If you are able to use the computer without prescription glasses, then you may want to try filtering lenses. The makers of this type of eyewear claim that it filters out "artificial" light and reduces the stress on your eyes by creating an enhanced and more-comfortable visual environment. There are early indications that this technology is effective at reducing irritation, dryness, tearing, and tiredness,[9] but by no means is there unequivocal proof that they will help. More research needs to be done.

---

8. *A field study of supplementary rest breaks for data-entry operators [GSSH00]*
9. http://commons.pacificu.edu/verg/2/

> **Tip 6** Use the 20-20-20 rule: Every 20 minutes, focus on something 20 feet (6 meters) away for 20 seconds.

If you stick with these suggestions and make them habits, there's a good chance you'll have fewer headaches and prevent CVS. But your eyes aren't the only culprit when it comes to headaches—there are many other triggers.

5.3 Avoiding Headache Triggers

The gray matter inside your skull does not have pain-sensitive nerve endings, but that doesn't mean headaches aren't in your head. Many of the blood vessels supplying blood and oxygen to the brain have pain receptors and the muscles surrounding your brain can also sense it. The source of this pain ultimately depends on the type of headache.

There are two macro categories of headache: primary and secondary. We're focusing on primary headaches, which are those most commonly experienced by programmers (secondary headaches are caused by injuries, tumors, and other things that shouldn't happen in the course of programming). But even within the primary category, there are several subcategories. They include tension, migraine, cluster, sinus, and rebound headaches. The most relevant to our discussion are tension and migraine.

The essential mechanism that causes tension and migraine headaches is not completely understood. But it's believed that several factors contribute to the overarching condition:

- The release of neuropeptides from the pain-sensitive cells near the brain stem.

- The swelling of blood vessels that supply blood to the brain.

- The leaking of neuropeptide chemicals from the cranial blood vessels, which causes the surrounding tissue to swell.

Regardless of the mechanism, we do understand the various triggers that can induce the pain. Table 1, *Headache triggers*, on page 72 describes the most significant of these.

Many of these triggers are difficult to avoid. You may not have enough control over your environment to affect them. But there are some you can influence—primarily those triggers you eat. The most surprising source of headaches is food and drink. In fact, the majority of headaches that are not caused by what goes into your eyes are caused by what goes into your mouth.

Trigger	Description
Weather	Low barometric pressure, high heat, high altitude
Hormones	Menstruation, pregnancy, menopause
Sensory stimuli	Perfume, cleaning products, bright light, smoke
Physical exertion	Aerobic exercise, weight-lifting, dehydration, sex
Lifestyle	Sleep loss, stress
Diet	Caffeine, MSG, aspartame, alcohol

Table 1—Headache triggers

The list we're about to discuss is only for your information—it doesn't mean that you should avoid these things entirely. Instead, when a headache occurs, take note of what you've recently eaten. If you begin to see a pattern in which the same foods cause your headaches, then you'll probably want to make changes to your diet.

Caffeine Most programmers are no strangers to caffeine. We even have an award that's sponsored by the popular Jolt Cola brand. Caffeine has its perks, but it can also induce headaches. Paradoxically, caffeine can also provide temporary relief for an existing headache, which has turned it into a bit of a folk remedy. The problem is that its relief is temporary and it will likely cause a rebound headache. Use caffeine with caution. If you have a headache, avoid it entirely.

Monosodium Glutamate (MSG) When you read MSG, you probably think of cheap Chinese buffets, but MSG is contained in far more foods than you probably realize. It's considered "natural" by the US Food and Drug Administration (FDA), so it may even appear in foods that are labeled "all natural" or "no artificial ingredients." MSG is essentially the chemical behind the taste we call *savory*, so it's often used to restore flavor in canned or preserved food. MSG has developed a reputation for contributing to numerous health conditions, but those concerns are most likely overblown. A 1995 report by the Federation of American Societies for Experimental Biology done for the FDA concluded that MSG is safe when eaten at normal levels.[10] However, the report did leave a lot of room for interpretation.

Many people insist—and some physicians concur—that MSG can induce or contribute to headaches. As with every other item on this list, you

---

10. *Executive Summary from the Report: Analysis of Adverse Reactions to Monosodium Glutamate (MSG) [RTF91]*

should pay attention to this ingredient. The hype may be unwarranted, but if consuming MSG aligns with your headaches, then it would be wise to avoid products that contain it in large quantities. That includes packaged foods such as soups, bouillons, salty snacks, gravies, processed meats, veggie burgers, or anything advertised as containing "natural flavoring."

Aspartame Many people claim that artificial sweeteners, especially aspartame, can trigger headaches. But not all artificial sweeteners have the same effect—and sugar shouldn't be a problem. If you find that consuming diet drinks aligns with your headaches, then try switching to a different beverage brand. A variety of tasty products exist, with a wide array of sweeteners.

Fermented Food You might be surprised at how long this list could be. A large amount of the food we eat is fermented: bread, coffee, chocolate, cheese, yogurt, pepperoni, olives, and pickles, to name a few. But the reasons they trigger headaches are not all the same. In some cases, such as cheese and fermented sausage, the culprit is a chemical called tyramine, which can induce headaches. But in many fermented beverages the culprit is alcohol. If you've ever had a hangover, this won't come as a surprise.

Some alcoholic beverages may be worse than others. Red wine, cognac, and other dark liquors contain high levels of congeners, which can contribute to headaches. Drinks like vodka, which are made with a strict distillation process, are lower in congeners and may not have the same affect. As a general rule, lighter-colored liquors have fewer congeners. Pay attention to what drinks align with your headaches, and you may find that some sit better than others.

Dehydration Dehydration contributes to headaches in many different ways. It creates a chemical imbalance by reducing the quantity of essential salts (sodium and potassium) in your body. It also leads to a drop in blood volume, which lowers the blood and oxygen levels in the brain. This causes blood vessels in the brain to dilate and swell, which results in the feeling of a headache. As a result, one of the best ways to prevent headaches is to drink plenty of water.

A recent study from the Institute of Medicine determined that adult men need roughly 3.7 liters (about 16 cups) of water per day and women need roughly 2.7 liters (about 12 cups) of water each day.[11] However, we get a

---

11. http://www.iom.edu/Reports/2004/Dietary-Reference-Intakes-Water-Potassium-Sodium-Chloride-and-Sulfate.aspx

great deal of water from our food. That's why the NIH recommends the 8x8 rule: eight 8-ounce glasses of water each day.[12] After a full day or work no one can ever remember if they're drinking the seventh or eighth cup of water. Break it down however you'd like, but try to get 64 ounces each day.

Tip 7	Staying hydrated can prevent headaches. To ensure your fluid levels are topped off, drink a large (16-ounce) glass of water with every meal, plus one at the end of the day.

Remember that you don't have to completely avoid the foods in the preceding list. They *contribute* to headaches but don't necessarily *cause* them. If you're in a situation that makes you more susceptible to headaches, then try to stay away from these foods. For example, if you just went for a brisk walk at high altitude, you might want to avoid caffeine for a while.

No matter how hard you try, though, you will get a headache every now and again. When it happens, you'll need to know what to do.

5.4 Treating Headache Symptoms

Dim the lights, lie down, close your eyes, and try to relax. That's the best way to treat a headache, because it has no side effects and won't cause a rebound headache. If possible, place a cool wet towel on your forehead. Despite its simplicity, this strategy has proven to be effective.[13]

Other studies have found that relaxation techniques such as mediation, tai chi, and yoga are effective at relieving headaches.[14,15] Some individuals prefer to do mild exercises at the onset of a headache—although this likely masks the pain until it can subside rather than actually reducing it.

But sometimes you just can't relax. You have a job, places to be, and things to do. When that's the case, it may be time to hit the medicine cabinet. In general it's okay to treat acute headaches with medication, but you should consult a doctor before taking any of the advice we're about to discuss.

The medications that are best at treating acute headaches have some kind of anti-inflammatory component. However, we'll steer clear of medications

---

12. http://www.nlm.nih.gov/medlineplus/ency/article/002471.htm
13. *Goldman's Cecil Medicine [GS11]*
14. *A randomized controlled trial of tai chi for tension headaches [AHHL07]*
15. *Effectiveness of yoga therapy in the treatment of migraine without aura: a randomized controlled trial [JSSK07]*

> ### Joe asks:
> # How Do You Know These Foods Are Triggers?
>
> The hard evidence that backs up some of these foods as headache triggers is pretty weak, and many researchers have pointed out that the tests themselves may be the reason for the lack of proof.[a] Isolating each of these foods while reproducing the real-world conditions that cause headaches is nearly impossible. The problem is further complicated because no single factor *always* causes a headache.
>
> For example, one study that tested the safety of MSG asked participants to fast prior to the experiment and then ingest modest amounts of the chemical (or a placebo).[b] In the real world, conditions are often different. You may be predisposed to headaches for other reasons (weather, stress, and so on), and consuming large amounts of MSG tips the scale. We just don't have that kind of study yet.
>
> However, some of the foods listed earlier—namely, caffeine and water—have shown strong correlations with contributing to and mitigating headaches, respectively.[c,d] Thus, it's best to use that list as a guide when investigating the cause of recurring headaches, but not as a definitive source.
>
> ---
>
> a. *Heal Your Headache: The 1-2-3 Program for Taking Charge of Your Pain [Buc02]*
> b. *Monosodium L-glutamate: A double-blind study and review [TK93]*
> c. *Headache caused by caffeine withdrawal among moderate coffee drinkers switched from ordinary to decaffeinated coffee: a 12 week double blind trial [SSL04]*
> d. *Caffeine as a risk factor for chronic daily headache: A population-based study [vK90]*

that also include caffeine (such as regular Excedrin). These drugs supplement the anti-inflammatory ingredient with caffeine so that it will enter the blood stream more quickly and provide faster relief. This is, of course, a double-edged sword, as those medications are likely to cause rebound headaches. You should favor the medications in Table 2, *Headache Medications*, on page 76.

In circumstances such as the following, however, a headache requires you to seek help from a doctor:[16]

- Your headache is explosive or violent.

- Your headache gets worse after a twenty-four-hour period.

- You have slurred speech, a change in vision, problems moving your arms or legs, loss of balance, confusion, or memory loss with your headache.

---

16. http://www.nlm.nih.gov/medlineplus/ency/article/003024.htm

Drug	Brands	Description
Ibuprofen	Advil, Aleve, Motrin	Ibuprofen is in a class of medications called non-steroidal anti-inflammatory drugs (NSAIDs). It works by stopping the body's production of a substance that causes pain, fever, and inflammation. There is an increased risk of heart attack or stroke when taking it (http://www.nlm.nih.gov/medlineplus/druginfo/meds/a682159.html)
Acetaminophen	Tylenol, Excedrin PM	Acetaminophen is in a class of medications called analgesics (pain relievers) and antipyretics (fever reducers). It works by changing the way the body senses pain and by cooling the body. Taking too much acetaminophen can cause liver damage (http://www.nlm.nih.gov/medlineplus/druginfo/meds/a681004.html).
Aspirin	Bayer, Bufferin	Aspirin is in a group of medications called salicylates. It works by stopping the production of certain natural substances that cause fever, pain, swelling, and blood clots. Beware of allergies (http://www.nlm.nih.gov/medlineplus/druginfo/meds/a682878.html).

Table 2—Headache Medications

- You have a fever, stiff neck, nausea, and vomiting with your headache.

- Your headache coincides with a head injury.

- Your headache is severe and just in one eye, accompanied by redness in that eye.

You should use your judgment when it comes to treating headaches. They are common, but they can also be an early warning sign of terrible things—like cancer and tumors.

5.5 Retrospective

Even when headaches don't threaten your life, they can still be killers—*productivity* killers. But now that you know what causes them, you're well equipped to keep them at bay. When they do strike, you'll be able to treat them effectively.

But simply treating your problems won't do any good if you let your eye health deteriorate. That's why your goal for this chapter is to get an eye exam.

Taking care of your eyes is important, but you can also prevent headaches by taking care of your body. Your new daily action item is to drink eight 8-ounce glasses of water each day. If you prefer, you can make this easier to remember by drinking a large glass of water with every meal, plus one at the end of the day.

We won't add anything new to your daily checklist in this chapter, but the 20-20-20 rule aligns very well with the existing recommendation to change positions every twenty minutes. Continue to carry out the practices you've learned about, and in the next chapter we'll increase the intensity of your hourly movement by adding some strength exercises.

Act On It

- Position your monitor 20 to 40 inches (51 to 101 cm) from your face.

- Adjust the light in your office and the brightness of your monitor to achieve a good equilibrium.

- Blink often to moisten your eyes and prevent CVS.

- Use the 20-20-20 rule to exercise your eyes.

- Pay attention to the foods you've eaten prior to getting a headache. They may be related.

- Take a anti-inflammatory drug (if your doctor says it's okay) to ease the pain of a headache. But don't do it often or if your headache persists.

- Get your eyes tested regularly to detect diseases that are asymptomatic.

CHAPTER 6

Preventing Back Pain

When the harpsichord came into wide use in the seventeenth century, many musicians were uncertain about the proper technique to use when playing it. They weren't sure where to sit on the bench, how high the bench should be, and how far from the keyboard they should position their bodies. Even worse, most musicians accepted that they had to tolerate a great deal of pain to become master keyboardists.

This began to change in 1753 when Carl Philipp Emanuel Bach (the son of Johann Sebastian Bach) published his *Essay on the True Art of Playing Keyboard Instruments [Bac49]*. He addressed many aspects of technique, including the positioning and fingering issues that had been a source of confusion to most players. It was so foundational that Mozart said Carl Philipp Emanuel Bach "is the father, we are the children."

Since the time of Bach, many other musicians and teachers have dismissed the notion that a life of pain is required to become a professional pianist, and our understanding of how piano players should position themselves has advanced greatly. Today, posture is one of the essential components of piano pedagogy at institutions such as The Juilliard School and the Royal College of Music in London.[1]

A professional pianist makes a full-time job out of practicing in front of a keyboard every day. In that way, programmers have a lot in common with pianists (beyond the parts of the brain we use).

A professional programmer typically spends more than forty hours a week sitting in a chair in front of a keyboard. Yet few of us have received instruction on how to position our bodies for this task, so it's no wonder that many programmers develop chronic back pain as a result of poor ergonomics—just

---

1.   http://www.alexandertechnique.com/musicians.htm

like those seventeenth-century harpsichord players. In fact, back pain is so common that it has become the number-two reason for doctor visits in the United States, behind headaches.[2]

Bad posture is not the only reason programmers suffer from back pain, however. Many types of back pain result from the gradual de-conditioning of the back muscles due to a lack of physical activity. Fortunately, reconditioning these muscles does not take much work, and in some cases you don't even need to leave your office.

In this chapter we'll develop a framework for assessing and treating various forms of back pain. We'll focus on muscular back pain, which accounts for seventy-five percent of clinical diagnoses and is the source of pain for most programmers. We won't address pain derived from injury or spinal damage, as that is not usually the result of sitting for prolonged periods (and the solutions are much more complicated). The good news is that muscle pain is often reversible by strengthening your body's core. Later in the chapter, we'll practice some exercises that will help you improve these muscles.

Let's begin by running some tests on your body to better understand the source of back pain.

6.1 Unit-Testing Your Core Muscles

There are many ways to take stock of back pain, but perhaps the best known is the Kraus-Weber Test.

The Kraus-Weber (K-W) Test of Minimum Muscular Fitness measures large muscle groups for strength and flexibility. The individual tests that make up the full K-W Test were originally created in the 1940s in an effort to understand why an increasing number of children were developing bad posture. Some time after the end of World War II, doctors began applying the tests to a new epidemic: back pain. Dr. Hans Kraus, who developed the tests, dedicated the rest of his life to finding causes, preventions, and cures for this problem that no one had heard of before the war.

In the first clinical application of the tests, eighty percent of more than 4,000 healthy subjects were unable to pass Dr. Kraus's test. As these people began to exercise, they performed better and their back complaints decreased. But eight years later they again failed the tests and their back pain returned because they had stopped exercising.

---

2.   http://www.jhu.edu/jhumag/0699web/pain.html

Modern research continues to demonstrate the efficacy of this test, and many doctors continue to use it as a the first tool in assessing back pain.[3,4,5]

The K-W Test is composed of six exercises, which must all be completed to pass the test. Some of the exercises may require a partner, so go find someone to help you, and let's do this now. If you have an existing back problem or other health condition, consult your doctor before proceeding. The tests are not demanding, but lawyers are ruthless.

Also, keep in mind that these are only tests. You should not perform them repetitively as you would other exercises.

Kraus-Weber Test 1

The first test is often called a straight-leg raise. You lie flat on your back with your hands gently touching behind your neck, and your legs extended and together. Keep your knees straight, and raise both feet so your heels are 10 inches (25 cm) above the floor, as shown in the following figure. If you can hold this position for 10 seconds, you pass this test.

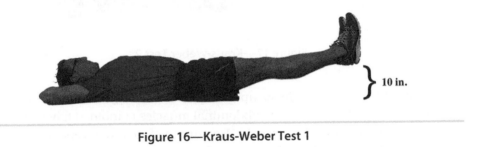

} 10 in.

Figure 16—Kraus-Weber Test 1

This exercise is designed to test the strength of your hip flexors (the muscles that bring your knees toward your chest) and lower abdominal muscles. We'll discuss these muscles in more detail in Section 6.1, *Understanding the Anatomy of the Back*, on page 86.

Kraus-Weber Test 2

This test is often called a straight-legged sit-up. Lie flat on your back again, but with your hands touching behind your neck. This time, you'll need an assistant to anchor your feet by holding your ankles in place, as shown in

3. *Reliability Of Kraus-Weber Exercise Test As An Evaluation Tool In Low Back Pain Susceptibility Among Apparently Healthy University Students [BAH08]*
4. *Assessment Of Muscular Fitness In School Children Using Kraus-Weber Tests [KDSB10]*
5. *End Back Pain Forever: A Groundbreaking Approach to Eliminate Your Suffering [Mar12]*

the following figure. If you don't have an assistant, you can position your feet below heavy furniture. Now attempt to roll your chest upward so that the upper half of your body is vertical, and perpendicular to your legs.

Figure 17—Kraus-Weber Test 2

If you are able to do a single sit-up, you pass this test, which is designed to determine if your hip flexors and abdominal muscles combined have sufficient strength to handle your bodyweight. Be sure to stop at one repetition—overdoing this exercise could make your problems worse.

Kraus-Weber Test 3

The next test is often called a bent-knee sit-up. As in the previous test, lie on the floor with your hands touching behind your neck and your feet securely anchored. But this time, have your knees flexed such that there is a ninety-degree angle between your thigh and calf, as show in Figure 18, *Kraus-Weber Test 3*, on page 83. Now attempt to bring your chest upward, just as you did in the previous test. If you can do this once, then you pass.

The purpose of this test is to assess the strength of the abdominal muscles alone. Don't feel bad if you didn't pass. It's one of the most commonly failed of the K-W tests because it isolates your abdominal muscles, which may have become very weak after years of sitting at a desk.

Figure 18—Kraus-Weber Test 3

Kraus-Weber Test 4

The fourth test is often called a Superman (because the position you end up in looks like you are flying). This time, turn over on your stomach, and place a pillow under your abdomen and hips. Then touch your hands together behind your neck as you did before. Have an assistant keep the lower half of your body stable by placing one hand on your lower back and one hand on your ankles, as shown in Figure 19, *Kraus-Weber Test 4*, on page 84.

You pass if you can lift your trunk off the floor and hold it steady for 10 seconds. This tests the strength of your upper-back muscles.

Kraus-Weber Test 5

This test is often called a reverse straight-leg raise. You remain on your stomach with the pillow under your abdomen and hips, and your hands behind your neck. Have your assistant place one hand on your lower back and one hand on your upper back to keep you steady, as in Figure 20, *Kraus-Weber Test 5*, on page 84.

You pass if you can lift your legs, with knees held straight, off the floor for 10 seconds. This tests the strength of your lower-back muscles. We'll describe how these differ from your upper-back muscles in Section 6.1, *Understanding the Anatomy of the Back*, on page 86.

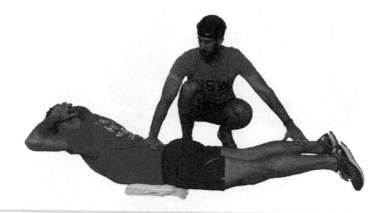

Figure 19—Kraus-Weber Test 4

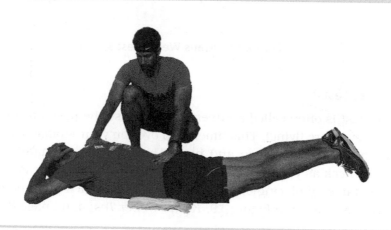

Figure 20—Kraus-Weber Test 5

Kraus-Weber Test 6

The last test is often called a toe-touch. This time, stand up straight with your feet together. Then slowly reach down as far as you can without bending at the knees, as shown in Figure 21, *Kraus-Weber Test 6*, on page 85. You pass if you can touch the floor.

Use caution when performing this test. Some experts believe that it puts excessive strain on the vertebrae and dipping your head below your heart could cause you to pass out. If you have reservations about this exercise, you can modify it by resting your butt against a wall with your feet 12 to 20 inches (30 to 51 cm) in front of you.

Figure 21—Kraus-Weber Test 6

When you come up, bend your knees so that when you raise your body you're using your leg muscles instead of your back muscles.

The toe-touch is another commonly failed exercise. It is designed to measure the flexibility of your back and hamstring muscles. If you failed, it's not because your arms are too short or your legs are too long, but rather because the back and hamstring muscles are too tense.

If you successfully completed all six of the K-W tests, then you pass. That means you've met the *minimum* level of muscular fitness.

If you failed even one of the six, you are below par. You are probably under-exercised or overtensed (or possibly both). In Section 6.2, *Strengthening Your Powerhouse*, on page 88, we'll define a set of exercises that is proven to correct those deficiencies and help eliminate your pain. But first let's examine the components of the human back to develop a better understanding of what your body was doing during these tests.

Goal 8

Pass the Kraus-Weber Test

Later in this chapter you'll learn some exercises that you can practice daily to improve the strength of your core muscles. After doing them for a few weeks, you should be able to pass all six of the K-W tests.

6.2   Understanding the Anatomy of the Back

Back pain may be on the rise because of our increasingly sedentary lives, but it's certainly not a new thing. As far back as 1500 BC the Egyptians recorded this kind of pain in their medical literature. It was not until recently, however, that muscles were considered as the source of the problem.

For a long time, the prescription for patients with back pain was bed rest or even surgery. In the worst cases, some doctors even used devices akin to the medieval rack to stretch the spine. But today it is widely accepted that most back pain can be attributed to weak core muscles, and the best cure is exercise.

The reason it took doctors a long time to understand the role of muscles in back pain is that muscular pain is difficult to isolate. Unlike the pain you get from a pin prick, which is very sharp and direct, the pain from a muscle spans out across the other muscles nearby or in the same group. This effect is called *referred pain*, and it's believed that this mechanism prevents further injury by signaling you to reduce all activity in that area.

To unravel the source of back pain, we need to examine the various muscle groups that support our backs. This will provide the proper framework for us to discuss what is happening when you do the exercises in Section 6.2, *Strengthening Your Powerhouse*, on page 88. We'll begin at the base of your spine.

Lower Back

The muscles in the lower back provide most of the support for your posture, but they are buried beneath a layer of silvery tissue and the lower portion of the muscles in the upper back. They include three groups: extensor muscles (as shown in the following figure), flexor muscles, and oblique muscles.

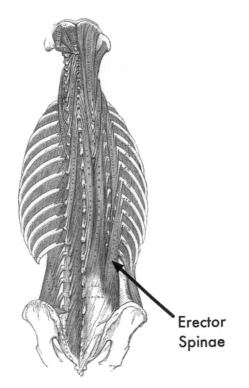

Erector Spinae

This group of muscles, called the erector spinae, travel the length of the back and provide tension that supports the spinal column.

Figure 22—The paired extensor muscles of the lower back

The extensor muscles are attached to the back of the spine and allow you to stand up straight or lift from the waist. This group includes some large paired muscles that are essentially a bundle of long fibers and tendons. You can think of these muscles like the fishing line that runs taut along a fishing pole. As the fishing line tenses, the pole bends—just as your spine bends when these muscles tense. If they are too tense, they can pull on your spine too much. If they are too weak, the spine won't be supported enough.

Next is the flexor muscle group, which attaches to the front of the spine. It includes your abdominal muscles, which enable the flexing, bending, and arching of the lower back. Weakness in these muscles are the number-one reason for failure of the K-W Test.

Finally, the oblique muscles are attached to the side of the spine and help rotate it to maintain proper posture.

When you're sitting in your chair at work, all of these muscles are supporting your spine. But research shows that slouching causes twice as much pressure and strain on these muscles as sitting up straight. In *Developing Better Posture*, on page 97, we'll discuss this in more detail.

Upper Back

Some of the lower-back muscles extend to the upper back, but the most significant pain-causing muscles of the upper back include the infraspinatus, teres major, and trapezius. These muscles rotate your shoulders, but they also support the spine.

Hips and Butt

The muscles that attach to the spine are the most important to our discussion, but there are many other supporting muscles in the hips and buttocks that can also cause back pain.

An example of this is the iliopsoas (shown in the following figure), which connects to the bottom of the spine and extends down through the hip, where it connects with the femur. This collection of muscles is used to rotate the hip, but if they become stiff or inflamed they can squeeze a set of spinal nerves called the lumbar plexus. This sensation is often mistaken for a herniated disk in the spine.

The exercises you'll learn about in the next section are designed to strengthen and increase flexibility in all of these muscles groups. That's why you'll see exercises that involve not only your back and abdomen, but also your shoulders and hips.

Let's get to work!

6.3 Strengthening Your Powerhouse

One of Dr. Kraus's early patients was President John F. Kennedy. The president had such terrible back pain that the Secret Service thought he might end up in a wheelchair before the end of his first term in office. He was already using crutches, but kept them out of public sight.

Dr. Kraus's first trip to the White House revealed that the president's back muscles were stiff and weak, his leg muscles were "as taut as piano wires,"[6] and his abdominal muscles had atrophied to the point that he could not do a single sit-up.

---

6. *JFK's Secret Doctor: The Remarkable Life of Medical Pioneer and Legendary Rock Climber Hans Kraus* [Sch12]

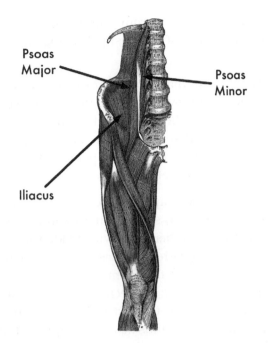

The term iliopsoas refers to the combination of the psoas major, the psoas minor, and the iliacus. Notice how these muscles connect to the lower spine, travel through the pelvis, and connect to the upper leg.

Figure 23—The iliopsoas muscles

Dr. Kraus's prescription was simple. He designed a set of exercises that the president would practice three times a week. Within a month of starting the exercises, Kennedy could almost touch his toes again. Not long after that, he was able to lift his two-year-old son into the air for an iconic picture.

Modern research upholds Dr. Kraus's view that exercise is the most effective treatment for the kind of back pain programmers commonly experience. In 2005 a group of researchers from the University of Toronto published a review of randomized controlled trials that found exercise programs designed to target the muscles we discussed earlier can improve pain and function in patients with chronic nonspecific low-back pain,[7] and a review in 2006 found similar results that included acute nonspecific back pain.[8] Unfortunately,

---

7. *Systematic review: strategies for using exercise therapy to improve outcomes in chronic low back pain [HvT05]*

8. *Outcome of non-invasive treatment modalities on back pain: an evidence-based review [vKM06]*

there isn't a scientific consensus around any single exercise program as a universal treatment, but some of the most promising methods include Pilates and yoga.

Pilates is an exercise system that emphasizes concentration, breathing, and controlled movement to improve the strength and flexibility of the body's *powerhouse*, which includes the abdominals, hips, and back. A number of recent studies have found that Pilates can improve pain and function in patients with chronic nonspecific lower-back pain.[9,10] As a result, many doctors have begun to prescribe it for their patients.[11]

But not every Pilates exercise is appropriate for every person. Depending on what is causing your back pain, some Pilates exercises could even make it worse. That's why many researchers are trying to identify subsets of exercises from Pilates and yoga, along with exercises they've designed themselves, as the basis for treatment. One of the foremost researchers doing this is Dr. Stuart McGill, a professor of spine biomechanics at the University of Waterloo in Canada. Dr. McGill has spent the last twenty years researching effective exercises for strengthening the muscles that support the spine, and he's concluded that the difficultly in creating a universal program lays in the fact that every individual has different needs. For some people, pain results from a lack of mobility. For others, pain results from a lack of stability. And very often, stability and mobility are at odds with each other when it comes to choosing appropriate exercises.

Despite the difficulty of defining a complete program, Dr. McGill has identified a set of exercises that he believes should be performed by most people on a daily basis.[12] Even extremely fit athletes can benefit from these exercises because they are designed to enhance the *health* of the back as opposed to its athletic performance. These two factors, health and performance, can be at odds with each other. Dr. McGill stated in a *New York Times* interview that he sees "too many people who have six-pack abs and a ruined back."[13]

Find a soft place on the ground, and try Dr. McGill's exercises right now. It's important to remember that these are therapeutic exercises as opposed to

---

9. *Pilates-based therapeutic exercise: effect on subjects with nonspecific chronic low back pain and functional disability: a randomized controlled trial [RLS06]*

10. *Two different techniques in the rehabilitation treatment of low back pain: a randomized controlled trial [DDCG06]*

11. http://www.nytimes.com/2005/09/15/fashion/thursdaystyles/15fitness.html?pagewanted=all

12. *Exercises for spine stabilization: motion/motor patterns, stability progressions, and clinical technique [MK09]*

13. http://well.blogs.nytimes.com/2009/06/17/core-myths/

explosive strength-training exercises—they should be done slowly and with control. If you're familiar with Pilates or yoga, you'll probably recognize many of them. Take some deep breaths, get relaxed, and we'll begin.

Mobility and Stability Exercises

Cat Back   Dr. McGill recommends beginning each routine with the cat-back exercise, which is intended to reduce spine viscosity (that is, internal resistance and friction) by lubricating the nerve roots where they exit the spine. It is essentially a warm-up for your back. Keep in mind that it is intended as a motion exercise, not a stretching exercise.

To perform the cat back, you'll need to get on all fours so that your weight is on your hands and knees. Then arch your back like a cat—at the same time, drop your head as though you are looking toward your belly button. Next, reverse the movement by lowering your back so it forms the letter *U*. As you do this, raise your butt and head—you should be looking straight forward. It is especially important that you perform this exercise slowly. Repeat five to eight times.

Double Heel Slide   Dr. McGill recommends following the cat-back exercise with a few hip-and-knee-mobility exercises. For this, we'll start with the double heel slide. Lie down on your back with your knees bent, your feet flat on the ground, and your arms at your side. Slowly extend both feet so that your legs are fully extended and on the ground. Then bring your feet back to the starting position and repeat the exercise five to ten times.

Single-Knee Flex   The next hip-and-knee-mobility exercise is the single-knee flex. Remain on your back in the same position, and inhale as you raise your right knee back toward your chest. When it is as far back as it can go, begin to exhale and slowly return your leg to the bent position. When your foot reaches the ground, slide it down so that your leg straightens. Then raise your knee again. Do this five to ten times with the right leg and then five to ten times with the left leg.

Curl-Up   This exercise has become so uniquely associated with Dr. McGill's program that many people refer to it as the McGill curl-up. It is the first of what Dr. McGill calls *the big three* exercises, which are designed to condition the muscles of your trunk to provide stability to the spine.

To perform the exercise, lie flat on your back with your left leg bent and your right leg straight. Then place your hands underneath the small of your back so that they fill in the gap created by the curve of your spine. Begin by lifting your head and upper shoulders off of the floor. Hold yourself in this elevated position for seven to eight seconds while continuing to breathe. Finally, return your shoulders to the ground. Perform the exercises four or five times, switch your legs, and then perform it another four or five times. If you need to increase the difficulty, try lifting your elbows off the ground with your shoulders.

The purpose of putting your hands below the small of your back is to prevent you spine from flattening out as you lift your shoulders. Dr. McGill claims that this kind of flexion can worsen back pain. Ultimately, it is this concept that makes the exercise unique.

Side Bridge　　The next exercise in the big three is similar to an exercise from Pilates. To perform the side bridge, lie on your side and prop up your body with your elbow and knees. Hold this position for seven to eight seconds while continuing to breathe, and repeat four or five times for each side. You should not try to increase the difficulty by increasing the duration of the exercise. Instead, increase the number of repetitions as necessary. This is true with all of the exercises in the big three.

Bird Dog　　This exercise is the last of the big three. It is similar to the Vyaghrasana (Tiger Pose) in yoga. To perform the exercise, you'll need to get on all fours. Then lift your right arm and left leg simultaneously and extend them until they are parallel with the ground. Hold this position for seven to eight seconds. Finally, lower your hand and knee, gently sweep the ground, and raise them again for another repetition. Switch sides after four or five repetitions, and repeat.

Shoulder Bridge   Another of Dr. McGill's favorite exercises for back health is the shoulder bridge. Back pain often causes people to use their hamstring muscles instead of their gluteals (butt) to extend the hip. The shoulder bridge, which forces you to squeeze the gluteal muscles without using the hamstrings, helps establish gluteal dominance during hip extension.

To perform the exercise, lie on your back again, with you knees bent and your feet flat on the floor. Then push your hips up so that your torso is flat, and squeeze your buttocks to provide support. Hold this position for five to ten seconds and then return to the starting position. Repeat the exercise five to ten times.

Bicycle Hamstring Stretch   The remaining exercises are not a part of Dr. McGill's big three, but they are important for increased flexibility in your hips, back, and legs. To perform the first of these exercises, lie on your back with your legs straight and your hands at your side. Bring your right knee to your chest, and then straighten your leg so that it is perpendicular to the floor. At first you may not be able to raise your straightened leg completely, but with time your flexibility will increase and you'll get closer. When you have straightened your leg as much as you can, point your toes toward the ceiling. Then slowly lower your leg while keeping it straight until your foot touches the ground. Return your knee to the bent position, and repeat the exercise until you've done it a total of six times. Then do six repetitions with your left leg.

Bicycle Calf Stretch   The next exercise is very similar to the previous one, but it uses a slightly different foot position to stretch your calf instead of your hamstring. You will follow the exact same motions, but point your heel, not your toe, toward the ceiling (Figure 24, *Bicycle Calf Stretch*, on page 96). Do this six times for each leg.

Dr. McGill recommends following an exercise routine like this one daily. You should always begin with the warm-up exercises, then pick at least one more from Dr. McGill's big three, and finally at least one of the flexibility exercises. In total, you should do about five of these exercises per day. Here's an example workout plan for the first three days of the week:

	Monday	Tuesday	Wednesday
Ex. #1	Cat back	Cat back	Cat back
Ex. #2	Double heel slide	Single knee flex	Double heel slide
Ex. #3	Curl-up	Side bridge	Curl-up
Ex. #4	Side bridge	Bird dog	Shoulder bridge
Ex. #5	Bicycle hamstring stretch	Bicycle calf stretch	Bicycle hamstring stretch

Table 3—Examples of Bodyweight-Exercise Workouts

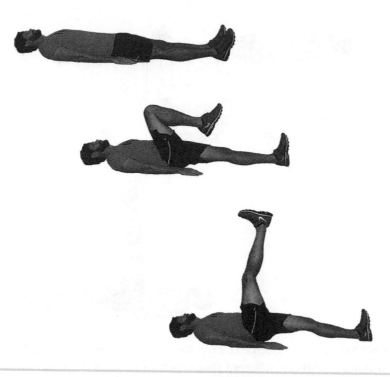

Figure 24—Bicycle Calf Stretch

If you have the time, you can do more exercise or more repetitions. After following a plan like this for a few weeks, try the K-W Test again. You'll probably find that your performance has improved. Continue to use these exercises until you are comfortably able to pass all six tests.

But don't stop there! After you are able to pass the K-W Test, continue to do these exercises. You will likely regress if you go back to being sedentary. If you feel you've outgrown them, then you can move on to the more-advanced exercises in Chapter 10, *Refactoring Your Fitness*, on page 147. But you can always come back to these as a simple and relaxing way to strengthen your powerhouse.

Having a strong core is an important part of eliminating back pain, but it's not the only thing you can do. Next we'll discuss some simple practices that don't require any time or money, but can still help your back.

6.4 Developing Better Ergonomics

Most programmers love technology, so it's no surprise when we spend hours online searching for the best office chair. A good chair can greatly improve your posture and help reduce back pain, but it's possible that the chair you have is perfectly sufficient. You might just be sitting incorrectly.

In this section we'll discuss some simple changes that can help eliminate back pain. They don't cost anything, and they may even save you from paying doctor bills.

Developing Better Posture

The correct posture is somewhat dependent on an individual's physical characteristics. But you can follow a few common rules to get in the best position. Many experts and health organizations, including Dr. Alan Hedge (whose research we discussed in Chapter 3, *A Farewell to Chairs?*, on page 29) and the United Kingdom's National Health Service (NHS), recommend the following general guidelines:[14]

Support Your Body   Adjust your chair height so that your back is properly supported. Your hips should be level with your knees so your are not sliding forward or backward in the seat. You'll also want to adjust your desk height so that your elbows are level with your wrists. This will help relieve strain on your shoulders that can ripple down your back.

Distribute Your Weight Evenly   As you sit in your chair, ensure that you are placing even amounts of weight on your front, back, and side supports. This will often require adjustments to the vertical alignment of the chair. Also be aware of unbalanced positions such as crossing your legs, hunching your shoulders, and leaning to one side. These are usually resolved by height and alignment adjustments to the chair.

Support Your Spine   It's important to use a lumbar support to take the load and strain off of the spine. Many chairs include an adjustable lumbar support, but sitting in the chair correctly (as described already) is usually sufficient. If you require additional support, you can use a rolled-up towel.

Keep Your Feet on the Ground   One of the most overlooked aspects of posture is the importance of keeping your feet on the ground. This helps support the weight from your legs and keeps you balanced. If your feet are not touching the ground but your position is good otherwise, then you may want to use a small footrest to prop up your feet.

If you've followed the guidelines from earlier in this chapter, your posture should look like the image in the following figure.

---

14. http://www.nhs.uk/Livewell/workplacehealth/Pages/howtositcorrectly.aspx

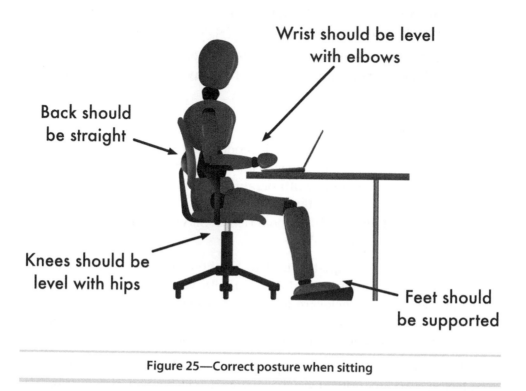

Figure 25—Correct posture when sitting

But no matter how good your posture, sitting in a single position for an extended period of time can cause back pain. That's why it's important to remember to get up and walk around occasionally.

Standing Up

One of the best things you can do for your back is to not sit at all.[15] Many programmers use a standing desk, which we discussed in Chapter 3, *A Farewell to Chairs?*, on page 29. But aside from spending as much as $1,000 on a fancy new desk or building your own, there are many free things you can do that will help you remember to get on your feet.

Stand Up During Meetings or Phone Calls   One of the best ways to get out of your chair is to stand up any time you don't need to be writing code. Make a habit of staying on your feet during meetings. You might even find that it's easier to stay awake this way!

---

15. *The Treatment of Acute Low Back Pain — Bed Rest, Exercises, or Ordinary Activity?* [MHAH95]

Stand Up During Your Breaks   In Chapter 8, *Making Exercise Pragmatic*, on page 121, we'll discuss how the Pomodoro Technique can provide several breaks in your day that you can use to get active. But even without exercise, using these breaks as an opportunity to stand up can reduce your back pain.

Go for a Walk at Lunch   The benefits of walking are undeniable, and the most relevant benefit to this discussion is that walking can help reduce back pain. Decades ago, doctors recommended bed rest for patients with back problems, but today we know that activity is the best prescription.

Staying active is a critical part of eliminating back pain. Whether it's standing up, walking, or practicing the exercises in this chapter, you need to get moving.

A Model for Good Health

The models demonstrating the exercises in this book are all programmers.

Michael Stephenson (the guy wearing glasses) has a story that's similar to Chad Fowler's. Michael is a programmer in Huntsville, Alabama. Six years ago, he weighed 240 pounds and wasn't taking care of his health, but after a massive transformation Michael is now an extremely fit athlete. He completed the Louisville, Kentucky, Ironman event in August 2012 and is a regular competitor at races throughout the year.

Erin Spiceland (the only woman among our models) is a programmer at Digium, the inventor and maintainer of the open source Asterisk telephony software. She is also the cofounder of EvenHealth, a website dedicated to fitness and health.

Jonathon Powell (the guy with the beard) is an Android programmer and a general fitness enthusiast. He can be found at the local YMCA most mornings playing basketball. Jonathon can dunk.

The last model is the author, who does a few of these exercises every day—despite being fit enough to run marathons.

6.5 Retrospective

If you do the exercises in this chapter for a few weeks, you'll begin to see improvements very rapidly. But if you revert to a sedentary lifestyle your back will only get worse. That's why we'll incorporate these exercises into your daily checklist. You should begin doing curl-ups, bridges, and other body-weight exercises on a regular basis to build strength in your trunk muscles. You can even work these into your hourly five-minute breaks.

DAILY CHECKLIST
☒ PLAN: Healthy stand-up
☒ WALK: 10,000 steps/day with 20 mins. brisk
☒ MOVE: 5 mins./hr. Change position every 20 mins.
☒ EAT: 5 servings of fruits or vegetables
☒ BUILD: 5 bodyweight exercises

You can do these strength exercises daily because they are not explosive. Every day, pick at least five of the exercises in this chapter, with at least two from *the big three*, and perform them as described. Rotate through the list so that you are constantly working your muscles in different ways.

You can even count this workout toward your twenty minutes of daily moderate activity. However, it's still good to do some walking in addition to your bodyweight exercises because each activity is designed to address different aspects of your health. After two weeks of doing the new exercises on your checklist, it will be time for your next retrospective. In this iteration, you'll have a new goal to assess: can you pass the Kraus-Weber Test?

If you keep up with the bodyweight exercises, you should be able to achieve this goal in just a few weeks. But don't get discouraged if it doesn't happen right away. The exercises are meant to be a lifelong habit, so keep with them as long as you are seeing improvement. In this way, it's a lot like your career.

If you don't continue to hone your programming skills, you'll eventually fall behind the technology curve.

Programming is a relatively new profession, but we can still learn from the past by embracing the lessons taught in other professions. Pianists take their posture very seriously, and we should too. Let's not follow their same progression and take 300 years to start paying attention to it.

In the next chapter we'll take some more advice from our musician friends. We'll discuss how to avoid certain kinds of pain that occur from overly repetitive motions—especially in our wrists.

Act On It

- Do a different group of bodyweight exercises in each workout. If you get tired of these exercises, try using new ones from Pilates or yoga.

- Experiment with your posture. It may be hard to use the correct position at first, but you'll eventually figure out what works best.

- Stand up if your back hurts. If you've already enhanced your workstation, then it should even be possible to keep writing code.

- Evaluate yourself with the K-W tests, but don't use them as regular exercises. Some maneuvers, such as the straight-leg sit-up, can make back pain worse when they're overused.

CHAPTER 7

Preventing Wrist Pain

No amount of pain was going to stop Ethan Kind from pursuing his passion. He was studying classical guitar at the Royal College of Music in London, and preparing for a career as a concert performer. The many hours of practicing every day were taking a toll on his body, but like many young people driven by a dream, he continued to work through the pain. Eventually he was diagnosed with *carpal tunnel syndrome* (CTS), but even that did not stop him.

"I ignored the pain and kept practicing," Ethan says. "I just practiced harder and harder, until I crashed and burned in my third year."

Ethan's crippling injury forced him to leave the school and return to his home in the United States. "When I came back to the States, I went into therapy and never returned to pursuing a concert career," he recounts.

Today Ethan is a teacher. He works with students and performers who are suffering from the same kind of pain that eventually ended his performance career, but now Ethan knows how to help them avoid burning out the way he did.

Before leaving the Royal College, Ethan was introduced to an educational process called the Alexander Technique, which aims to eliminate tension in the body by changing the way a person moves or holds a position. This technique is popular among musicians, stage actors, singers, and other performers. Ethan Kind, who is now a certified professional Alexander Technique instructor, has even applied the methodology to computer users.

In this chapter you'll learn about the Alexander Technique, and how musicians like Ethan use it to prevent pain. The most common type of pain they are trying to avoid is found in the wrists, and it leads to the infamous carpal tunnel syndrome that Ethan suffered from. We're going to look at what this condition does to your body, and how to prevent it through exercise and posture adjustments.

Let's begin by getting some feedback on the current condition of your body.

7.1 Unit-Testing Your Wrists

We'll apply three very common tests to the nervous tissue in your wrists. All of the tests work by trying to elicit a tingling sensation in your fingers. If you feel this sensation, it's a sign of neuroregeneration, or the regrowth of damaged nerve tissue. This means that there has been some damage to your nerves.

The tests progressively apply more pressure to the main nerve that causes wrist pain. If you experience pain in one of the tests, do not proceed to the next one. Let's begin with the gentlest of the tests.

Tinel's Sign

In 1915, a French neurologist named Jules Tinel noticed that it was possible to generate a "pins and needles" feeling by tapping on a recently injured nerve. Tinel and other researchers determined that this sensation was a sign of young axons in the process of growing. It wasn't until 1957, however, that an American hand surgeon named George Phalen began applying the test to diagnose carpal tunnel syndrome (he also developed a test of his own, which we'll discuss in a moment).

The test is old, but it's still in heavy use today as one of the first steps in diagnosing wrist pain. Let's give it a try.

Place your right hand and lower right arm on a flat surface with your palm up. Your arm should be relaxed, and your hand should be open, as shown in Figure 26, *Tinel's Sign*, on page 105. Then, with the index finger of your other hand, percuss (tap) the center of the base of your wrist (this is where the median nerve passes through the carpal tunnel, which we'll discuss later in the chapter).

The intensity with which you percuss should be just "enough to cause the expected response."[1] The expected response is a tingling feeling in your fingertips, but the pressure should never be so intense as to cause mechanical simulation of the nerve (that is, to make your fingers move). More importantly, it should never hurt.

The test is positive when you feel a tingling or "pins and needles" sensation in the tip of your thumb, index finger, middle finger, or ring finger. A positive

---

1. http://www.turner-white.com/pdf/hp_jul00_tinel.pdf

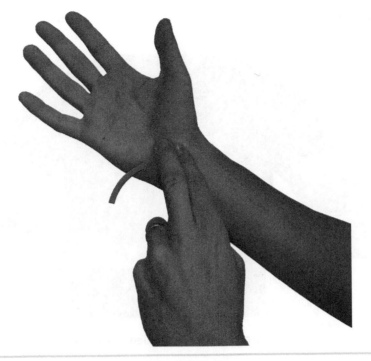

Figure 26—Tinel's Sign

test means that there is damage to the nerves in your wrist that may be carpal tunnel syndrome.

Tinel's Sign is an effective test and it's an important part of making a complete diagnosis, but it is not as sensitive (in the statistical sense) as the next two tests.

Reverse Phalen's Maneuver

Phalen, who popularized Tinel's Sign, eventually developed a test of his own. The test he designed worked well, but in the last twenty years a modified version has proven to work better.[2] That's why we'll be using a reverse Phalen's Maneuver.

Unlike Tinel's Sign, Phalen's Maneuver does not use percussion. Instead, it requires that you hold your hands in forced flexion for a short period of time.

Bring your arms in front of you and press the palms of your hands together such that they are flat and pointing upward, as shown in the following figure.

---

2. *Reverse Phalen's maneuver as an aid in diagnosing carpal tunnel syndrome [WBA94]*

Hold this position for sixty seconds and then slowly release. Stop immediately if you feel pain.

Figure 27—Reverse Phalen's Maneuver

After releasing your hands, pay attention to any tingling, numbness, or burning sensations in your thumb, index finger, middle finger, or ring finger. These sensations or the inability to hold the position for sixty seconds convey a positive test result and suggest that you might have carpal tunnel syndrome.

Carpal Compression Test

The last test is the carpal compression test. It is performed by applying direct pressure to the center of the base of your wrist (the same place you percussed with Tinel's Sign) for thirty seconds, as shown in Figure 28, *Carpal compression test*, on page 107. If you experience pain or numbness in your thumb or fingers during that period, then it is a positive result (and you should stop applying pressure).

This test is considered to have the highest level of accuracy of all the manual evaluation procedures.[3] But together, these three tests are all still used to detect carpal tunnel syndrome.

---

3.   *A new diagnostic test for carpal tunnel syndrome [Dur91]*

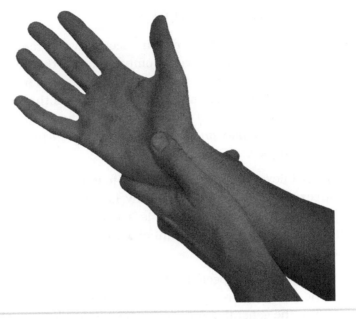

Figure 28—Carpal compression test

Unlike most of the tests in this book, you do not want to pass any of these. If you do end up with a strong positive result or you think you already have carpal tunnel syndrome, then you probably need to see a doctor.

The chance that you will have a positive result is actually very small. Only ten percent of programmers will have wrist pain severe enough to be detected by the test. That's why the discussion in this chapter will emphasize the prevention of carpal tunnel syndrome and wrist pain instead of the treatment. Understanding how the condition happens and knowing how to properly position your body are the best ways to avoid extreme measures like surgery.

Goal 9

Get a negative result on Phalen's Test

It's a good idea to test yourself with Phalen's Maneuver periodically, and that's why we'll make it part of your retrospective. If you ever get a strong positive result, see a doctor.

7.2 Understanding the Causes of Wrist Pain

The tests we performed in the previous section were replicating the basic mechanism that causes wrist pain: compression of the median nerve. The median nerve is a major sensory thoroughfare that runs from your shoulder to your finger tips. Along its journey, the nerve passes through a small canal in your wrist called the carpal tunnel, as shown in Figure 29, *The median nerve median nerveimage anatomymedian nerve carpal tunnel syndrome (CTS)anatomy*, on page 109.

When your wrist flexes or pressure is applied to it, the carpal tunnel compresses and squeezes the median nerve. Many factors affect the severity of the compression, but the most common is a congenital predisposition—some people just have a smaller carpal tunnel. Other factors include swelling due to trauma, injury, or obesity.

What you may not have expected is that people who use a keyboard for more than seven hours a day are not any more prone to developing carpal tunnel syndrome than the general population.[4,5] Keyboard users are, however, more likely to experience general wrist pain and hand numbness. These symptoms are not as severe as CTS, but they can benefit from the same solutions.

There are countless treatment options for carpal tunnel syndrome and wrist pain. They include exercises, braces, salves, steroid injections, and even surgery. The most effective are braces and steroids,[6] but those treatments are intended for patients with severe carpal tunnel syndrome (if that's you, then go see a doctor). Because this chapter is specific to the prevention of pain, we'll discuss some simpler steps you can take: exercise and posture adjustments.

7.3 Using Exercise to Prevent Pain

One of the most promising exercise systems for treating wrist pain appears to be yoga. In 1998, a group of researchers at Hahnemann University in Philadelphia published a study that tracked forty-two people with CTS. The patients in the experimental group received a yoga-based intervention two times per week that consisted of eleven yoga postures designed for strengthening, stretching, and balancing each joint in the upper body.[7]

---

4. *The frequency of carpal tunnel syndrome in computer users at a medical facility [SWSW01]*
5. *Carpal tunnel syndrome and keyboard use at work: a population-based study [Atr07]*
6. *A systematic review of conservative treatment of carpal tunnel syndrome [PAF07]*
7. *Yoga-based intervention for carpal tunnel syndrome: A randomized trial [GSKA98]*

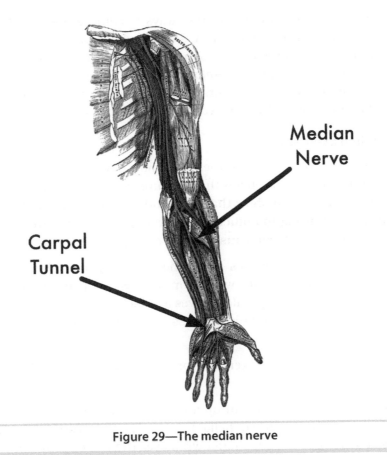

Figure 29—The median nerve

After eight weeks, the researchers found that the yoga group had significant improvement in grip strength and pain reduction while the control group saw no significant change. The yoga group also showed more improvement on Phalen's Test than the control group. However, neither group showed significant differences on Tinel's Sign. The Hahnemann study was seminal in its use of yoga as a CTS treatment, but more research is starting to back it up.[8]

Yoga is not without dangers. A number of publications in the last few years have warned of the injuries suffered from the improper practice of certain poses.[9] The injuries run the gamut from sore shoulders to paralysis. For that reason, it's best if you learn yoga under proper instruction and supervision. See Goal 10, *Take a yoga class*, on page 113.

---

8. *Non-surgical treatment (other than steroid injection) for carpal tunnel syndrome [OMM08]*
9. http://www.nytimes.com/2012/01/08/magazine/how-yoga-can-wreck-your-body.html

In the meantime, there are many other ways to achieve the benefits of yoga without incurring the dangers. In fact, some studies have shown that general exercise and physical fitness are just as effective at treating wrist pain (we'll discuss this more in Chapter 10, *Refactoring Your Fitness*, on page 147).[10] For the purpose of this chapter, we'll practice some simple exercises that you can do in just a few minutes from the comfort of your desk.

Nerve-Gliding Exercises

If you read a lot of tech blogs then you may have seen videos of people demonstrating unusual stretches that are supposed to help relieve wrist pain. There is some science to show that this kind of static stretching helps, but in some cases applying too much pressure to the stretch (often by putting your bodyweight into it) can cause further damage.

Instead, a system of exercises called nerve-gliding has shown the most improvement in patients with wrist pain or CTS.[11,12] These exercises are a form of dynamic stretching, which moves a muscle, nerve, or tendon through a range of motion. This puts less stress on the joint, and appears to also increase strength.

Let's try a few nerve-gliding exercises for your wrists. You can do all of these right at your desk.

Jazz Hands   Hold your left arm up and to your side with your elbow bent, as if you are about to wave "hello" to someone. With your left hand, make a loose fist. Your thumb should wrap over the top of your fingers. Then gently open the hand and stretch the fingers as far as your can. In particular, your thumb should be perpendicular to your forearm.

---

10. http://health.nytimes.com/health/guides/disease/carpal-tunnel-syndrome/print.html
11. *Can we use nerve gliding exercises in women with carpal tunnel syndrome? [Pin05]*
12. *Effectiveness of hand therapy interventions in primary management of carpal tunnel syndrome: a systematic review [MTSB04]*

Slowly close your fist again, and repeat the exercise five to ten times for each hand. You can do both hands at the same time if you would like (but only for this exercise, not the others).

Shadow Puppets   Hold your left arm up and to your side with your elbow bent, as you did in the previous exercise. Make a loose fist again, but this time extend your middle and ring fingers. Then rotate your wrist as if you are drawing circles in the air with those two fingers.

Make two or three circles going clockwise, and two or three circles going counterclockwise. Then repeat the exercise with the other hand.

The Egyptian   Extend your right arm to the side, with the palm of your hand facing the ceiling. Then bend your hand backward, as if you are trying to point your fingers toward the ground. This is the starting position. To perform the exercise, bend your elbow to a ninety-degree angle.

Straighten your elbow again, and then repeat the exercise three to five times for each arm.

Shoulder Shrug   Extend your right arm to the side at a forty-five-degree angle. Then bend your hand backward so that your fingers are pointing behind you. This is the starting position. To perform the exercise, gently shrug your shoulder upward.

Drop your shoulder slowly, and then repeat the exercise three to five times for each arm.

Head Tilt Extend your right arm to the side at a forty-five degree angle and bend your hand backward as you did in the previous exercise. Then gently lean your head to the left, bring it back to center, and then lean it to the right.

Perform the exercise three to five times for each arm.

In these exercises, you're gliding your median nerve through its range of motion, which classifies them as mobility exercises. The median nerve is very long (traveling from the neck to the fingers), which is why the exercises use all of the joints in your arm. The exercises can be done individually or they can all be done as a group up to four times per day. At the end of the chapter we'll add them to your daily checklist.

Research suggests that nerve-gliding increases the lubrication of the tendons and nerves in your arm, but exercise alone is not sufficient to keep these tissues pain-free. You'll also need to ensure that you're not putting unnecessary strain on them. To do this, you need to work on your posture. That's where our musician friends can help.

Ethan Kind eventually relieved his pain by employing a method called the Alexander Technique. Now he teaches this method to students who suffer symptoms similar to his. But the technique can be applied to more than just musicians; it's an excellent tool for programmers, as well. After we discuss your next goal, we'll dive into the Alexander Technique.

Goal 10

Take a yoga class

There's plenty of research showing the health benefits of yoga, but it needs to be practiced under proper instruction and supervision. That's why it's best for you to learn about it outside of this book.

The following poses that are most likely to improve and prevent wrist pain:

- Bharadvajasana (twisting your torso while sitting in a chair)

- Dandasana (sitting while extending your torso)

- Garudasana (arms interlocked and extended in front of your body)

- Half Uttanasana (ninety-degree forward bend at the waist)

- Namaste (pressing your hands together in prayer position)

- Parvatasana (extending your arms over your head with fingers interlocked)

- Tadasana (standing straight up)

- Urdhva Hastasana (extending your arms over your head)

- Urdhva Mukha Svanasana (dog pose with a chair)

- Virabhadrasana 1 (arms overhead with hands in prayer position)

7.4   Reducing Tension with the Alexander Technique

Many of Ethan Kind's students are under the same intense pressure that he experienced in college. That pressure leads to stress, which can eventually drive the students away from the thing they were so passionate about to begin with.

"I have taught a whole lot of hurting performers who felt like they had lost their love of classical music," Ethan states. "I make them aware that it may be a combination of poor technique and intense pressure to be great on their instrument that is making them feel like the thrill is gone."

Ethan believes that the pain his students experience is the result of tension in the body. Relieving that tension requires practice and training with a structured methodology—just like learning to play an instrument. "As I show them how to play or sing without hurting they realize they never really lost their love for classical music," Ethan explains. "It was how they treated themselves that was polluting their love for their instrument and its music."

Most programmers are familiar with the kind of pressure Ethan describes. We are driven by deadlines, and are often required to work strange hours. A common stereotype is that programmers enjoy drinking caffeine and working into the wee hours of the night, but in most cases we are driven to these unhealthy extremes by external pressures. Like music-making, programming is a craft that requires dedication and practice. The similarities between programming and playing music make the Alexander Technique beneficial for practitioners of both disciplines.

At its core, the Alexander Technique is about breaking bad habits, which relates in many ways to the discussion in Chapter 1, *Making Changes*, on page 1. It's a methodology for recognizing problems and actively intervening to correct them. The process has three steps.

Observe You must not only identify problems in your posture and movement, but also observe them. Many Alexander Technique instructors use mirrors to help students see the errors they are making.

Inhibit You must stop the behavior you recognize as being problematic, which is much harder than it sounds. The bad habits you have developed have taken years to learn. You can't unlearn them in just a moment.

Direct Finally, you must direct yourself to replace the problematic behavior with a new behavior that works better.

Let's apply these steps to a common problem for programmers. Say, for example, that you notice a pain in your right wrist. You've read the earlier parts of this chapter, so you know that it's probably related to some excessive flexion of your wrist or possibly your fingers. To observe the problem, you set up a small video camera and film your hands while you work for thirty minutes.

After playing back the video, you notice that several times per minute your right hand and its ring finger are flexing to the outside as they reach for either the `Return` key or the semicolon key (two very commonly used but ill-placed keys for programmers). The flexion is necessary because your arms are tired and you are resting your wrists on the desk, which prevents them from moving fluidly and possibly compresses the carpal tunnel even more. Now you need to inhibit this movement.

To stop an action that has become second nature, you must override the part of the brain that has memorized the behavior so that it can be performed subconsciously. In Chapter 1, *Making Changes*, on page 1, we discussed why the brain does this (essentially to save clock cycles), but now we need to pull the behavior back out and consciously control it. You can start by pausing and taking a breath before pressing `Return`. It will take some practice, but eventually the pause will allow you to be aware of when you press the `Return` key.

Once you have control over your bad habit, you must order yourself to execute a new behavior in its place. In this case, you need to order your body to reach for the `Return` key by rotating at either the elbow or the shoulder instead of the wrist. These upper joints are further away from the keyboard and thus require less flexion to bring your finger to its target (they also carry more weight, so it may take time to strengthen them).

This process may seem self-evident, and to some degree it is. What makes it novel is the structure it adds to the process of breaking habits. As you begin to use it in a number of different places, you'll probably find that the process itself becomes habit.

In *An Alexander Technique Approach to Using a Computer [Kin11]*, Ethan Kind sums up a lot of what he's learned from helping both musicians and computer users over the years; he makes a few simple suggestions for improved posture and movement. To begin, Ethan recommends that when you are typing, your wrists be held slightly higher than your knuckles. You can test this by placing a ruler on the back of your forearm such that it extends over the hand (see Figure 30, *Checking your wrist posture with a ruler*, on page 116). There should be a small gap between your knuckles and the ruler, as shown in the following figure. You may need to adjust your chair or desk height to achieve this position, but you should not need wrist supports.

Ethan strongly discourages the use of any kind of device that supports the wrist from below. He believes this encourages the collapse of your forearm, which puts pressure on its tendons and compresses the median nerve. Furthermore, it forces you to increase the amount of movement in your fingers, which is also something he considers harmful. According to Ethan, you should avoid curling and uncurling your fingers as much as possible when you type.

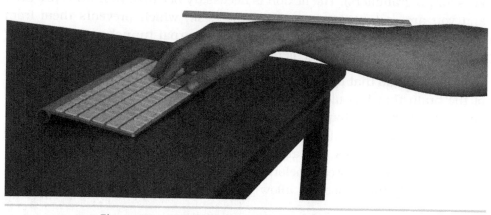

Figure 30—Checking your wrist posture with a ruler

Try to keep them gently curved and move them from the shoulder or elbow (just like a pianist would). For this reason it is important that your arms remain mobile (that is, don't rest them on the arms of your chair). Relaxed mobility is a key element of the Alexander Technique.

The science behind the Alexander Technique is mixed, but it's generally accepted as an effective approach to relieving pain. In particular, its proven to be very cost-effective method—especially when compared to surgery, steroid injections, and even doctor visits.[13] Unfortunately, the majority of research on the Alexander Technique has been performed on specialized groups, such as women older than sixty-five and patients suffering from Parkinson's Disease.[14,15] But in all cases, the results have been positive.

What's undeniable about the Alexander Technique is that if you are successful in using it to change your bad habits, then you are on the path to better health. That's why it's an important part of the curriculum at many major performing-arts schools.[16]

7.5 Restricting Movement with Braces

If neither the exercises described earlier nor the Alexander Technique have helped rid you of wrist pain, then you might be a good candidate for wrist braces.

---

13. *Management of chronic pain in primary care [ST11]*
14. *Functional reach improvement in normal older women after Alexander Technique instruction [DT99]*
15. *Management of chronic pain in primary care [SSC02]*
16. http://www.juilliard.edu/youth-adult/evening-division/courses/detail.php?course_code=EVDIV%20060

Braces should not be your first line of defense against wrist pain. Most doctors will recommend exercise before orthotics.[17] If you've jumped to this section in the hopes of a quick fix, then back up.

Braces are an effective treatment for wrist pain,[18] but they do have one drawback. Immobilizing the wrist will eventually weaken the muscles around the joint, which could lead to worse pain when not using the brace. In some sense, your body may become addicted to the brace.

The best kind of brace to start with is not a brace at all. Instead, you'll want to try a compression sleeve, as shown in the following figure. This helps support the wrist but allows for some range of movement. The best time to wear a device like the one in the figure is while you are working (that is, doing the activity that causes the pain).

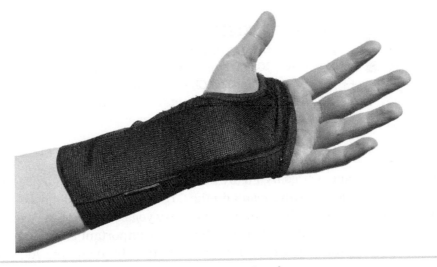

Figure 31—Compression sleeve

If you decide that compression is not enough and you want to use an immobilizing brace, then you should start by wearing it only while you sleep. One study, done at a hospital in Italy, found that patients who wore an immobilizing splint only at night showed significant improvement on Phalen's Test.[19]

---

17. *Is surgical intervention more effective than non-surgical treatment for carpal tunnel syndrome? A systematic review [Shi11]*

18. *Conservative interventions for carpal tunnel syndrome [Mic04]*

19. *Neutral wrist splinting in carpal tunnel syndrome: a 3- and 6-months clinical and neurophysiologic follow-up evaluation of night-only splint therapy [Pre06]*

Before doing anything with a brace, splint, or compression sleeve, be sure to consult your doctor. You should also try to relieve your pain by introducing the exercises and techniques described earlier in the chapter. Only then should you move on to a brace.

7.6   Retrospective

Most people can avoid wrist pain, but it requires active intervention. In this chapter you've learned some new techniques and exercises that can help with this. We'll introduce nerve-gliding to your daily checklist as part of your movement every hour. You can add these activities to the mobility exercises you learned about in the previous chapters. (As you probably know, ++ is the increment operator in languages like C++, and we'll use it to represent an enhancement to an item on the checklist.)

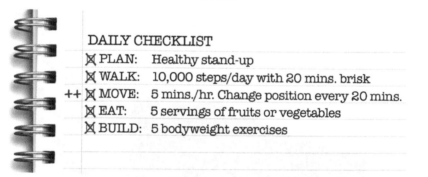

DAILY CHECKLIST
- ⌧ PLAN: Healthy stand-up
- ⌧ WALK: 10,000 steps/day with 20 mins. brisk
- ++ ⌧ MOVE: 5 mins./hr. Change position every 20 mins.
- ⌧ EAT: 5 servings of fruits or vegetables
- ⌧ BUILD: 5 bodyweight exercises

You've also set some new goals (Figure 32, *Goals for your wrists*, on page 119). If you want to avoid a positive result on the CTS tests, then you'll need to add some activities to your daily routine. You can try yoga or just do the exercises from this chapter. No matter what you choose, it's important that you remain physically active and pay attention to your posture by using the Alexander Technique.

Be conscious of your body movements and position. Don't allow bad habits to cripple you and keep you from doing the job you love. Use the Alexander Technique to recognize and control the actions that are causing you pain. But don't stop with your wrists.

You can use the Alexander Technique for positioning and movement in many other parts of your body. As you work your way through the rest of the book, you'll learn about some other physical bad habits you may have developed over the years. Each time you discover one of these, try to use the Alexander Technique as a tool for becoming conscious of the habit and to overcome it.

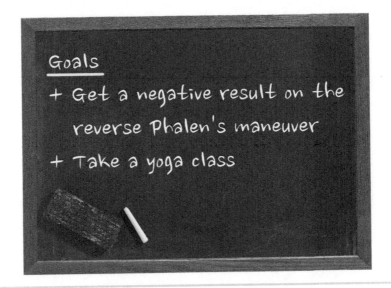

Figure 32—Goals for your wrists

Adding yoga and the nerve-gliding exercises to your routine is a great first step, but there are more-comprehensive exercises you can do in addition to these. In the next chapter you'll learn how to set up a complete exercise plan that is likely to help your wrist pain and is certain to improve your overall health.

Act On It

- Do some nerve-gliding exercises to lubricate the tendons and nerves in your arm, and ultimately reduce wrist pain.

- If you enjoy your yoga class, make it a regular practice. You can even count it toward the twenty minutes of moderate activity on your daily checklist.

- Use the Alexander Technique to observe, inhibit, and direct any motion that you repeat numerous times each day.

CHAPTER 8

Making Exercise Pragmatic

Natsuki Terada, an elite Japanese marathon runner, was finishing a race near Tokyo in January 2011 when he made a mistake. With 300 meters to go, Natsuki surged to the front in a move that appeared to secure him the victory, but moments later he made a wrong turn on the course. The rest of the field blew past him and he had to claw his way back just to finish in third place.

Natsuki's mistake may seem dimwitted, but he has a good excuse. Studies have shown that high-intensity exercise (seventy to eighty percent of HR_{max}) can reduce cognitive functions by shunting blood away from the prefrontal cortex. A marathon runner who is in the final throes of a race is operating at an intensity that's more than ninety percent of his or her HR_{max}.

For that reason, you probably shouldn't write code while running a marathon. But even your daily exercise routine can interfere with your job if you don't coordinate the two activities. If you do coordinate them, you may actually improve your ability to write code. That's because immediately after exercise, blood shifts rapidly back to the brain, which makes it the perfect time to focus on tasks that require complex analysis and creativity.

In this chapter, you'll learn some strategies for adding exercise to your day in a way that makes you healthier and smarter. We'll discuss how you can use the Pomodoro Technique to structure your workouts and how playing video games can be healthy. You'll also learn some ways to make exercise more rewarding by getting feedback on your progress.

This chapter's goal is to make exercise fun, attainable, and pragmatic by including it in your day in a way that makes sense. For programmers, that means it needs to align with your career goals and job routines as well as your health goals and fitness habits.

8.1 Exercising Your Brain

Let's test your brain power. You'll need a timer and something to write on. Set the timer for one minute. In a moment, you'll be given the name of a common object—then you can start the timer. During that minute, write down as many alternative uses for that object as you can think of. For example, if the object is a newspaper you might write down that it could be used to house-train a puppy, line a birdcage, pack dishes, and so on.

Okay, here's your common object: a ruler.

How many uses did you think of? If you're good at programming, then you probably did pretty well (five to ten ideas). That's because this type of brain function, called cognitive flexibility, plays an essential role in problem-solving. Cognitive flexibility is characterized by an ability to shift thinking and produce a steady flow of creative thoughts within different contexts. It's important to our discussion because there's a great deal of evidence showing that cognitive flexibility is enhanced as blood flows back into the brain after exercise.

According to a 2007 study from the *International Journal of Sports Medicine*, a single thirty-five-minute session on a treadmill is enough to provide a short-term improvement in cognitive flexibility.[1] The experiment in the study asked forty adults to think of alternative uses for common objects just as you did a moment ago. Then, half of the subjects watched a movie while the other half ran at sixty to seventy percent of HR_{max}. Thirty-five minutes later, both groups were tested again, and then after twenty minutes they were tested one more time. The movie-watchers showed no change in their ability to answer the questions, but the runners showed a significant improvement.

This study and many others like it suggest that going for a brisk walk, taking a slow jog, or playing basketball at lunch could pay dividends in your afternoon pair-programming session (as long as you take a shower). But even small workouts can pack a big punch as long as they don't interfere with your job. For this, we can use a process model that provides structure to both your workouts and your programming work.

8.2 Taking Healthy Pomodoro Breaks

In the late 1980s, Francesco Cirillo was struggling through his first years at college. His productivity was low and his study habits lacked any kind of structure. Even worse, he couldn't focus on individual tasks because the

---

1. *The effect of a single aerobic training session on cognitive flexibility in late middle-aged adults [NTAA07]*

magnitude of the big picture was distracting him. Francesco needed a system that would help him concentrate—so he created the Pomodoro Technique.

The Pomodoro Technique is a method of working on a single task for a short, well-defined period of time. The basic activity loop goes like this:

1. Set a timer for twenty-five minutes.
2. Start working on a task.
3. Stop when the timer ends (even if the task is not done).
4. Take a five-minute break, and then return to Step 1.

Try it right now. Pick a task you've been agonizing over, set your timer, and get to work. You'll probably find that having a preset time box lessens the fear of failing at the task, which might be what kept you from starting on it in the first place. Instead of failing, you take a break.

Francesco named the technique after the tomato-shaped kitchen timer he used in college (pomodoro is the Italian word for tomato), and he called each iteration a Pomodoro. But it's the break between Pomodoros where we're going to build on this technique. Instead of surfing the Internet or getting a cup of coffee, you'll do something physically active. The goal is to get your body moving every twenty-five minutes.

We'll call this a Pomodoro workout. Set aside a block of time—two or three hours. Then pick two or three programming tasks you want to do during that time. You'll also need to pick two or three exercises you want to do. They could be walking, nerve-gliding, curl-ups, or any of the other activities you've learned in this book. You'll begin the workout with a programming task. Set your timer for twenty-five minutes and get to work. When the period ends, set your timer for five minutes and switch to your first exercise. After the timer goes off, return to your computer and start the process over again. Repeat this until the block of time you've allotted yourself is over (see Figure 33, *A Pomodoro workout*, on page 124).

According to Staffan Nöteberg, the author of *Pomodoro Technique Illustrated: The Easy Way to Do More in Less Time [Nö09]*, this kind of physical activity during Pomodoro breaks is ideal. He even does it himself. "I always leave the office chair during my Pomodoro breaks," Staffan says. "Normally I take a one-minute walk."

However, Staffan emphasizes the importance of time-boxing your breaks in addition to your work periods. That is to say, you probably shouldn't go for a three-mile run between iterations. "Your breaks shouldn't be longer than five minutes to be able to continue quickly from where you left off," he emphasizes.

Code Review
(25 mins.)

Walk
(5 mins.)

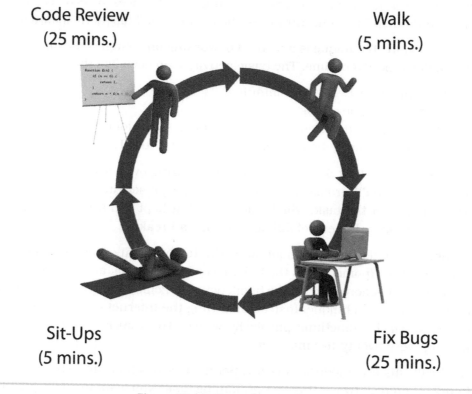

Sit-Ups
(5 mins.)

Fix Bugs
(25 mins.)

Figure 33—A Pomodoro workout

Keeping your breaks short doesn't render them useless, though. Small spurts of exercise in between Pomodoros can have profound effects on your health. In fact, these microactivity breaks may be more important to your health than longer workouts.

A 2008 publication from a group of researchers at The University of Queensland in Australia found that getting thirty minutes of exercise per day was less effective at preventing type-2 diabetes, cardiovascular disease, and obesity when it was done in one lump sum—especially when another fifteen hours of the day were spent sitting. Surprisingly, subjects who split up their exercise across the day were at lower risk for those health issues. The study suggests that long periods of nonexercise can actually counteract the benefits of regularly going to the gym.[2] But as you learned in Chapter 3, *A Farewell to Chairs?*, on page 29, just five minutes is enough to mitigate these dangers.

---

2.   *Too much sitting: a novel and important predictor of chronic disease risk? [OBB09]*

To make things even better, Staffan believes that the mental benefits of doing physical activity during your breaks align well with the other goals of the Pomodoro Technique. "One of the benefits of regularly taking short breaks is that you recharge your brain," Staffan asserts. "When you return to your desk, it's not uncommon that you have three awesome new ideas about how to solve the problem you were struggling with before the break. If you focus on something non-theoretical, like push-ups, it'll probably help even more."

When you do a Pomodoro workout, there's a lot happening in your brain. Neurons are being recruited and new pathways are being created. In Chapter 2, *Bootstrapping Your Health*, on page 13, you learned how exercise promotes the production of BDNF, which strengthens this process. However, an ideal plan for the best type, duration, and frequency of exercise that builds brain power has not been identified. That kind of research just hasn't been done yet. It may happen in the next decade, but until then the Pomodoro Technique can provide excellent structure that blends with your career goals and your health goals.

Most programmers who use the Pomodoro Technique like that it pairs well with large-scale methodologies such as Scrum, agile, and spiral (all of which use time-boxed iterations). Given that, and how well Pomodoro also aligns with the goals in this book, it's a sure win for staying healthy, smart, and productive. It can also help rebuild your habits. But if you're going to make fitness a habit, you're also going to require a reward. For that, you'll need some feedback.

Goal 11

Do a Pomodoro workout

Get a timer and do a Pomodoro Technique workout. In the breaks between iterations you can do some of the activities you've learned thus far in the book. Table 4, *An Example Pomodoro Workout*, on page 126 shows an example plan. It includes four iterations with three breaks for a total of two and a half hours.

You can make your Pomodoro Technique workout any length you'd like, and you can do it at any time of day. You can also fill your breaks with whatever activity you prefer. Some people prefer to only walk during their breaks. Later in the book you'll learn some more exercises that you can add to your workouts.

Work	Break	Duration
Write code (sitting desk)		25 min
	Walk stairs	5 min
Fix bugs (standing desk)		25 min
	Nerve-gliding	5 min
Refactor code (sitting desk with exercise ball)		25 min
	Curl-ups	5 min
Code review (standing desk with balance board)		25 min
TOTAL		*2.5 hours*

Table 4—An Example Pomodoro Workout

8.3   Keeping a Log

The best way to get feedback on your health is to keep an exercise log. This simple tool can track your progress, but it can also help make your exercise routine more effective.

In 1988, researchers at Stanford university undertook a study to find out what strategies best encourage the adoption and maintenance of moderate-intensity, home-based exercise training.[3] The strategies used in the experiment included making phone calls to the participants, having an instructor demonstrate the exercises, and having the participants self-monitor by recording their workouts in a journal. After six months, the researchers found that the self-monitoring group not only was better at sticking to their exercise regimen, but also reported doing more exercise and had bigger improvements in overall fitness.

Other studies have shown similar results for subjects that are trying to lose weight.[4] In any case, keeping a log of your workouts is a scientifically proven method for making workouts a habit.

Your log can take many different forms. It can be a mobile app or a Moleskin notebook, but for it to be effective you'll need to follow some guidelines:

---

3.   *Strategies for increasing early adherence to and long-term maintenance of home-based exercise training in healthy middle-aged men and women [KTHD88]*

4.   *Experiences of Self-Monitoring: Successes and Struggles during Treatment for Weight Loss [Bur09]*

Be Specific Record the number of times you did each exercise, how long it took, your heart rate during and after, the weather conditions, who you were with, how you felt, and anything else you think is important. If you don't include details, then the log won't make your progress visible.

Be Consistent Put an entry in your log every day—even if you didn't exercise. Write down "rest day" if it was intentional, or be honest if it wasn't it. The Stanford study actually had two groups: one that self-monitored on a daily basis and one that self-monitored on a weekly basis. The group that monitored daily had better results and showed more improvement.

In addition to keeping a daily log, try to use the same methods for each entry. Record the same types of detail and put it into the same structure. Think of it as a science experiment in which you don't want the way you record the results to affect the findings.

Read Your Log To get the most out of your log, you have to read it. Look back on what you've done and feel proud. This can be a great motivator, but more importantly, it can provide data that you can use to adjust your workouts. If you try something new and your progress starts to flatten out, then you may need to undo that change. If you develop an injury, the log book might reveal the cause—did you increase intensity or distance too quickly? Look for trends, make changes, and iterate.

One way to keep an exercise log is to use the Healthy Programmer companion iPhone app. As you check items off on the daily checklist, the app will automatically update your log for you. The app also contains a list of all the exercises presented in the book. You can simply tap on the ones you've done, and it will add them to your log entry for the day. It also has room for general notes and such, as shown in Figure 34, *The log-book feature on the companion iPhone app Healthy Programmer iPhone appexercise log toolsexercise logs toolsHealthy Programmer iPhone app iPhone appslogs*, on page 128.

No matter what tool you use, start your log right now. Write down what you've done today for your health. This log will be a key element in making fitness a habit—but it's not the only way of getting feedback. Feedback can be fun.

8.4 Playing Games with Your Health

Video games get a lot of bad press, but they've also inspired a number of people to do great things. Chad Fowler is one of them. "*Doom* is the reason I am a computer programmer," he says. "I loved *Doom* so much that I wanted to learn about programming—to understand how they did it."

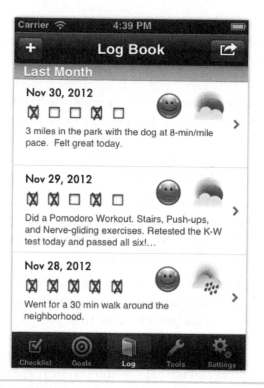

Figure 34—The log-book feature on the companion iPhone app

Games are fun, entertaining, and often provide rewards, which makes them ideal motivators. That's also why they make great tools for getting fit. Chad enjoys gaming so much that he needed to find a way to keep playing even when he was trying to lose weight. For this, he used his talent as a professional hacker.

"I had never done anything with electronics, and I felt that it was a sad skill hole for me," Chad recalls. "I got an Arduino and a bunch of electronics stuff, and I bought an exercise cycle." Chad arranged the bike so it would fit under a desk, and then put his programming skills to work. "I disconnected the sensor from the onboard computer and created a circuit so I could plug it up to the Arduino, [which I] plugged into my computer via USB. I wrote a simple little driver for it in Ruby that would normalize and report RPMs out. Then I could easily write Ruby programs that would use the RPM information and do stuff like turn on the screen saver every time it went below a certain level."

"I also made a rule for myself that if I wanted to play video games, I had to be on that pedaling desk," Chad continues. "That was interesting, I would graph my RPMs over time while I was playing games. Depending on the intensity of the game, it would vary wildly."

Chad's pedaling desk was a fun but artificial way of combining gaming with exercise. In addition to his roll-your-own approach, a number of gaming systems integrate physical activity into the games themselves.

Motion-controlled video game platforms like Nintendo's Wii, Microsoft's Xbox Kinect, and Sony's PlayStation Move use sensors to detect movements in a player's body. This allows you to play a boxing game, for example, by actually throwing punches. There's a diverse array of games like this that includes tennis, bowling, and even activities that aren't sports-oriented—like dancing, or flying through the air with Peter Pan.

All of these games get you up and moving, but their effectiveness as exercise tools has often been questioned. To address this, a group of exercise scientists at the University of Wisconsin–La Crosse put the Wii to the test.[5] They created a study in which participants played Wii games for ten minutes at a time while the researchers monitored oxygen uptake, heart rate, and rating of perceived exertion (RPE).

The games chosen for the study included golf, bowling, baseball, tennis, and boxing. As you might expect, they each delivered different results in terms of their effectiveness as exercise. The boxing game yielded the highest energy expenditures, with the participants recording a mean heart rate of 139 BPM. Some of the players even got as high as ninety-four percent of their HR_{max}, which suggests it's a more effective exercise than walking. In fact, the study found that the intensity required to play the boxing game is high enough to actually improve some people's cardiovascular endurance. The tennis and baseball games also delivered good results by bringing the players' mean heart rate to about sixty percent of HR_{max}, which makes it equivalent to a brisk walk. But bowling and golf just barely got the players' heart rates above their resting levels.

According to the researchers, the games are most effective when the players actually try to simulate the movements of the real sport. This provides the best possible workout, and the participants suggested that it made the games more fun. Having fun is precisely the goal of this kind of activity.

Games are fun because they provide a more tangible and immediate reward than activities like walking. That's because games have feedback systems

---

5. http://www.acefitness.org/getfit/studies/WiiStudy.pdf

such as scores, levels, and progress bars that tell players how close they are to achieving the games' goals.

Feedback and goals are two essential traits of any game, but the rules of a game are just as important. Consider a game like golf (the actual kind of golf, not the Wii version). If there were no rules and you simply wanted to achieve the goal of putting the ball in the hole, then the game would be trivial. You would probably pick the ball up and drop it into the cup, which would not be all that fun. But golf is fun because the players have agreed upon a set of rules that make the game more challenging.

The rules of a game create obstacles that a player must overcome, and doing so stimulates creative and strategic thinking. As we discussed in Chapter 4, *Agile Dieting*, on page 47, these brain functions produce dopamine, which rewards the thinker. Thus, playing a game that requires physical activity may provide a double dose of chemical rewards.

One aspect of games that the Wisconsin study did not examine was the impact of having an avatar. It turns out that this is an important factor in motivating the players of any game that requires physical activity. A study at Stanford University in 2009 compared the exercise behavior of video game–players who had an avatar and those who did not.[6] The avatar in this study was customized to lose weight as the participants exercised harder. In one group, the avatar even gained weight when the participants failed to exercise.

The experiment in the study had the participants do a number of arm and shoulder movements with two-pound weights. All groups started by doing a required set of twelve repetitions and were then given a rest. The participants with avatars that lost weight as they performed the exercise voluntarily chose to do more repetitions after the break. Furthermore, a follow-up survey done twenty-four hours later found that these participants were more likely to have engaged in other exercise outside of the experiment.

The findings of the Stanford study further bolster the importance of feedback. The participants who saw their avatars lose weight were motivated by having a visual representation of the progress they were making. However, this study has not yet been replicated—more research needs to be conducted before drawing broad conclusions from its results.

Both Wii golf and actual golf are excellent activities that you can use to make your workouts fun, but there are plenty of other games to choose from. Sports

---

6. *Virtual self-modeling: The effects of vicarious reinforcement and identification on exercise behaviors* [FB09]

such as basketball and soccer provide a much higher level of intensity, which in turn yields a better workout. We'll discuss team activities like these in Chapter 11, *Teaming Up*, on page 173, and you'll even learn how to play more-accessible games that do not require as much finesse and skill (like dodgeball). Many games require a group of people to be played properly, but in lieu of getting a group of friends together in person, you can play games with your virtual friends.

8.5 Taking Your Fitness to the Web

The explosion of social-media applications in the last few years has led to a number of fitness-related websites and services. Many, like Strava, encourage competition among users. According to its website, Strava "makes fitness a social experience, providing motivation and camaraderie even if you're exercising alone." It also provides a challenge.

Strava lets you record a run or bike ride with any GPS device, and then upload it to the Strava website. Once your data is in the cloud, you can track your progress and compare it to other users'. Some route segments allow you to compete for titles like King of the Mountain. There are also general Strava challenges, which range from the attainable to totally ridiculous.

Xavier Shay, a programmer at the mobile-payments company Square, knows a bit about these extreme challenges. He's an accomplished runner—having completed the San Francisco Marathon, among other things—and a Strava user.

"There was this challenge on Strava [to run] 200 miles [in] a month," says Xavier. "The marathon was week three, so I still had to pull out 80 or 90 kilometers the next week. I went for a recovery run [the Sunday after the race]. Then on Wednesday I ran a half marathon." In addition to the challenge, Xavier managed to grab Strava's King of the Mountain title for Bernal Heights in San Francisco. It's a 100-meter climb near his office.

Not everyone can lay down the miles like Xavier, but even he needs motivation. Xavier doesn't consider himself a competitive person, so typical motivators don't work for him. But the Strava challenges and titles aren't a competition to him—they're a game.

Xavier's 200-mile month left him a little broken down—he probably over did it. Strava definitely targets athletes like Xavier who have aggressive goals, but many other services are designed to appeal to a wider spectrum of fitness enthusiasts. Among these is DailyBurn, which was started by programmers.

Andy Smith, one of DailyBurn's cofounders, was working as a programmer on government contracts in 2007, but he wanted to get into the commercial world and work directly with consumers. He also wanted to scratch his own itch. "I wanted a tracking app that was easy to use and useful for tracking sets and reps in the gym," he says. "It's grown quite a bit from there."

"DailyBurn lets you stream interactive video workouts to your computer, mobile device, TV, etc." he describes. "They are best-in-class videos (not just some trainer on YouTube) and let you have access to world-class trainers. It's way better than DVD workouts because you can work out anywhere, it's customized to you, and the variety is outstanding."

The most important advantage of DailyBurn over traditional DVD workout videos is that it provides you with feedback. "We have a full tracker site with tracking tools, including mobile," Andy explains. "And we are releasing a new diet program soon that I think will be a big hit."

Keeping a log, gaming, using online workout trackers, and employing other fitness gadgets are means of getting feedback during and after exercise. This kind of feedback is extremely important because it's immediate, whereas the other benefits of being healthy are not.

Goal 12

Sign up for an online fitness service

Go sign up for an online service like the ones we've discussed. You can choose one of the websites mentioned here or any of their competitors—the important thing is that you get started. The best service for you depends on your ability level. If you're ready to tackle some tough challenges, then try Strava. If you're just getting started or need more guidance, then try DailyBurn. You can find a list of other recommended sites that cover a wide range of ability levels at http://healthyprog.com.

8.6 Retrospective

In this chapter you've learned a few ways to make your workouts fun and pragmatic. The Pomodoro Technique provides a structured system that aligns with your fitness goals and your career goals, but it also provides the essential components of a habit. The cue is the Pomodoro timer, the routine is whatever activity you choose to do during your iteration, and the reward is twofold: you'll be healthy and productive.

Your first goal for this chapter is to do just one Pomodoro Technique workout. You'll find that in just a couple of hours you can knock out many of the items on your daily checklist and get your real job done. Given how many studies suggest exercise boosts creative thinking, you might even do your job better. You second goal is sign up for an online fitness service.

You also learned that games, trackers, and fitness tech can take the edge off of exercise by making it more fun. This is due, in part, to the feedback they provide. If you've been keeping track of your daily checklist, then you are well on your way. You should incorporate the checklist into your log, but you should also include as much additional detail as possible. Remember to be specific, be consistent, and read your log book often. This will give you the best results. You can even record your Pomodoro Technique workouts.

The structure of the Pomodoro Technique is essential to making your exercise routine pragmatic, but eventually you'll need a different kind of structure to ensure that your workouts are holistic and balanced. The powerhouse exercises and nerve-gliding activities are excellent for solving specific health problems, but being truly healthy requires a program that covers every aspect of physical fitness. In the next chapter, you'll learn how to do that.

Act On It

- Use a Pomodoro Technique workout to add some activity to your day.

- Get some exercise before a code review or pair-programming session to enhance your cognitive flexibility.

- Keep a log of your exercise. Write down what you did (or didn't do) every day. You can do this easily with the companion iPhone app.

- Play games. Whether it's Wii tennis or real tennis, games will make fitness fun.

- Set your own goals and think of them as challenges. This is the best way to motivate yourself.

CHAPTER 9

Thinking Outside the Cube

Last year I attended a software conference in Helsinki, Finland. Finland is a beautiful country with a fantastic culture, but it was a little depressing that the midday sun never rose higher than the buildings. Finland is located along the arctic circle, so the sun doesn't even rise at all on some winter days. Conversely, there are summer days when it doesn't set. People tell me you get used to these extremes, but it must take a few millennia.

The region around Finland was first settled in 8500 BC,[1] and since that time the Finnish culture has learned to embrace those precious sunlit summer days. Festivals and outdoor activities expose the Finns to as much sunlight as possible when it's available. In this way, the Finns can synthesize enough vitamin D to keep their bodies healthy through the winter months. But in an increasingly indoor world, the country has taken more-extreme measures—such as mandating the fortification of certain foods with vitamin D.[2]

As a programmer, you may face some of the same health concerns as the Finns. Most offices and cubicles create a synthetic arctic circle for software developers—I'm not talking about the air conditioner, though. We get to our desks early in the morning and often leave around the time the sun is setting. As a result, we may be putting our health at risk by limiting our exposure to unfiltered sunlight. In this chapter, we'll explore a few ways that you can ensure your vitamin D levels are topped off without putting yourself at risk for skin cancer. For some people this requires a dietary change, but it can also mean getting outside more often.

---

1. *People, Material Culture and Environment in the North [Her04]*
2. *Impact of national fortification of fluid milks and margarines with vitamin D on dietary intake and serum 25-hydroxyvitamin D concentration in 4-year-old children [PLI07]*

Vitamin D isn't the only reason we need to leave our cubical environment, though. Some studies suggest that increased exposure to the outdoors can have positive impacts on blood pressure, heart rate, and the immune system. It's important for programmers to have a strong immune system because working in an office environment puts us in contact with lots of people (and the residue they leave behind). We'll finish this chapter by discussing other ways to build immunity and ultimately how to treat a cold if you happen to catch one. In most cases, the solution is to let our bodies get back to what Mother Nature intended. And she definitely didn't intend for us to spend our day indoors writing code.

9.1   Dosing on Vitamin D

Vitamin D is an organic compound that is naturally present in very few foods, but humans are able to synthesize the vitamin when ultraviolet radiation penetrates the skin. Our bodies are even capable of storing the excess we produce in our liver and fat so that it can be released later—this is what allowed the Finns to survive at their extreme northern latitudes for so many generations. But vitamin D deficiency is no longer unique to Finland. One study found that as many as fifty-one percent of Australian office workers have a vitamin D deficiency,[3] and Australia is not known for lack of sunlight.

Go get some vitamin D right now. Step outside, roll up your sleeves, and expose as much of your skin to the sun as possible. If it's sunny and you can stay outside for ten minutes, you'll probably synthesize enough vitamin D to meet your quota for one day. Sunlight through your office window doesn't count, however, because the glass will filter the radiation.

Spending ten minutes in the sun while exposing the skin on your shoulders and legs will provide enough radiation to produce about 10,000 international units (IUs) of the vitamin if you're fair-skinned. It will be considerably less if you are dark-skinned or wearing long sleeves and pants. If you wanted to get the same amount of vitamin D from your diet, you'd have to drink about twenty quarts of milk (don't do this), and even that is only because milk is vitamin D–fortified in most countries.

The National Institutes of Health (NIH) and the Institute of Medicine (IOM) recommend that most people ingest 600–800 IUs of vitamin D per day (increasing with age),[4,5] but getting vitamin D as a dietary supplement may

---

3.   *Serum vitamin D levels in office workers in a subtropical climate [VWvK11]*
4.   http://www.iom.edu/Reports/2010/Dietary-Reference-Intakes-for-Calcium-and-Vitamin-D.aspx
5.   http://ods.od.nih.gov/factsheets/VitaminD-HealthProfessional/

not have the same health benefits as synthesizing it from sunlight. There are early indications that daily supplements increase the risk of kidney stones and have little effect on preventing bone fractures. As a result, a panel assigned by the U.S. Department of Health and Human Services recently recommended against taking vitamin D and calcium supplements.[6]

Despite the warnings, the popularity of these supplements has increased because the number of individuals who are not getting enough vitamin D is on the rise. Among the U.S. population, only twenty-three percent of adolescents and adults have levels that are considered "adequate" or "normal," according to a survey sponsored by the NIH.[7] Nearly all non-Hispanic blacks (ninety-seven percent) and most Mexican Americans (ninety percent) are characterized as having "insufficient" levels.

We clearly need to increase the vitamin D in our bodies, but doing it safely is tricky. Radiation from the sun is dangerous in and of itself, and too much exposure to ultraviolet light can lead to skin cancer. Determining how much sun is too much depends on your skin pigmentation, your latitude, the time of day, cloud cover, clothing, sunscreen, and more. In general, the ten minutes we discussed earlier should be safe for people with fair skin. If you are of Hispanic origin or already have a tan, you many need double the amount of time. If you have very dark skin, you may need as much as six times the sun exposure.

Tip 8	Fair-skinned individuals need about ten minutes of unprotected sun exposure each day to produce sufficient levels of vitamin D. People of Hispanic origin need about double the exposure, and people with even darker skin may need six times the exposure.

Thus far, we've discussed how to get vitamin D but we haven't addressed the bigger question of why it's needed. Answering this question presents a good opportunity to discuss some common mistakes when making decisions about your health.

9.2   Shedding Light on the Vitamin D Hype

Open a browser and enter the term "vitamin D benefits" into your favorite search engine. You'll likely find reports that link vitamin D to curing cancer; strengthening

---

6.   http://www.uspreventiveservicestaskforce.org/uspstf/uspsvitd.htm

7.   http://www.cdc.gov/nchs/nhanes.htm

the immune system; averting depression; improving pain; clearing up psoriasis; lowering your blood pressure; and lowering your risk of developing diabetes, heart disease, and kidney disease. Here are a few example headlines:

- The Benefits of Vitamin D: Weigh Less, Smile More[8]
- Vitamin D Prevents Breast Cancer[9]
- Vitamin D Solved Pain Problem[10]
- Vitamin D Reduces Body Fat[11]
- Does Vitamin D Improve Brain Function?[12]

Indeed, there is some evidence to support a few of these claims, but a consensus is still many years away. In the worst cases, there is conflicting evidence and the publications have used a single study to draw a broad conclusion. The vitamin D media frenzy is a good example of how we can fall prey to the hype that surrounds promising results even when they lack sufficient evidence. That's why Dr. David Angus used vitamin D to illustrate the importance of skepticism in his book *The End of Illness [Ang12]*.

Dr. Angus points out that it is nearly impossible to perform a reliable study of vitamin D because it cannot be controlled in any given person. As a result, the only research that exists is observational (although a promising nationwide clinical study is underway, and results are expected around 2015).

Studies have shown that a vitamin D deficiency can result in impaired bone mineralization, which may lead to rickets in children and osteoporosis in adults. It can also manifest itself in your teeth, which is why an increase in cavities is often a sign that you have insufficient levels of vitamin D in your body.[13] But it's not understood if a dietary vitamin D supplement can prevent these conditions, and that's why Dr. Angus recommends obtaining the vitamin by synthesizing it yourself—a process that evolution has perfected over millions of years.

The human body is very good at taking care of itself. We call this homeostasis, and it's responsible for managing vitamin D synthesis, blood pressure, body temperature, blood sugar, and many other things. But as anyone with diabetes will tell you, we can disrupt this system by messing around with our natural environment. Sitting in front of a computer all summer is one way to do that.

---

8. http://www.foxnews.com/health/2012/08/17/benefits-vitamin-d-weigh-less-smile-more/
9. http://www.naturalnews.com/027204_cancer_Vitamin_D_breast.html
10. http://www.app.com/article/20121211/NJLIFE04/312110033/Vitamin-D-solved-pain-problem
11. http://www.digitaljournal.com/article/338739
12. http://www.scientificamerican.com/article.cfm?id=does-d-make-a-difference
13. *Diet, nutrition and the prevention of dental diseases [MP04]*

Creating the best environment for your body requires attention to your unique health needs. Every person's needs are different, and you must consider each factor your body brings to the party when making decisions about your health. Do you have fair skin or dark skin? Are you young or old? Are you male or female? Do you have a family history of skin cancer? Do you live in Australia or Finland? You must weigh all of these instead of drawing broad conclusions from a single study.

That being said, you won't live long enough to collect as much data as you'd probably like to. You have to make decisions about your health based on the information you have at hand. Right now it tells us that having sufficient levels of vitamin D appears to be generally beneficial, and the best way to get the vitamin is to synthesize it yourself. More studies will be done on vitamin D in the coming years, but until then you must heed Dr. Angus's advice and be skeptical when reading headlines.

Dr. Angus's book is about more than just vitamins and skepticism, though. It's also about changing the perception of the human body. We must view the body and its health as a complex system instead of individual entities. When you turn one knob, it can have profound and unexpected consequences on other parts of the system. A vitamin D deficiency is a good example, and that's probably why we are starting to see it linked to such a wide range of illnesses. After we discuss your next goal, you'll learn how perceiving your body as a system and treating it accordingly can keep you from getting sick.

Goal 13

Learn about your family medical history

Ask your parents and grandparents what caused their parents' deaths. Did they suffer from any health conditions that you didn't know about? Understanding your genetic predisposition to cancer, heart disease, and stroke can help you make better decisions about your health. Write down this information and pass it on to your next of kin. Some software tools for doing this are listed at http://healthyprog.com.

9.3 Boosting Your Immune System

The immune system works exactly the way Dr. Angus describes the human body—it requires the harmonious interaction of many components to function well. In that regard, *boosting* immunity is a process of creating balance that will allow the immune system to function at its best. The most obvious ways to do this include healthy living and following the recommendations made earlier in this book: monitor your blood pressure, exercise regularly, don't smoke, and eat well. But there are many other "knobs" you can turn, and a few of them have been shown empirically to improve the function of your immune system.

Get Enough Sleep   We don't know the exact number of hours one should sleep at night—it probably differs from person to person—but we do know that losing sleep, such as by staying awake for twenty-four-hour periods, has a negative impact on the immune system.

One of the first studies to demonstrate this came from the University of Lübeck in Germany.[14] Researchers vaccinated participants against hepatitis A. One experimental group slept after the shot while another group stayed awake. Both groups were tested four weeks later, and the experimental group showed a twofold increase in certain antibodies.

In general, a good amount of sleep is probably between seven and nine hours, and going without sleep is really bad.

Drink Enough Water   We've already discussed the relationship between hydration and headaches, but hydration affects your immune system, as well. Dehydration creates a chemical imbalance in your body that prevents the immune system from functioning at it's best. So keep drinking eight glasses of water each day (follow the 8x8 rule), and remember to stay hydrated during and after exercise.[15]

Avoid Antibiotics (If Your Doctor Approves)   Antibiotics kill good bacteria (probiotics) as well as bad bacteria. Probiotics in your gut influence your immune system's development by correcting deficiencies and increasing the number of natural antibodies. Exactly how the probiotics interact with the immune system is not completely understood, but most research suggests it's bad to kill them.[16] The point is, if your doctor doesn't say you need antibiotics, then don't take antibiotics.

Eat Fermented Foods (Maybe)   Some studies suggest that eating fermented foods, such as yogurt, can replenish the belly with probiotics like

---

14. *Sleep enhances the human antibody response to hepatitis A vaccination [LPFB03]*
15. *Effect of exercise, heat stress, and hydration on immune cell number and function [MDMN02]*
16. *Antibiotic overuse: Stop the killing of beneficial bacteria [Bla11]*

Lactobacillus and Bifidobacterium.[17,18] However, more research needs to be done.

Get Your Vitamin D   As discussed earlier, the effects of a dietary vitamin D supplement are not completely understood. But it is clear that vitamin D plays an important role in the immune system. In fact, a deficiency in vitamin D has been shown to increase the risk of infection.[19] Your ten minutes of unprotected sun exposure each day should help improve your immune function and restore balance in your health.

Getting outside certainly has health benefits, but staying indoors—much like sitting—is worse than breaking even. It can even make you sick.

9.4 Dealing with the Common Cold

Vitamin D production drops in the winter in part because we spend more time indoors, but that's also why viruses and colds spread like wildfire during those same months. Being indoors increases our contact with people who may carry contagious viruses like the common cold.

There is no cure for the common cold, and there isn't even conclusive evidence to suggest that echinacea, zinc, vitamin C, or any other remedy can shorten the duration of being sick. There is mixed evidence regarding these compounds, and a deficiency can weaken your immune system, but those are extreme cases. The best thing you can do is try to prevent catching a cold in the first place and then treat the symptoms if you get one. The following are some prevention tips.

- Wash your hands with soap and water. When water is not available, the Centers for Disease Control and Prevention recommends using alcohol-based products made for disinfecting your hands.

- Clean your desk. Some cold viruses (such as the rhinovirus) can survive for up to three hours. Cleaning surfaces like your desk with a virus-killing disinfectant can help prevent viruses from spreading.

- Don't touch your face. Cold viruses enter your body through the mouth, nose, and eyes. Keeping your hands away from these orifices can reduce your risk of getting sick.

---

17. *Regulatory effects of a fermented food concentrate on immune function parameters in healthy volunteers [SSSS09]*
18. *Daily ingestion of fermented milk containing Lactobacillus casei DN114001 improves innate-defense capacity in healthy middle-aged people [PMCM04]*
19. *Vitamin D and the immune system [Ara11]*

- Spend time outside. We'll discuss in the next section how this can boost your immune system even without sunlight, but it will also reduce your level of contact with other people who may carry a contagious virus.

Treating the symptoms is even less glamorous. Get some rest, and take an anti-inflammatory drug if your doctor says it's okay. We all wish there were a better answer here, but there isn't! You should see a doctor, but in most cases (such as the very common rhinovirus) antibiotics won't help.

It's also a good idea to stay away from your office to avoid spreading the bug to coworkers. If you feel well enough to go outside, then do that too. As we've already discussed, being outdoors and exposing yourself to sunlight has many benefits to the immune system. But the way you spend your time outdoors may also have an impact on your health. Here again, we can learn from the Finns.

9.5 Thinking Under the Trees

An important part of Finnish culture, stemming from the population's need for sunlight, is the human connection to nature. It's expressed in everything from religion to art to the economy. In fact, Finland is one of the world's leading wood producers, which has led to a significant national investment in forestry conservation and research. In keeping with the Finnish tradition, these studies often include forestry's connection to humans.

The Finnish Forest Research Institute (Metla) has done much of this work in conjunction with researchers in Japan, a country that might have an even deeper national tradition of connecting to nature. In fact, Japanese scientists have been studying the benefits of what they call *forest-bathing* for several decades.

Forest-bathing is a Japanese tradition of taking a leisurely excursion into the woods while embracing the smells and sounds of its relaxing environment. Japan's forestry agency has created official forest-bathing trails, and the country has even spent $4 million on forest-bathing research since 2004.[20] This investment has revealed some of the profound effects that the outdoors can have on our well-being. A simple walk through the woods might strengthen the immune system, lower blood pressure, and reduce stress more than walking on city streets.

---

20. http://www.outsideonline.com/fitness/wellness/Take-Two-Hours-of-Pine-Forest-and-Call-Me-in-the-Morning.html?page=all

In one study, a group of middle-aged Tokyo businessmen (and women) spent three days hiking in the woods.[21] The researchers took blood and urine samples during and after the trip to measure natural killer (NK) cell activity. NK cells are essentially white blood cells that instruct other cells, such as tumor cells and virus-infected cells, to self-destruct. After two days in the woods, the participants in the study had a fifty-six percent increase in NK activity. One month later they were tested again, and still had a twenty-three percent increase over their initial levels. Similar studies in urban environments have not shown the same results.[22]

Most people don't have time to spend three days in the woods, however, and that's why the author of this study repeated the procedure over a one-day period. He found a similar increase in NK activity that was sustained for seven days following the excursion.[23] Other studies have shown that as little as fifteen minutes in the woods can lower your heart rate and blood pressure as well as decrease the production of cortisol, a hormone that's used to measure stress.[24,25]

> **Tip 9** Doing your twenty minutes of walking or moderate activity in the woods may be more beneficial than doing it in an urban setting.

According to Hiro Asari, a software developer at Red Hat and a native of Japan, forest-bathing is especially important to those of us who spend most of our time in offices or urban environments. "You can walk on the city blocks, too, but you would rather walk in the woods if all things are equal, wouldn't you?" asks Hiro rhetorically. "Imagine a lush summer day, the sun shining through the dancing leaves. The air is filled with energy and oxygen, and you feel invigorated." The benefits of forest-bathing are obvious to Hiro, but researchers are still trying to understand the exact mechanism that makes a walk in the woods more beneficial than an urban stroll.

---

21. *Effect of forest bathing trips on human immune function [Li10]*
22. *Visiting a forest, but not a city, increases human natural killer activity and expression of anti-cancer proteins [LMKI08]*
23. *A day trip to a forest park increases human natural killer activity and the expression of anti-cancer proteins in male subjects [LKIH10]*
24. *The physiological effects of Shinrin-yoku (taking in the forest atmosphere or forest bathing): evidence from field experiments in 24 forests across Japan [PTKK10]*
25. *Effect of forest bathing on physiological and psychological responses in young Japanese male subjects [LPTO11]*

Some studies have attempted to isolate the scents and sounds of the forest to produce results in the laboratory that are similar to those found in the woods. In a few cases, they've tested the phytoncides that give evergreen plants their smell.[26] The results are promising, but not entirely surprising. Since the 1990s, researchers have been studying other fragrant chemicals—such as pinene, which is found in pine resin and sagebrush, for its antimicrobial properties; and limonene, which is given off by citrus trees, as a possible tumor suppressor in cancer patients. Some of the forest-bathing researchers recommend picking up pieces of wood and breaking them in half to release oils that you can smell. Others recommend listening to birds chirp—even when you aren't in the forest.[27]

All of this evidence has led to the growth of a new field, nature therapy,[28] which is beginning to reveal the psychological, neurological, and chemical effects of spending time outside. Despite this, nature-based recreation in the United States has dropped by thirty-five percent in recent years,[29] and more than half of the world's population now lives in urban environments.

Regardless of where you live, it's likely that you work inside. That's why getting out of the office is your next goal.

Goal 14

Take an outdoor vacation

Schedule a trip to go camping, hiking, fishing, canoeing, rock-climbing, or to participate in any other outdoor activity. A trip to a national park or a forest may boost your immune system, lower your blood pressure, and reduce stress more than a vacation to a city.

9.6 Retrospective

Life inside your cube or office exposes you to contagious viruses and depletes your vitamin D levels, but don't be fooled by claims that vitamin D will cure any particular ailment. The most important reason to go outside is to restore balance in your health. This will empower your body to operate at its best.

---

26. *Phytoncides (wood essential oils) induce human natural killer cell activity [LNMM06]*
27. *Enhancing the benefits of outdoor walking with cognitive engagement strategies [Duv11]*
28. *Nature Therapy and Preventive Medicine [LLTT12]*
29. *Evidence for a fundamental and pervasive shift away from nature-based recreation [PZ08]*

You must think of your body as a system, and some parts of that system include the unique concerns related to your family history. That's why your first goal in this chapter is to ask your relatives some questions. Then you can schedule a vacation. Cities are fun, but studies have shown that they do not provide the same health perks at the great outdoors.

+ Learn about your family health history
+ Take a vacation in the great outdoors

Many other health benefits to getting outside, such as fending off depression, are not covered in this chapter. But being outdoors is not the only thing you can do to stay happy. General physical fitness may play an equally important role in your mental well-being. We'll discuss that in the next chapter.

Act On It

- Get at least ten minutes of sunlight exposure per day to allow for sufficient vitamin D synthesis. You'll need even more time in the sun if you have dark skin.

- Learn about your family medical history. It can affect your health decisions.

- Go for a walk in the woods instead of in an urban setting. This has been shown to reduce stress, blood pressure, and heart rate while boosting the immune system. Record the location of your walks in your exercise log.

- Work outside. If it's a nice day, schedule a meeting in the park instead of the office.

- Stop and smell the roses—literally. Some natural scents, such as ever-green, may promote the production of anticancer proteins.

- Turn off your iPod. Bird songs and the sounds of the forest may be responsible for some of nature's health benefits.

- Schedule a vacation to visit a national park or other outdoor location. Three days in an outdoor setting has been shown to produce an increase in certain types of white blood cells.

- Think of your body as a system. For it to function well, you must keep it balanced. A good diet and plenty of exercise are two of the things it needs.

CHAPTER 10

Refactoring Your Fitness

John Gill is responsible for several advances in mathematics and computer science,[1,2,3] but he's better known for his contributions to the sport of rock-climbing. Gill had an epiphany while taking a gymnastics class at Georgia Tech that led to a new style of climbing called *bouldering*. He saw how gymnasts practiced on their equipment, and began to think of the small cliffs in the North Georgia mountains as apparatuses instead of rocks.

Gill saw boulders, short but difficult climbing routes, as puzzles, and he began to look at himself as a gymnast instead of a mountaineer. To improve his bouldering skills, he supplemented his climbing regimen with exercises that emphasized all-around physical fitness; including cardio, strength, endurance, and flexibility. His athleticism not only revolutionized the sport, but also changed Gill's perspective on everything from mathematics to daily life. As he told John Krakauer in *Eiger Dreams: Ventures Among Men and Mountains* [Kra09], "you'll never feel the joy of movement if you're struggling."

Physical fitness is not a number on a scale, your cholesterol level, or even the absence of disease. It is a state of well-being. Thus far in the book, we have focused on those other yardsticks of wellness: risk of disease, weight, pain, and so on. But physical fitness (the state, not the exercise that leads to it) is just as important because it affects your concentration, mood, mental health, and ability to enjoy life. It's what allowed Gill to enjoy movement.

In this chapter you'll learn how to measure physical fitness, and how to become physically fit by following the same daily checklist you've been using.

---

1. *Computational Complexity of Probabilistic Turing Machines [Gil77]*
2. *The use of attractive fixed points in accelerating the convergence of limit periodic continued fractions [Gil75]*
3. *Compositions of analytic functions of the form Fn(z) = Fn−1(fn(z)), fn(z) → f(z) [Gil88]*

It will require a commitment to more-intense exercise, but that doesn't mean it will take more time. You'll just need to add some new activities to your regimen.

The exercises in this chapter are more strenuous than those in the previous chapters, so you need to consult a doctor before doing them. You should also be doing some walking or running (at least fifteen to twenty minutes at a time), and you should be able to pass the Kraus-Weber Test in Chapter 6, *Preventing Back Pain*, on page 79. If you do not meet all of these criteria, then do not move on. Work your way up through those other goals and then return to this chapter. If you have met those goals and your doctor gives you the green light, then you're ready to get started. The first thing you'll need to do is get warmed up.

10.1 Warming Up

It's important to prepare your body before intense exercise by increasing the blood flow to your muscles and the range of motion in your joints. Both of these are factors in reducing injuries, but they also help you perform better. The science behind good warm-ups is mixed, but it's generally accepted that ten to fifteen minutes of light-intensity movement is ideal.[4]

Some of the exercises you learned about in Chapter 6, *Preventing Back Pain*, on page 79 are excellent ways to get warmed up. You can also use those exercises as a warm-up before playing basketball or tennis, going skiing or rock-climbing, or doing anything else that requires a lot of complex movement. Perform the following exercises in order once, then repeat them in the reverse order. As before, do them slowly and with control.

- Cat back
- Double heel slide
- Single knee flex
- Flutter kick[*]
- Arm circles[*]

The two exercises with an asterisk are new, but don't worry—neither of them is hard. They are described here.

Flutter Kick   For this warm-up exercise you'll need to sit on the edge of a chair with your legs straight out. Then alternately kick your legs twenty-five to fifty times as though you are swimming.

---

4.   *The First 20 Minutes: Surprising Science Reveals How We Can: Exercise Better, Train Smarter, Live Longer [Rey12]*

Arm Circles   Stand up with your feet shoulder width apart and your arms out to your side. Then rotate both arms in the same direction so you're make circles in the air with your hands. Do this twenty-five to fifty times, and then reverse the direction of the circles and do another twenty-five to fifty circles.

When you're done with the warm-up, you'll be ready to assess your current level of fitness. After we discuss your next goal, we'll cover exactly what it means to be fit.

Goal 15

Take a rock-climbing class

You don't have to ascend mountains to go rock-climbing. Short bouldering problems like those pioneered by John Gill can exercise every aspect of your fitness in just a few minutes. A bouldering problem is a puzzle that must be solved by practicing the movements and angles required to complete the route. This kind of complex motion can have a unique effect on your mind.

If you know how to ride a bike, then you're already familiar with the relationship between physical movement and the brain. Your ability to quickly recall how to balance while pedaling is known as *motor memory* (also known more commonly, but less accurately, as *muscle memory*). Studies have shown that a single bout of exercise can improve the brain's ability to learn new motor skills,[5] which means bicycling may stick so well because the exertion of pedaling strengthens the neurochemical pathways that are created when learning the movement.

The theory behind this, according to Dr. John Ratey, is that aerobic exercise elevates neurotransmitters and creates new blood vessels that pipe in growth factors like BDNF. The complex movements strengthen the synaptic connections, which expand the network and spawn new cells.[6]

The new cells provide benefits that go beyond sports, though. The prefrontal cortex can co-opt them for other situations, which may explain why kids who learn to play the piano improve their academic scores.[7]

Thus, exercise that combines aerobic activity with more-complex movements—like rock-climbing, karate, tennis, wrestling, and gymnastics—may be better at improving cognitive function than general activity alone. Be sure to warm up first, but after twenty minutes of climbing you'll be well on your way to completing the items on your daily checklist. That's because rock-climbing incorporates multiple dimensions of fitness.

10.2 Understanding the Dimensions of Fitness

If you went to grade school in the United States, it's likely that you participated in the Presidential Physical Fitness Test. At the very least, you might remember seeing the Terminator (Arnold Schwarzenegger) shaking hands with President George H.W. Bush after being appointed chairman of the President's Council on Fitness, Sports and Nutrition (PCFSN).[8] The PCFSN was founded by President Dwight Eisenhower after Dr. Hans Kraus, who we discussed in Chapter 6, *Preventing Back Pain*, on page 79, sounded the alarm about the poor state of youth fitness in the United States.[9]

---

5. *A single bout of exercise improves motor memory [RSLK12]*
6. *Spark: The Revolutionary New Science of Exercise and the Brain [Rat08]*
7. *Enhanced learning of proportional math through music training and spatial-temporal training [GPS99]*
8. http://www.fitness.gov/
9. http://www.fitness.gov/about-pcfsn/our-history/

Today, the organization administers a test that measures middle-school students for their level of fitness in five health-related dimensions. It's designed for people who are much younger than most programmers, but its classification system is universal. The five dimensions are listed here.

Body Composition   The relative amounts of fat, muscle, bone, and other parts of the body. It's often measured with a skin-fold caliper, but it can also be done using underwater weighing to achieve more-precise results.

Cardiovascular Fitness   The ability of the circulatory and respiratory systems to supply oxygen during sustained physical activity. It's often referred to as aerobic fitness or just endurance. It can be tested with various forms of running, but in the laboratory it's done with complicated equipment that measures the ratio of oxygen and carbon dioxide a person breathes and exhales (essentially $VO2_{max}$).

Flexibility   The range of motion available to a joint. Each joint has its own level of flexibility so there is no general test as with the other components.

Muscular Endurance   A muscle's ability to continue to perform without fatigue. It is measured through repetitive exercises of a specific muscle group (like doing pull-ups or push-ups).

Muscle Strength   The ability of a muscle to exert force. It is usually measured by testing a single repetition of a particular exercise (like doing a single bench-press at maximum weight).

Each of these five components represents a dimension of fitness relating to health as opposed to athletic skill. Forty years ago, that distinction was not made, but it's important to us because you're not trying to become a world-class athlete. You just want to be healthy.

Now let's determine whether you have satisfactory abilities in each of these dimensions.

10.3 Unit-Testing Your Fitness

The five tests listed next are designed to measure each of the dimensions of fitness. They are based on the adult version of the Presidential Physical Fitness Test.[10] We'll discuss how to carry them out and what your goals should be. Later in the chapter, we'll discuss how to get better at them. Let's begin with the one you've been dreading since grade school—it's not as bad as you remember.

---

10. http://www.adultfitnesstest.org/

1.5 Mile Walk/Run Test

For this test, you'll need to mark out a 1.5-mile (2.4-km) course. You can do this with the odometer on your car, or you can just use a treadmill. You'll also need a stopwatch. During the test, walk at a brisk speed or run if you feel capable. In either case you'll get the best result by keeping your pace as even as possible.

This test is measuring your cardiovascular fitness, as described earlier. A casual walker will complete this in twenty minutes, so your first milestone is to surpass that time. As you become more comfortable, you should strive to bring your time closer to twelve minutes for a man and fourteen minutes for a woman, but don't worry about your time yet—in fact, you won't even need a watch to measure your first goal.

Instead of starting with a specific time, we'll use something more universal. Your next milestone is to *run the entire mile and a half* without stopping to walk at all. Once you can run the entire distance, you'll probably find your desired time is right around the corner. We'll base this goal on the fiftieth percentile of people in the United States for your sex and age. Those numbers are as follows:

Age Group	20–29	30–39	40–49	50–59	60+
Men	11:58	12:24	13:12	14:23	15:56
Women	14:04	14:34	15:34	17:19	19:04

Running for an entire mile and a half may be daunting, but with a little practice you can get there in just a few weeks. We'll discuss this plan later in the chapter.

Push-Ups Test

The next test is a measurement of muscular strength and endurance. When most people think of strength training, they imagine oiled-up behemoths pumping iron. But extremely heavy weights are not necessary to build muscular strength. In fact, one of the strongest athletes in modern history, Herschel Walker, never lifts a single dumbbell. Instead, he does 1,500 push-ups per day![11]

The reason Walker is able to use push-ups as a substitute for weight-lifting is that it exercises many different muscles in the upper body. This also makes it a great tool for measuring overall strength.

---

11. http://www.youtube.com/watch?v=46o0to59LIY

Start the exercise by lying prone on the floor or ground. Position your hands in line with your chest about 6 inches more than shoulder-width apart on each side.

The best position for your hands is a matter of personal preference and depends on your physiology (that is, the length of your arms and the ratio of upper arm to lower arm). Finding the best position will require experimentation. In general, if your arms are too far apart you won't be using the muscles of your upper arms enough. If your arms are too close together you'll be using those upper-arm muscles too much.

To perform the exercise, press against the ground and lift your chest up until your arms are fully extended. Be sure to keep your body flat as you come up, such that there is a straight line from head to toe. If you sag at the hips or put your butt in the air, then you have not done a proper push-up.

Now set a timer for one minute and do as many push-ups as you can before the timer stops. You can rest with your body on the ground, but do not get up or rest on your knees.

Your goal is to reach the fiftieth percentile of Americans for doing push-ups in one minute. As with the run, this number depends on your sex and age. The following table shows the estimated standards.

Age Group	20–29	30–39	40–49	50–59	60+
Men	33	27	21	15	15
Women	16	14	12	9	6

It's not uncommon to find that doing even a single push-up is difficult. Don't be discouraged, though. You'll learn how to get better. Later in the chapter we'll discuss some variations on this exercise that will help you improve very rapidly.

Half Sit-Ups Test

The next exercise is the half sit-up. You'll begin with your back on the ground and your legs bent. You may want someone or something to anchor your feet. Roll your shoulder blades up until the small of your back has just left the ground. Finally, ease back down to the starting position.

Keep in mind that this is a good exercise for measuring abdominal strength, but it can cause problems when performed on a regular basis. We'll discuss better abdominal exercises later in the chapter.

Now set a timer for one minute and see how many half sit-ups you can do before time runs out. You can rest with your back on the floor, but don't get up, roll over, or stretch your legs out. The following table shows the estimated fiftieth-percentile scores. That's your goal again.

Age Group	20–29	30–39	40–49	50–59	60+
Men	39	31	27	27	16
Women	25	21	21	19	13

That completes the muscular tests. Let's move on.

Sit-and-Reach Test

The next test is designed to measure flexibility. It's similar to the toe-touch exercise in the K-W Test, but it uses more precision in measuring the results—and less gravity.

To set up the test, you'll need some masking tape and a tape measure that is at least 20 inches (50.8 cm) in length. Extend the tape measure on the ground, and put a piece of masking tape over the 15-inch mark. Sit on the ground with your legs on either side of the tape measure, 12 inches (30.5 cm) apart, with the zero mark of the tape measure toward your crotch. Line up your bare feet with the 14-inch (35.5-cm) mark on the tape measure (they are really supposed to be at the 15-inch or 38-cm mark, but they will probably move when you perform the exercise).

To perform the test, place your open hands together so one is on top of the other. Slowly lean forward and touch your fingertips to the farthest point you can reach on the tape measure, as shown in the following figure. Exhale as you do this, and do not use a fast or sudden motion (you'll get hurt).

Figure 35—Sit-and-reach test

Perform the movement three times, with rests in between, and then record your best measurement. The following table shows the fiftieth percentile of Americans for each age group and sex.

Age Group	20–35	36–49	50+
Men	14.4 in (36.6 cm)	12.6 in (32.0 cm)	10.2 in (25.9 cm)
Women	14.8 in (37.6 cm)	13.5 in (34.3 cm)	11.1 in (28.2 cm)

Your goal is to sustain a level of flexibility that is at or beyond the fiftieth percentile for your sex and age group.

Body-Composition Test

The final test is not an exercise at all, but a measurement of body composition. The primary purpose of this test is to determine what percentage of your body is fat, which is a strong indicator of your risk for developing many different kinds of health issues.

The most-accurate methods of measuring body composition are very difficult, and in some cases expensive. They include densitometry (underwater weighing), dual-energy X-ray absorptiometry, anthropometry (skinfold assessment with calipers), and bioelectrical impedance analysis. All of these require special equipment, and most of them are not "do-it-yourself" options.

The best at-home technique for this test is the *body mass index* (BMI). It's a notoriously unreliable heuristic for measuring body fat (Chad Fowler calls it "bullshit"), but there are ways of compensating for its flaws by incorporating other factors. We'll use waist circumference (see Figure 36, *How to measure waist circumference*, on page 157).

To perform this test you'll need a scale and a tape measure. The first two components are weight and height. You probably don't need to be told how to measure these. The third component is waist circumference. You'll need to wrap the tape measure around your abdomen, just above your hips, as shown in the preceding figure. Note where the two ends of the tape measure meet and record the distance between them.

Next we'll use the weight and height measurements to calculate your BMI. The formula depends on the units used to measure the variables. The most common are as follows:

$$BMI = \frac{mass(kg)}{(height(m))^2}$$

$$BMI = \frac{mass(lb)}{(height(in))^2} x703$$

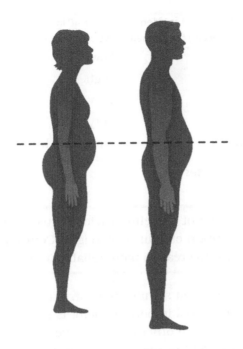

Image courtesy of the National Institute of Diabetes and Digestive and Kidney Diseases, National Institutes of Health

Figure 36—How to measure waist circumference

As stated earlier, BMI alone is unreliable. However, it is possible to estimate percentage of body fat based on it.[12] The formula for doing so is as follows (where *A* is your age in years, and S indicates your sex—1 for men and 0 for women):

$$PercentageBodyFat = (1.20 * BMI) + (0.23 * A) - (10.8 * S) - 5.4$$

Don't put too much stock in that. Instead, consider Table 5, *Risk of type-2 diabetes*, on page 158, which incorporates waist circumference to determine your risk of type-2 diabetes, hypertension, and cardiovascular disease (as determined by the NIH).[13]

Your body-composition goal for this chapter has nothing to do with percentile. Instead, you want to be at low risk for the aforementioned diseases. That means you should strive for a BMI below 25.

---

12. *Body mass index as a measure of body fatness: age- and sex-specific prediction formulas* [DWS91]

13. http://www.nhlbi.nih.gov/guidelines/obesity/e_txtbk/txgd/4142.htm

BMI	WC <= 40 in (101.6 cm) for Men WC <= 35 in (88.9 cm) for Women	WC > 40 in (101.6 cm) for Men WC > 35 in (88.9 cm) for Women
18.5–24.9	Low	Low
25–29.9	Moderate	High
30–34.9	High	Very high
35-39.9	Very high	Very high
> 40	Extremely high	Extremely high

Table 5—Risk of type-2 diabetes

> **Tip 10** BMI alone is not a useful metric because it doesn't account for the distribution of your bodyweight. Combine it with waist circumference to create a more reliable indicator of health risks.

Your diet is probably the most significant contributing factor to your results on this test, but the next most important factor is physical activity. If you do what's needed to improve the other aspects of your fitness, you'll naturally start to see improvement on this test. Let's move on and discuss exactly what that requires.

Goal 16

Reach the fiftieth percentile for the adult version of the Presidential Physical Fitness Test

Your goal for this chapter is to achieve a score on the adults' Presidential Physical Fitness Test that surpasses fifty percent of people in your age and sex group. That means the goals will be different for each person. You can get your exact ranking by entering your scores online.[14]

The fiftieth percentile for a thirty-year-old man is as follows:

- 12:00 minutes for the 1.5-mile run/walk
- 31 half sit-ups in one minute
- 27 push-ups in one minute
- 14.4-inch (36.6-cm) sit-and-reach

---

14. http://www.adultfitnesstest.org/dataEntry.aspx

For a thirty-year-old woman it's as follows:

- 15:00 minutes for the 1.5-mile run/walk
- 21 half sit-ups in one minute
- 14 push-ups in one minute
- 14.8-inch (37.6-cm) sit-and-reach

In all cases, you'll want to achieve a BMI that is below 25.

10.4 Upgrading Your Hardware

What do you do when the number of users accessing a web application exceeds the system's capability? You can scale up (improve the hardware of a single computer) or scale out (add more computers). When it comes to your body's ability to meet the demands of daily life, you have only one option: scale up.

Scaling up your body requires pushing yourself to uncomfortable limits, but as with most discomfort in life you can't simply describe this as pain. Exercise—especially at the levels we are about to discuss—can improve mental health, happiness, and general mood. It can also reduce stress (or improve your tolerance for stress, depending on how you look at it). In any case, exercise requires that you think beyond the immediate discomfort. Your brain will be telling you that it hurts, but you must trust in the science that indicates the cumulative effect is actually less discomfort. Of course, sometimes it may hurt because you are close to injuring yourself! Be careful at first, and after some time you'll be able tell the difference between discomfort and pain in your activities. Eventually you will begin to enjoy the movement.

Each activity we're about to discuss is intended to improve your score on the physical-fitness test. Remember to warm up before all of these exercises, as you should before any intense physical activity.

Upgrading Your Aerobic Capacity

As we discussed earlier, the first twenty minutes of physical activity is the most important. Walking is a great way to start, but if you want to meet the fiftieth percentile goal for the 1.5-mile run/walk, you'll need to increase the intensity. Like every other activity, you should do this incrementally.

The following table outlines a seven-week plan that is based on a 5k training regimen designed by the Sports Medicine Council of British Columbia.[15] It's been tweaked to work for your 1.5-mile effort. The plan requires three exercise

---

15. *The Beginning Runner's Handbook: The Proven 13-Week Run/Walk Program [Mac12]*

sessions per week. Each session alternates between walking and running at a predefined interval. As the program goes on, time spent running increases and time spent walking decreases.

	Session 1	Session 2	Session 3
Week 1	Run for 1 min. Walk for 2 mins. Do this 8 times	Run for 1 min. Walk for 2 mins. Do this 7 times	Run for 1 min. Walk for 2 mins. Do this 9 times
Week 2	Run for 2 mins. Walk for 2 mins. Do this 9 times	Run for 1 min. Walk for 2 mins. Do this 8 times	Run for 2 mins. Walk for 2 mins. Do this 8 times
Week 3	Run for 3 mins. Walk for 2 mins. Do this 7 times	Run for 2 mins. Walk for 2 mins. Do this 7 times	Run for 3 mins. Walk for 2 mins. Do this 7 times
Week 4 (Recovery Week)	Run for 3 mins. Walk for 2 mins. Do this 6 times	Run for 2 mins. Walk for 2 mins. Do this 6 times	Run for 2 mins. Walk for 3 mins. Do this 6 times
Week 5	Run for 3 mins. Walk for 1 min. Do this 7 times	Run for 2 mins. Walk for 1 min. Do this 7 times	Run for 3 mins. Walk for 2 mins. Do this 7 times
Week 6	Run for 5 mins. Walk for 1 min. Do this 4 times	Run for 2 mins. Walk for 1 min. Do this 7 times	Run for 3 mins. Walk for 1 min. Do this 7 times
Week 7	Run for 10 mins. Walk for 1 min. Do this 2 times	Run for 3 mins. Walk for 1 min. Do this 7 times	Run for 5 mins. Walk for 1 min. Do this 4 times

You can track the progress of this program with the companion iPhone application (see Figure 37, *Run/Walk Plan*, on page 161). You can add each session to your log, and the app will remember which ones you've completed.

At the end of week seven, you should be ready to run an entire mile and a half without stopping. In fact, you'll probably be surprised at how quickly you recover after doing it. All you must do is add these sessions to your daily routine. On the four days of the week not covered by the plan, you should still get your twenty minutes of walking or moderate activity. A part of that twenty minutes should be devoted to scaling up your strength.

Figure 37—Run/Walk Plan

Upgrading Your Strength

The only way to significantly improve your strength is to put your muscles under stress and then allow them to recover—a process called *adaptation*. During exercise, you're creating microtears in the skeletal muscle fibers by progressively *overloading* them with each movement. The tears are actually a good thing because you get stronger, or adapt, when your body repairs them. If you don't overload a muscle, then you probably aren't stressing the fibers enough, which means they won't tear and you won't get stronger.

The exercises used in the fitness test are sufficient to overload your muscles, but it's important to add variety to your repertoire because overusing certain exercises (especially the half sit-up) can lead to injury. It's also a great way to rapidly improve strength. If you can do only two or three push-ups at a time, try using one of the modified versions here:

Wall Press   The wall-press is a version of the push-up that requires less strength. Stand about two feet away from a wall and position your hands against it just as you would put them on the floor for a full push-up. Then ease your chest into the wall by bending your elbows. Maintain a straight line from your head to your toes, as the following image shows:

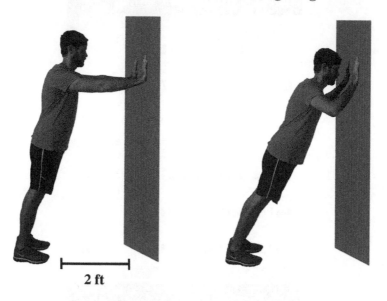

2 ft

Each time you do the exercise, try moving your feet a couple of inches farther away from the wall. After a few weeks your muscles will adapt. When you are doing push-ups starting three feet out from the wall, you can try moving on to the next variation.

Half Push-Ups   To perform a half push-up, start in the same position as a full push-up, but put your weight on your knees instead of your toes. Be sure to maintain a straight line from your head to your knees, as in Figure 38, *Knee push-up*, on page 163.

To perform the exercise, press against the ground and lift your chest until your arms are fully extended, as with the full push-up. Lower yourself back to ground, and that completes one repetition. Eventually your muscles will adapt again and you can move on to repetitions of the full push-ups.

For all of these exercises, each set should consist of ten to twelve repetitions, but the number you do isn't as important as making sure your muscles are overloaded for about thirty to sixty seconds. Some researchers believe that you must actually reach a state of *momentary muscle failure*,[16] which is the

---

16. *Low-load high volume resistance exercise stimulates muscle protein synthesis more than high-load low volume resistance exercise in young men [BWSA10]*

Figure 38—Knee push-up

point where you cannot complete another repetition without significant rest. But this idea is still somewhat controversial.

Regardless, if you repeat the same exercise over and over again for days, your improvement will begin to taper off as your muscles adapt. That's why progressing an exercise like the push-up through its variations is important, but you should also add variety to every exercise in your workouts—including the half sit-up.

The exercises you learned in Chapter 6, *Preventing Back Pain*, on page 79 are excellent for improving abdominal strength. But as you seek to achieve higher levels of fitness, you'll need to add new exercises to your regimen. Studies that monitor muscle activity with electromyography equipment have shown each of the following exercises to be very effective at activating the muscle groups in your trunk.[17,18]

Bicycle Maneuver   Lie flat on your back with your hands gently touching behind your head. Lift your feet off the ground so your knees are making a ninety-degree angle (see the following image). Then alternate extending your left and right legs as though you are pedaling a bicycle. As you do this, turn your upper body so that one elbow meets the opposing knee. A full pedal (that is, extending each leg once) counts as a single repetition. Do this ten to fifteen times per set.

---

17. *Muscle activation of different core exercises [ODSH10]*
18. *The effects of different sit- and curl-up positions on activation of abdominal and hip flexor musculature [PDWB08]*

Double Knee Flex   Lie flat on your back with your hands at your sides and your knees bent. Press your lower back on the floor as you contract your abdominal muscles. Your hips will slightly rotate and your legs will reach toward the ceiling with each contraction (see the image). Exhale as you contract and inhale as you return to the starting position. Repeat this ten to fifteen times per set.

Squats   A few studies have found that the best way to strengthen your abdominal muscles is to stabilize your trunk in exercises that predominantly activate other muscles.[19] One example is the squat, shown here, which is another excellent exercise to add to your battery of strength workouts.

---

19. *Trunk Muscle Activity Increases With Unstable Squat Movements [AB05]*

The key to doing a squat correctly is to lead it with your butt. Start by standing up straight, with your feet shoulder-width apart. Then lower yourself by pushing your butt out behind you. The bending of your knees will naturally follow this movement. Continue downward until your thighs are parallel to the floor. Try to keep your knees over your toes by placing your weight on your heels. You can put your arms in front of you as a counterweight to balance yourself. Finally, return to the standing position, and repeat the movement for a total of ten to twelve times per set.

Given all of these different exercises, you'll need a plan for carrying them out. Like everything else in this book, it should be iterative. Fortunately, an iterative approach to strength training, called circuit training, has been established as an effective means of improving muscular strength.[20,21]

A circuit workout combines several exercises in sequence. Each circuit, or single iteration through the sequenced exercises, is followed by a short break and then another round of the exercises. Many studies have tried to identify specific arrangements of exercises that are most effective,[22] but designing a

---

20. *Effects of three distinct protocols of fitness training on body composition, strength and blood lactate [PPBM10]*
21. *The effect of heart rate controlled low resistance circuit weight training and endurance training on maximal aerobic power in sedentary adults [KYSB00]*
22. *Effect of concurrent endurance and circuit resistance training sequence on muscular strength and power development [CCLC08]*

good circuit is still somewhat of an art. In general, a circuit should challenge many different muscle groups and combine aspects of strength, power, stamina, agility, flexibility, and endurance.

The following table presents a sample circuit that uses the exercises you've learned.

Exercise	Circuit Workout (complete 2 or 3 times)
Squat	10–12 reps, 1 set
Curl-up	15–20 reps, 1 set
Push-up	8–12 reps, 1 set
Bicycle maneuver	15–20 reps, 1 set
Double knee flex	15–20 reps, 1 set
BREAK	2–3 minutes

Don't limit yourself to the exercises we've discussed, though. There are numerous calisthenics, resistance exercises, and bodyweight exercises you can use. You can even include shuttle runs, jump tests, and other kinds of movements that address more than just strength. The ones in this chapter are designed specifically for the fitness test, but in the long term you should seek out as much variety as possible.

Regardless of the exercises, you should always follow a few guidelines when composing a circuit workout:

- Include between five and nine exercises per circuit
- Each exercise (station) should take no more than thirty seconds
- Each circuit should take between twelve and fifteen minutes
- Take two to three minutes of rest between circuit iterations
- Adjacent stations should challenge different muscle groups
- The entire workout should last between thirty minutes and one hour

Try rearranging the exercises each time you do the circuit. You'll prevent your muscles from adapting and keep the workout challenging.

> **Tip 11**   Get the most out of each workout by combining exercises into a circuit.

Remember that adaption is the process of creating microtears. Because your body needs to repair these microtears, it's important that you rest your muscles. For activities that are as intense as push-ups and squats (which, unlike running, can be done for only a short period of time), you'll need at least a full day of recovery. Thus, you should do these more-intense workouts only two or three times per week. You can continue doing the easier, more-therapeutic bodyweight exercises from Chapter 6, *Preventing Back Pain*, on page 79, on the other days.

Conditioning your muscles is essential to fitness, but it might even extend your life. A 2002 study from researchers at York University in Canada sampled 8,116 people between the ages of twenty and sixty-nine.[23] The study participants completed a fitness test that measured sit-ups, push-ups, grip strength, and sit-and-reach flexibility. The researchers tracked the participants for thirteen years and adjusted for age, smoking status, body mass, and other factors. They found that subjects who completed the fewest sit-ups were twice as likely to die during the study. No pattern of increased risk was found for push-ups and flexibility, but the men with the weakest grip strength had a fifty percent increase in their risk of death.

An even larger study from Sweden, which was published in the *British Medical Journal*, tracked more than one million teenage boys over a twenty-four-year period and found similar results.[24] A 2008 study from the same journal tracked 8,762 men between the ages of twenty and eighty, and also found that muscular strength was inversely and independently associated with death from all natural causes.[25]

These studies don't necessarily imply causation between muscular strength and mortality, but it is clear that strength and fitness can enhance your health and increase your overall quality of life.[26] Another side effect of these bodyweight exercises is that they can actually increase flexibility. That's good, because the more traditional approach to increasing flexibility won't have the effect you might expect.

Upgrading Your Flexibility

If you look around at the starting line of a local 5k race, you'll probably see a number of people leaning up against a light pole while stretching their calves or their quadriceps. Most of them will tell you that they're trying to loosen up before the race, but unfortunately they are probably only making their muscles weaker.

---

23. *Musculoskeletal fitness and risk of mortality [KC02]*
24. *Muscular strength in male adolescents and premature death: cohort study of one million participants [OSTR12]*
25. *Association between muscular strength and mortality in men: prospective cohort study [RSLM08]*
26. *Musculoskeletal fitness, health outcomes and quality of life [KBQ01]*

A study done at Florida State University in 2010 tested male distance runners by having some stretch before running and having others just sit around.[27] The men who stretched followed a sixteen-minute routine that had them hold five different stretches for twenty to thirty seconds each. When the two groups ran for one hour, the group that stretched covered less distance and used more calories. The researchers concluded that "stretching should be avoided before endurance events." Other studies have found that basketball players are not able to jump as high after stretching, and that muscles can be up to thirty percent weaker after stretching.

Most people stretch before physical activity because they were raised doing so. If you go to a children's soccer game you'll see kids warming up with the same stretches the runners at the 5k race used. Stretching can make you feel more flexible, but it turns out that the feeling is only mental. You're just temporarily increasing your tolerance for the discomfort of the stretch. A consistent routine of stretching over a long period of time can increase flexibility,[28,29] but the short-term effect of each stretch is negligible.

> **Tip 12**   Skip the static stretching before your workouts. Use dynamic stretching, like the warm-up in this chapter, to loosen your muscles before playing sports or working out.

The point of this discussion is that you probably shouldn't simply stretch before your workouts. Instead, warm up with dynamic stretching (light activity that moves your joints through their range of motion). The warm-up you did at the beginning of this chapter is perfect for this, and you should do it before going for a run or playing sports. But leave the static stretching until the end of any workout.

If you've met your goal of taking a yoga class, then you'll have learned some exercises you can use to increase flexibility. But even without yoga, you already have the tools you need. The bodyweight exercises you've learned about in this book will improve your flexibility as well as your strength. If you do these exercises consistently, you'll see small improvements in flexibility over a period of weeks.

---

27. *Effects of static stretching on energy cost and running endurance performance [WHKU10]*
28. *The effect of time and frequency of static stretching on flexibility of the hamstring muscles [BIB97]*
29. *Current concepts in muscle stretching for exercise and rehabilitation [Pag12]*

You don't have to achieve extreme levels of flexibility, however. In fact, if you are sufficiently flexible, then you may not need to do any stretching. Flexibility is primarily defined by your genes—so you can put aside those dreams of becoming a circus contortionist (unless you already are one). That's okay. You need only enough flexibility to allow your joints to move safely through a range of motion without getting injured. If you notice a decrease in the flexibility of a particular muscle or joint, it may be an early warning sign of a problem.

Scheduling your workouts is completely up to you. Some people like to set aside an entire lunch hour and knock out all of them. Other people like to spread them across one or two Pomodoro Technique workouts. As with your diet, it's important that you pick a schedule that works for you. If you're not a morning person, then don't work out in the morning. You may recall that Chad Fowler preferred to go to the gym at 11:00 PM when he first got started.

Fitness should be fun. If you are not enjoying your workouts, then make changes and iterate. Eventually you'll find a routine that works for you.

10.5 Retrospective

If learning a musical instrument is beneficial to your intelligence, then it's likely that rock-climbing is too. The science of motor memory and fitness suggest that the link between movement and the brain is more than incidental. It may have evolved as a means to strengthen the tasks we learned in primitive days—like climbing trees, cracking nuts, and building tools. Today we can use it to improve our ability to write code.

Beyond their application to programming, fitness and movement can improve your wellness. Life is more enjoyable when you aren't struggling through each day, and that's why the goals and exercises in this chapter are designed to improve each aspect of physical fitness.

You can add the bodyweight exercises you learned in this chapter to your daily checklist as part of your hourly movement. Or you can put them together in a circuit workout a few times each week. Either way, you'll begin to see improvements on the fitness test. Circuit workouts and the time you spend on the seven-week running program count toward the twenty minutes of daily activity on your checklist, as well. In the end, your health regimen shouldn't take much more time than it did before—but it will be harder.

DAILY CHECKLIST

- ☒ PLAN: Healthy stand-up
- ++ ☒ WALK: 10,000 steps/day with 20 mins. brisk
- ☒ MOVE: 5 mins./hr. Change position every 20 mins.
- ☒ EAT: 5 servings of fruits or vegetables
- ++ ☒ BUILD: 5 bodyweight exercises

We've also added two new goals in this chapter. The President's Council on Physical Fitness has found that reaching the fiftieth percentile on the fitness test puts you at lower risk for heart disease, diabetes, and many other health issues. If you find the rock-climbing class enjoyable, you can use the sport to help improve your scores on the test in addition to practicing the workouts described in this chapter.

Improving your fitness will take determination, but it doesn't have to be done in solitude. In the next chapter we'll discuss how getting your coworkers involved can provide benefits for you, them, and the company you work for.

Act On It

- Warm up before intense physical activities—it will prevent injuries and help you perform better.

- Participate in sports that require complex movement. This will strengthen your motor memory, which can be co-opted for other tasks, such as programming.

- Know your BMI. This metric gets a bad rap, but when combined with other metrics it becomes a reliable gauge of your risk of developing many diseases.

- Use the run/walk plan in this chapter to improve your aerobic capacity. After seven weeks, you'll be able to run an entire mile and a half without stopping.

- Do two or three circuit workouts each week, and incorporate the more-intense resistance exercises discussed in this chapter.

- Add new resistance exercises to your workouts. If you do the same exercises over and over, your muscles will adapt and your workouts will become less effective.

- Save the static stretching until the end of your workout.

CHAPTER 11

Teaming Up

"I tend to get absorbed in my work and spend long hours at a stretch in front of a computer," says Mark McCraw, a programmer at the SAS Institute in North Carolina. "The longer I go, the more I hunch towards the screen. This [led to] weird nerve-related side effects like my arm occasionally going numb. Scary stuff, at first."

Fortunately for Mark, SAS has one of the most remarkable health and wellness programs in the world. "The on-site healthcare center referred me to the on-site physical therapist, who quickly identified the problem, helped me schedule an appointment with the ergonomics specialists at SAS, and put me on track with a physical-therapy program—all visits on-site—that resolved my issues. In some cases, I didn't even have to leave my office," he remembers. "Having all of these services on-site and easily accessible makes all the difference."

Not everyone is lucky enough to have these kinds of facilities, but on-site services are just one way that a work environment can help you stay healthy. In this chapter you'll learn how to make health and fitness effective for you and your coworkers by simply talking about it. You'll also learn how to organize and sustain a team to play dodgeball, a surprisingly healthy and inclusive game. Finally, you'll learn how you can get your employer involved in your health and how it can be mutually beneficial.

With very little cost, a software company can receive a huge return by investing in the wellness of its employees. Often the least expensive activities have the biggest impact. Mark's favorite services at SAS are just that kind of thing.

"I sometimes attend lunchtime seminars on particular nutritional trends that interest me," he says. "I also occasionally participate in lunchtime intramural sports leagues." These kinds of activities are not that different from code reviews, user groups, hack nights, and many other social forms of learning. They're also easy to organize—so easy that you can set one up on your own.

Let's begin this chapter by discussing the simplest kind of wellness program: the one you build for yourself.

11.1 Message-Passing

Your first goal for this chapter is to host a lunch-and-learn seminar for your coworkers. Pick a chapter from this book and share it with your friends.

You don't even have to prepare the material yourself. You can download slide decks for a few of this book's chapters from http://healthyprog.com. Each deck contains bullets with the main points of the chapter, and notes for the presenter. You need only to familiarize yourself with the materials, practice a few times, and you'll be ready to present.

Teaching a subject from this book may inspire others, but it will also help you to better understand the content. One of the best ways to gain deeper knowledge on a topic is to teach it to someone else.

This idea has been around since at least the first century, when the Greek philosopher Seneca wrote, "docendo discimus" (Latin for "by teaching we are learning"). Since that time, a number of empirical studies have shown the value of teaching as an aid to learning. In fact, some research has even connected the act of speaking about a subject to an enhanced understanding of it. This is often called the Vygotsky Connection, after the Russian psychologist who first identified the link.[1]

> | Tip 13 | Talking about health issues is one of the best ways to strengthen your commitment to staying healthy. |

If you're uncomfortable speaking in front of groups, an alternative is to ask your coworkers to read a particular chapter and then have a round-table discussion. In either case, you'll want to follow up by getting your bosses involved. They'll be surprised by how inexpensive and effective it can be.

If you're an employer, read the rest of the chapter with an open mind. But if you're an employee, use this information to explain why the people you work for should care about and sponsor your health. The advantage for you goes beyond small perks. Having an employer with a good wellness program makes

---

1. *Mind in Society: The Development of Higher Psychological Processes [Vyg78]*

you statistically more likely to remain healthy. Let's discuss your next goal, and then get to the pitch.

Goal 17

Give a healthy lunch seminar

Pick a chapter from this book, and organize it into a thirty-minute session that you can present to your coworkers. Try to convince them to make some of the same changes you've made. If you succeed, you'll find that having coworkers with the same desire to be healthy creates an invaluable support mechanism. You can download sample presentations from http://healthyprog.com.

11.2 Investing in Your Health

Healthy workers are good workers, and regardless of whether you're an employer, a manager, or just a another member of the team, having healthy coworkers can make your job better. That's why employees at companies with effective wellness programs are less likely to quit.

A study by Towers Watson and the National Business Group on Health found that companies with wellness programs like the one at SAS experience significantly lower rates of voluntary attrition. SAS reported voluntary turnover of just four percent after introducing its program.[2] That's remarkably low when compared to the average turnover rate of twenty-five to thirty-three percent at other Fortune 500 software companies.[3]

> SAS Institute reported a 4% voluntary turnover rate after introducing its wellness program.

Mark agrees with this assessment: "It's unbelievably refreshing to know that the company cares so much about the wellness of its employees. It means a lot to me, and has been a definite factor in my career choices." Mark also believes that the program has ultimately made him more productive. "I'm sure I would not have pursued things until the problems were much worse," he says. "[It] saved me countless hours and helped me prevent all kinds of future medical problems."

The results at SAS are not an anomaly, and in some cases the payoff is even more tangible. In 2002, Johnson & Johnson (J & J), a multinational manufacturer of

---

2. http://sloanreview.mit.edu/the-magazine/2012-winter/53205/do-it-yourself-employee-health-care/

3. *Shortage of Skilled Workers and High Turnover in the Information Technology Workforce: What Are the Possibilities for Retention?* [HCMS04]

medical and pharmaceutical products, began looking at the cost-effectiveness of its wellness program.[4] J & J found that since the program's inception in 1995, it had helped to reduce the number of employees who smoked by two-thirds, the number of people who were physically inactive by one-half, and the number who had high blood pressure by one-half. These were all signs that the program was a success, but the most surprising part of the study was the money.

J & J's wellness program had saved the company $250 million on healthcare costs over a decade. This was attributed to a reduction in healthcare premiums, worker's compensation payouts, injury leave, and even an increase in government-sponsored grants and tax incentives. The return on investment for J & J was $2.71 for every dollar spent.[5]

As more companies begin to sponsor wellness programs, more research is being done with regard to their efficacy for both employees and businesses. The results have consistently shown that companies with wellness programs have healthier and happier employees. But not all programs are equal. For example, providing discounts at fitness clubs and posting nutrition information in the cafeteria are simply not enough.

> Johnson & Johnson's wellness program saved the company $250 million over a decade.

According to Dr. Leonard Berry, a professor at the Mays Business School at Texas A&M University, the best programs follow a certain formula. In a recent study published by the Harvard Business Review, he outlined six pillars of effective wellness programs.[6] As discussed next, these pillars have great practical application.

Get the Boss Involved Programs that include embedded experts and wellness champions are more effective than ones that do not, but the most important form of inspiration and leadership can be found at the *C* level (CEO, CFO, COO, and so on). According to Dr. Berry's study, participation of the CEO is a determining factor in a program's effectiveness. In some of his examples, the participation was as simple as the CEO asking employees, "How's your health?"

Use Carrots, Not Sticks Unsurprisingly, the least effective wellness programs use force to improve health. In the worst cases, companies require mandatory health screenings and education courses that may not be beneficial to everyone. Positive incentives are more effective—for example,

---

4. *Long-term impact of Johnson & Johnson's Health & Wellness Program on health care utilization and expenditures [OLGB02]*

5. http://hbr.org/2010/12/whats-the-hard-return-on-employee-wellness-programs/ar/1

6. *What's the Hard Return on Employee Wellness Programs? [BMB10]*

offering a $50 discount on medical insurance to employees that pledge not to use any tobacco products.

Get Personal Many companies make the mistake of creating a wellness program that focuses on only one aspect of health. In most cases, companies will offer a discounted gym membership but place no emphasis on healthy eating. The best programs include support for exercise, nutrition, depression, stress, and even spiritual issues. But it's difficult to have a program that covers everything. That's why the next-best solution is to personalize the program. In some cases, this could be as simple as out-sourcing the wellness program to inexpensive but well-rounded websites like DailyBurn (see Chapter 8, *Making Exercise Pragmatic*, on page 121, for more on this site).

Make It Free As mentioned before, a discount at a gym is a useless incentive. In fact, it's usually a sign that the company isn't committed to the program or your health—your contribution is like an insurance copay, which is actually intended to deter you. Instead, the most effective wellness programs are the ones that are the most accessible. A free gym membership is great—having on-site services is even better. The program at SAS is the gold standard, but on-site services can be small, too. Square (a company we'll discuss later in the chapter) has partnered with a business that does on-site blood tests for employees. That kind of partnership is actually one of the other essential components Dr. Berry's study found.

Partner Up The most effective wellness programs tend to have some level of partnership between the company looking to offer an employer health program and the companies that provide the health services. That's how many small companies, like Comporium (around 1,000 employees), have managed to develop exceptional programs. Comporium leveraged the resources of the YMCA, one of its vendor partners, to design a "metabolic makeover" program for Comporium employees.

Send a Strong Message The last pillar of effective wellness programs costs almost nothing: sending a strong and consistent message to employees that health and wellness is important. The message is a key element because the goal of these programs is to overcome the apathy most employees have toward their health. For some companies, the message can be as simple as putting a bicycle rack next to the entrance of the office. This acts as a constant reminder that healthy living is encouraged. A more elaborate reminder at the Lowe's Home Improvement headquarters is a dramatic spiral staircase intended to make taking the stairs more appealing.

Having a great wellness program doesn't have to cost your company a lot of money. If a business truly cares about the well-being of its workers, then the huge return on investment should only be a bonus.

However, apathetic employees can make even a great wellness program go bad. That's because health and fitness are contagious. Unfortunately, laziness is also contagious. If you want to succeed at achieving your health goals, then you're going to need buddies. But finding and engaging with others is the fun part.

11.3 Playing Well with Others

"Why do I run? It makes my brain work better," says Xavier Shay. "It feels freaking incredible. The massive endorphin rush just puts you on top of the world. When you're finished with a run in the morning, you've already won the day no matter what else happens." Despite this powerful endorsement of running and Xavier's years of experience, he still needs to find ways of motivating himself.

"My training is better when I run with other people," Xavier explains. "The social thing is huge. That's one of the main reasons I run with the group."

Xavier, as you may recall from Chapter 8, *Making Exercise Pragmatic*, on page 121, is a programmer with Square in San Francisco. The group he's talking about is an official Square running group. "We go out running twice a week," he says. "We do Tuesday and Thursday nights after work. Last week, we had ten to fifteen people come out. There are people there from Support, Engineering, Events, and Marketing. Day to day my job doesn't have much to do with them—so it's a good social opportunity, too."

Square is the quintessential West Coast startup. One of the founders, Jack Dorsey (of Twitter fame), saw an opportunity for businesses to accept credit cards by attaching a small plastic square to their phones. Now the company is worth an estimated $3.25 billion.[7] Like many tech startups, Square competes for good employees by providing unique benefits.

"We offer a monthly health benefit that can be applied to whatever you'd like," Xavier says. "If you need a massage, you use it to pay for a massage. If you want to put it toward a gym membership, you put it toward a gym membership. Whatever—it's up to you."

For Xavier, however, these tangible perks are the least important aspect of the program. It's the camaraderie that keeps him motivated.

---

7. http://www.nytimes.com/2012/08/08/technology/starbucks-and-square-to-team-up.html?_r=1

Starting a running group at your workplace is an extremely simple but effective way to build a healthy team. It usually just takes a single email to get the ball rolling. However, one problem with a running group is that it can be somewhat exclusive. Most people who are just getting started with fitness will fall behind and eventually drop out. Even worse, the people who need the exercise the most might be too intimidated to join the group.

Remember that fitness should be fun, and for most people games are more fun than running. That's why SAS invested in a massive swimming pool for its recreation center that allows people to play aquatic basketball, lacrosse, and Ultimate Frisbee. According to the program's director its a "gymnasium on water."

You probably don't have access to a facility like the one at SAS, but that shouldn't stop you from enjoying fitness. You can easily rent pools, gyms, and basketball courts at local recreation centers. In most cases, a facility will welcome the opportunity to make it a recurring rental—especially if you use it during work hours (when recreational venues are often empty) instead of the evening.

Tip 14	Many gyms and churches are empty during the workday. Getting access to these facilities may be easier and cheaper than you expect.

Once you have a venue, you'll need a game that everyone can play. Basketball is good because most people know the rules, but it also favors skilled players—often excluding the people who need the exercise the most. That's why dodgeball is a better game.

How to Play Dodgeball

Dodgeball is no joke. There are competitive leagues, self-described professional teams, official rules, and an intercollegiate championship (Saginaw Valley State University was the most recent winner). But the best part about dodgeball is that it has a low barrier to entry. Dodgeball is a simple sport when compared to running (which takes a long time to get used to) and basketball (which takes finesse and coordination). That makes it a perfect game to play with coworkers who have a wide range of physical talent (or lack thereof). Furthermore, the game's rules prevent a minority of players from dominating a particular matchup.

The game has just two prerequisites, which are usually easy to satisfy.

- A gym. Usually these can be rented from a local fitness center or even a school. As an alternative, you can use a tennis court without a net. The following figure shows the official dimensions of a regulation court, but any size is acceptable.

- Lots of rubber balls. You'll need the big soft kind that you used in grade school. They can be purchased online for about $40 per half dozen.

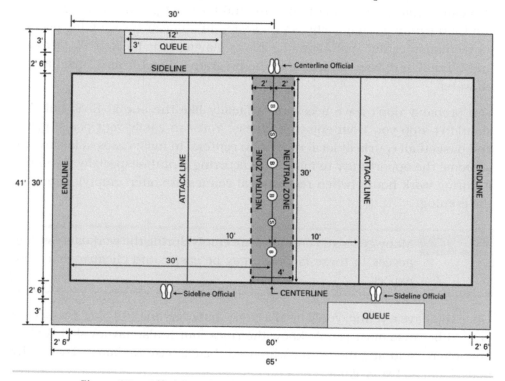

Figure 39—Official National Dodgeball League court diagram

You'll also need to know how to play the game. The basic instructions and rules are as follows:

Starting the Game Line up the foam balls along the court's centerline. The number of balls to use depends on the number of players and the size of the court. Competitive teams use ten players per team (with six on the court at a time), and six balls that are shared by both teams. Some divisions prefer to use various ball sizes, with smaller balls used for offense and bigger ones preferred for defense. Again, this is totally up to you.

Once the balls are lined up, each team should take one end of the court and stand at the baseline (endline) on that side. The game begins by having an neutral party blow a whistle or give some other indication that play should commence. When this happens, players from both teams rush toward the centerline and try to grab the balls.

Playing the Game The game is played by throwing balls at members of the opposing team in an attempt to eliminate them. When a player is hit by a ball and the ball is not caught before touching the ground, then that player must leave the court.

If a player catches a ball before it hits the ground, then the opposing player who threw the ball is eliminated. Furthermore, the team that caught the ball can reinstate the player on its bench that has been out of the game the longest.

Players can defend against thrown balls by blocking them with other balls. Any player that does this will not be eliminated as long as the thrown ball does not touch him or her.

Winning Conditions The game is over when all of the players on one team have been eliminated. The remaining team wins the game.

There are numerous variations on these rules, and even more subtleties that must be addressed (such as the boundaries of the court, and the result of a ball hitting an obstacle in the gym, like a backboard). But the elements we've outlined are the essentials. Ultimately, you and your coworkers should define the set of rules that works for you. Dodgeball is a very flexible game.

The absolute best characteristic of dodgeball, however, is that it won't leave weaker players in the shadows. Games like basketball, which have only one ball and one goal, tend to favor the hotshots and ball hogs. But dodgeball, which has a better distribution of balls and targets, provides a level playing field for all competitors. That doesn't mean it's easy, though. You'll get one heck of a workout trying to nail your coworkers with a rubber ball.

> **Tip 15**   Pick games that people with a wide range of abilities can enjoy.

Your next goal is Goal 18, *Start or join a team with your coworkers*, on page 182. Give dodgeball a try, but don't limit your team to just one sport. Many other games use the same rubber balls and court as dodgeball. Bombardment, Protect the Pin, and Capture the Flag can all be substituted if you get bored with playing the same game again and again. The point is to have fun while getting fit.

Goal 18

Start or join a team with your coworkers

If your company already has an active running group or intramural league, then your goal is to join in. But if one doesn't exist, you'll need to get the ball rolling. Use the guidelines in this chapter to develop a team that is healthy and fun.

Ad-hoc or impromptu gatherings are a great, but there are more "formal" ways to start a team. GitHub, a software company in San Francisco, has sponsored a dodgeball tournament for the last two years.[8] Companies—Square, Engine Yard, Heroku, and others—enter teams in the tourney while GitHub takes care of the venue and organization.

11.4 Building a Better Team

Whether you start a running group, dodgeball team, or some other kind of health-minded activity, you'll need to ensure that your coworkers faithfully participate. As it turns out, your own excitement is the best motivator.

Psychology has shown us that the enthusiasm level of teammates and leaders directly impacts the enjoyment level of people who participate in fitness-related activities. In one experiment done by researchers at Northern Arizona University and Wake Forest University, ninety male and female adults were asked to attend an aerobics class. All of the classes were led by a graduate student who was told to act either excited or disinterested. In addition, a trained group of planted students participated in the classes and were told to act the same way as the instructor.[9] After the workout session, the subjects in the study were asked how much they enjoyed the class. Those in the classes with the enthusiastic instructor and students reported an enjoyment level twenty-two percent higher than that reported by the other classes. They were also fourteen percent more likely to be involved in a fitness class again in the future.

We see the same trend in software teams. A reluctance from one developer to write clean code infects the rest of the team with a "why bother?" attitude. Eventually, the quality of the product suffers. But when a single person shows

---

8.   http://dodgeball.github.com/
9.   *Effects of leadership style and group dynamics on enjoyment of physical activity [FRG00]*

the initiative to refactor troublesome components or fix pesky bugs, it inspires others to improve the system's health.

> **Tip 16**   Your enthusiasm may be the best motivator for other people.

If you're sincere in your passion to get healthy, other people will see it. You'll be inspiring them to stay involved, and they'll inspire you back. But expressing enthusiasm isn't the only way to foster a strong team. The following are some recommendations for keeping people involved:[10]

Give the Team a Name   People tend to perform worse when participating as part of a team. It's a phenomenon called "social loafing." But studies have shown than when the team has an identity of its own, the participants tend to elevate their game—often performing better than they would have as individuals.[11] Two great ways of giving your team an identity are to name it and to create a logo.

Compete with Other Teams   Nothing inspires greatness like competition, but it also fosters strong teams. A great way to get some competition is to join a formal league (such as the National Dodgeball League), but there are other low-key options. Try scheduling a dodgeball game against a team from another company or get your running group to participate in a charity event.

Set Group Goals   Just like your personal goals, team-oriented goals are an effective way of developing new habits. If you have a running group, then set a monthly mileage target. For dodgeball, keep track of which players have the most "kills." You can even set up a Most Valuable ~~Programmer~~ Player award.

Above all, remember to have fun. If something isn't fun, then change it.

11.5 Retrospective

Peer pressure is a powerful influence that gets a bad rap. When used responsibly, it can encourage individuals to make positive changes in their lives. If you are able to convince your coworkers that being healthy is enjoyable, then you'll probably benefit by having them support you in return.

---

10. http://www.mayoclinic.com/health/walking/SM00062_D
11. *Social Loafing and Swimming: Effects of Identifiability on Individual and Relay Performance of Intercollegiate Swimmers [WNBL89]*

Organizing games and activities in which your coworkers can participate is a great way to get people onboard. In fact, you should ask one person each day about their health. The question can be as simple as "Did you go to the gym today?" If you know the person more intimately, you may be comfortable asking directly, "How's your health?" The purpose of these questions is to plant a seed that will hopefully grow into an interest in being healthy.

We added two new goals in this chapter: give a healthy seminar to your coworkers and join a group. For the seminar, you can choose one of the prepared presentations that are based on the chapters of this book, or you can create one yourself. Pick a subject that you are passionate about and share it with the people around you. You'll be fostering a healthy community from which you can build your new group.

Even with the help of your coworkers or your employer, your wellness is your own responsibility. Being healthy is a state that must be maintained, and it requires lifelong attention. In the next and final chapter, we'll discuss how to take care of your health even after you're done reading this book.

Act On It

- Talk about health issues. Ask your friends what they are doing to stay healthy. Tell your coworkers what you are doing. Be proud of your effort and share your success.

- Show your enthusiasm. You should be proud of your health, and if other people see your pride, they will follow.

- Talk to your employer about health issues. If your company is concerned about its employees' productivity, then it may be willing to follow the advice in this chapter.

- Get active with your coworkers. Set up games and groups that people can join. But be sure to include as many people as you can by picking activities that are broadly accessible.

CHAPTER 12

Onward, Healthy Programmer

Everyone knows that exercise is good for your health, but sixty years ago that connection had not been made scientifically. The first hint came in the 1950s, when Dr. Jeremy Morris began a study of the life expectancies associated with different kinds of jobs. He collected data on double-decker-bus conductors and drivers in London and found that the conductors, who walked the stairs many times each day, were much less likely to suffer from heart disease than the sedentary drivers. The connection he discovered changed the mission of his life's work, and he become a prolific advocate for general fitness.

Dr. Morris remained physically active until his death in 2009 at the age of ninety-nine. He lived long enough to witness the radical shift in society that he started. He saw the birth of aerobics in the 1960s and the running craze in the 1970s, which continues today. Surely, he must have been proud of these changes, but it's unlikely that he was satisfied. There is still much progress to be made.

Our society isn't out of the woods when it comes to physical-activity levels—far from it. With every decade, our jobs get easier and our daily lives require less physical effort. According to Dr. David Angus, this has contributed to the dramatic increase in obesity in the United States over the last twenty years.[1] In addition, heart disease remains the leading cause of death in most developed countries.[2,3] Likewise, you've made changes in your life but you aren't out of the woods. If you revert to a sedentary lifestyle, the benefits of the work you've done will dissipate. That's why good fitness and nutrition have to be maintained as lifelong habits.

---

1. *The End of Illness [Ang12]*
2. http://www.ons.gov.uk/ons/taxonomy/index.html?nscl=Causes+of+Death
3. http://www.cdc.gov/nchs/fastats/lcod.htm

Programmers often say that the hardest part of software development begins when a product is released. The real work, maintenance, continues until the last user uninstalls your software—it's a lot like your health. You must sustain a state of wellness for the rest of your life, and you need to continue setting goals, iterating, and making small improvements.

12.1 Continuous Improvement

In the early 1980s, the Ford Motor Company was struggling. It had losses totaling $3 billion, and much of its failure was due to the poor quality of the products it sold. One exception, however, was a line of cars containing transmissions assembled in Japan instead of the United States. Ford's engineers disassembled several of these units and found that the consistency of the Japanese-built parts far exceeded even the tolerance levels defined in the assembly's specifications. As a result, the Japanese cars ran more smoothly and had fewer failures than the same car models containing American-built transmissions.

The astonishing quality the Japanese factories delivered has been largely attributed to their use of a process called *kaizen*, which literally means "good change," but in this context it's more aptly translated as "continuous improvement." Kaizen is a philosophy of facilitating perpetual long-term improvement by focusing on small incremental changes rather than sudden radical changes. Its tenets, however, are universal and can be applied to more than just car-manufacturing.

In many ways, the iterative development processes we use as programmers have their roots in *kaizen*. We continuously improve the quality of our software products by embracing change, and we facilitate this by measuring improvement at a very fine granularity. Fixing just one or two bugs each iteration is sufficient if we do it continuously. We can apply this same approach to our health.

Each new day is a chance for you to make small incremental improvements to your health. That's why it's important to make sure that every twenty-four-hour period brings some kind of new personal achievement. Try to find some small nugget of improvement in every workout or every meal. It doesn't have to be a big change to be a personal best. In each Healthy Stand-Up, you should be able to reflect on accomplishing something that you haven't done before.

Maybe you did one more push-up today than in any previous workout. Or maybe you managed to avoid digging into the office candy bowl for the first time. If you're coming back from an injury, then maybe you've set records relative to your time away from exercise. These small improvements may seem insignificant, but they are quite the opposite. Just as with building software or running an assembly line, making positive changes to your health happens with the tiniest of steps.

> **Tip 17** Set a new personal record every day.

A side effect of setting personal records is that you'll never do the exact same thing two days in a row. You must constantly raise the bar by doing slightly better than the day before. Sometimes the bar will fall down—maybe you'll get injured or life will get in the way—but it's important to pick yourself up and keep moving. Remember that each day brings a new chance for improvement.

You've probably set a lot of personal records by following the plan in this book without even realizing it, but now it's time to pay attention to them. Each time you set a new record, be sure to write it down in your log. After a while, you'll recognize patterns and you'll be able to set new goals for yourself—and that's your final goal.

Goal 19

Set new goals

Your health goals shouldn't stop with the ones listed in this book. Set new goals for yourself by picking areas of fitness and nutrition that interest you. A few ideas are listed here:

- Learn taekwondo
- Run a 5k
- Run a marathon
- Get a DNA test
- Bike to work
- Bench-press your bodyweight
- Go vegan for a month
- Hike a section of the Appalachian Trail

After setting a few such goals and achieving them, you'll have a better idea of where you want to take your health. Maybe running isn't for you, but you won't know until you try. Many people think they hate running, but end up setting their sights on a marathon after running their first 5k. On the other hand, some people give up on fitness because they hate running. If that's you, then try some different activities you enjoy—you don't have to run to be healthy.

Fitness should be fun, and it will be if you find the right activities. Sometimes the best way to make it enjoyable is to include your friends. But often you'll have to change more than just your own habits to get other people involved.

12.2 Creating Social Habits

You probably wake up, go to the office, get a cup of coffee, and check your email every morning. Your life is loaded with cues, routines, and rewards. By now there's a good chance you've started to change many of them, but it didn't happen instantly. Change can take a long time, and in some cases you may not recognize a difference until a year or more after you've started making progress—especially when it comes to diet and weight loss.

Patience is essential to changing your health, but it can dry up. That's when we must rely on the encouragement and support of our friends and family. It's important to have them involved in your health at every stage in the journey. On the other hand, if you surround yourself with people who are indifferent toward health, it will make each challenge that much harder.

At the beginning of the book you met Chad Fowler, who made tremendous changes in his life—but he didn't do it alone. He had the support of his wife, friends, and coworkers. Even so, he still had to fight the cues that led to his old habits—and they were everywhere. Whether Chad was working in an office or traveling to customer sites, he had to deal with smokers, free pizza, and a general apathy toward physical activity. But he found some of the unhealthiest environments at technology conferences.

"At conferences, [there's a] rhythm of waking up as late as possible and rushing to the first session, drinking a bunch of coffee and Coke, and eating all the crap they bring, and then going to the bar afterword, and then going to dinner, and then going to the bar, and repeat." Chad says. "I changed that behavior. A bunch of us did together."

Chad decided that the best way to fight those conference habits was to replace the unhealthy routines with better routines. "At RailsConf 2009 in Vegas, we had a group that would meet and go to the gym together every day. Some people would even lead workout sessions," he recalls. Eventually the ad hoc workouts turned into formal 5k races at events like RubyConf (a conference Chad organizes).

Chad's strategy was perfect. The key to changing habits, as you'll recall from Chapter 1, *Making Changes*, on page 1, is to keep the same cues and rewards while replacing the routine with something new. But the power of social habits is equally important. To develop and change social habits, you must get involved in the community.

The next time you go to a software conference, participate in a 5k (even if you walk it). If there isn't a race being held, set one up yourself. Most conference organizers would love to include a healthy event like a 5k, but simply don't have time to manage it. If you're a people person, maybe it can be one of your new goals.

Ultimately, changing social habits is a process of giving people the opportunity to make better choices. In this way, it's not that different from changing your own habits—except you must think bigger. If you are able to change social habits, then you'll be making a small contribution to the movement that Dr. Jeremy Morris started in 1950.

12.3 The Joy of Being Healthy

The spirit of Dr. Morris's research continues today. Dr. Peter Katzmarzyk, of the Pennington Biomedical Research Center, is studying the epidemiology and public-health impact of obesity and physical inactivity. Dr. James Levine, of the Mayo Clinic, is leading an emerging field called inactivity studies, which is challenging many long-held beliefs about human health and obesity. These experts are changing our perception of how physical activity can improve our lives, and we'd be wise to listen.

Exercise is what our bodies were meant to do. Without it, we become less human. It may feel that the opposite is true at first—for example, you may feel like an outsider in your first 5k. But after some time, you will grow into your new level of fitness. You'll find activities, sports, and a diet that suit your individual needs. Be sure to give each new experiment some time, but after a while you should enjoy your new habits.

| Tip 18 | Being healthy should be fun. Keep iterating and changing until you find what makes you happy. |

Every recommendation in this book is designed to be not only fun, but also productive. Exercise and nutrition do not need to interfere with your duties as a programmer. In fact, your lifestyle can enhance your ability to do your job well. That's why staying healthy is the best way to ensure you keep doing this job you love for years to come.

Goals

- Goal 1, *Change one habit,* on page 11
- Goal 2, *Buy a pedometer,* on page 19
- Goal 3, *Find your resting heart rate,* on page 22
- Goal 4, *Check your blood pressure,* on page 37
- Goal 5, *Enhance your workstation,* on page 43
- Goal 6, *Count your calories for one day,* on page 57
- Goal 7, *Get an eye exam,* on page 69
- Goal 8, *Pass the Kraus-Weber Test,* on page 86
- Goal 9, *Get a negative result on Phalen's Test,* on page 107
- Goal 10, *Take a yoga class,* on page 113
- Goal 11, *Do a Pomodoro workout,* on page 125
- Goal 12, *Sign up for an online fitness service,* on page 132
- Goal 13, *Learn about your family medical history,* on page 139
- Goal 14, *Take an outdoor vacation,* on page 144
- Goal 15, *Take a rock-climbing class,* on page 149
- Goal 16, *Reach the fiftieth percentile for the adult version of the Presidential Physical Fitness Test,* on page 158
- Goal 17, *Give a healthy lunch seminar,* on page 175
- Goal 18, *Start or join a team with your coworkers,* on page 182
- Goal 19, *Set new goals,* on page 189

Examples

A2.1 Examples of Fruit/Vegetable Servings

These are examples of what counts as a single fruit or vegetable serving on the daily checklist (according to the UK's National Health Service).[1]

Green Vegetables
- 2 spears of broccoli
- 4 heaping tablespoons of kale
- 4 heaping tablespoons of spinach
- 4 heaping tablespoons of green beans

Cooked Vegetables
- 3 heaping tablespoons of carrots
- 3 heaping tablespoons of peas
- 3 heaping tablespoons of corn

Salad Vegetables
- 3 sticks of celery
- 5 slices of cucumber
- 1 medium-sized tomato
- 7 cherry tomatoes

Small Fruits
- 2 plums
- 2 kiwis
- 7 strawberries
- 14 cherries

---

1. http://www.nhs.uk/Livewell/5ADAY/Pages/Whatcounts.aspx

Medium Fruits
- 1 apple
- 1 pear
- 1 banana
- 1 orange

Large Fruits
- 1/2 grapefruit
- 1 slice of papaya
- 1 large slice of pineapple
- 2 slices of mango

Beans
- 3 tablespoons of baked beans (max 1/day)
- 3 tablespoons of chickpeas (max 1/day)

Juices and Smoothies
- 150 ml of unsweetened 100% juice (max 1/day)
- 80 g pulped fruit/veggies (max 2/day)

Vegetables That Don't Count
- Potatoes
- Yams
- Plantains

A2.2 Example Day

This table is an example of a typical day when following the plan in this book.

Time	Activity
7:30 AM	Healthy Stand-Up
7:45 AM	Grapefruit with breakfast (first serving of fruit/veggies)
8:30 AM	Start a Pomodoro Technique workout
8:55 AM	First Pomodoro break: five-minute walk
9:25 AM	Second Pomodoro break: five minutes of nerve-gliding
9:55 AM	Third Pomodoro break: five-minute walk
10:30 AM	Snack: apple (second serving of fruit/veggies)
12:00 PM	Smoothie with lunch (third and fourth servings of fruits/veggies)
3:00 PM	Five sets of bodyweight exercises (ten minutes)
6:00 PM	Broccoli with dinner (fifth serving of fruits/veggies)

Further Reading

A3.1 Books

Brain Rules: 12 Principles for Surviving and Thriving at Work, Home, and School [Med09]

The Power of Habit: Why We Do What We Do in Life and Business [Duh12]

Exercise Therapy in the Management of Musculoskeletal Disorders [WGH11]

Low Back Disorders [McG07]

Back RX: A 15-Minute-a-Day Yoga- and Pilates-Based Program to End Low Back Pain [Vad04]

A3.2 Publications

Effects of Exercise on the Brain

Effects of acute bouts of exercise on cognition [Tom03]

Endurance running and the evolution of Homo [BL04]

High impact running improves learning [WBMV07]

Be smart, exercise your heart: exercise effects on brain and cognition [HEK08]

Hours spent and energy expended in physical activity domains: results from the Tomorrow Project cohort in Alberta, Canada [CLFO11]

Reducing occupational sitting time and improving worker health: the Take-a-Stand Project, 2011 [PKLP12]

The Benefits of Microbreaks and Short Bouts of Exercise

Exercise and working memory: an individual differences investigation [SB07]

Plasticity of Executive Control through Task Switching Training in Adolescents [ZEPK12]

The Effects of Sitting, Standing, and Leisure Activity

Role of nonexercise activity thermogenesis (NEAT) in obesity [KL05]

Objectively measured physical activity and mortality in older adults [BH06]

The energy expenditure of using a "walk-and-work" desk for office workers with obesity [LM07]

Nonexercise activity thermogenesis–liberating the life-force [Lev07]

Neuroregulation of nonexercise activity thermogenesis and obesity resistance [KTB08]

Differences in daily energy expenditure in lean and obese women: the role of posture allocation [JWSF08]

Exercise intensity influences nonexercise activity thermogenesis in overweight and obese adults [AHKB11]

Incidental physical activity is positively associated with cardiorespiratory fitness [MR11]

Health risks, correlates, and interventions to reduce sedentary behavior in young people [STMH11]

Sedentary behaviors and subsequent health outcomes in adults a systematic review of longitudinal studies, 1996-2011 [TOND11]

Prolonged sitting: is it a distinct coronary heart disease risk factor? [DTH11]

Effect of intensity and type of physical activity on mortality: results from the Whitehall II cohort study [SDKB12]

Nonexercise activity thermogenesis: a way forward to treat the worldwide obesity epidemic [ML12]

Leisure time physical activity of moderate to vigorous intensity and mortality: a large pooled cohort analysis [MPMB12]

Dynamic Sitting — How Much do We Move When Working at a Computer? [HR03]

Alternative Workstations May Be New But Are They Better? [Hed11]

Headaches, Computer Vision Syndrome, and Eyes

Phototoxic retinopathy [VVT01]

Action spectra for the photoconsumption of oxygen by human ocular lipofuscin and lipofuscin extracts [PRZL02]

Blue-blocking IOLs decrease photoreception without providing significant photoprotection [MT10]

A comparison of symptoms after viewing text on a computer screen and hardcopy [CRPB11]

General Exercise for Back Pain

Evaluation of a specific home exercise program for low back pain [DNLD02]

United Kingdom back pain exercise and manipulation (UK BEAM) randomised trial: cost effectiveness of physical treatments for back pain in primary care [UK 04]

Comparing yoga, exercise, and a self-care book for chronic low back pain: a randomized, controlled trial [SCEM05]

Pilates for Back Pain

Laboratory gait analysis in patients with low back pain before and after a pilates intervention [dMd09]

Effects of Pilates-based exercises on pain and disability in individuals with persistent nonspecific low back pain: a systematic review with meta-analysis [LPLW11]

Comparing the Pilates method with no exercise or lumbar stabilization for pain and functionality in patients with chronic low back pain: systematic review and meta-analysis [PODM12]

Muscular Strength and Mortality

Musculoskeletal fitness, health outcomes and quality of life [KBQ01]

Musculoskeletal fitness and risk of mortality [KC02]

Association between muscular strength and mortality in men: prospective cohort study [RSLM08]

A prospective study of muscular strength and all-cause mortality in men with hypertension [ALRS11]

Muscular strength in male adolescents and premature death: cohort study of one million participants [OSTR12]

Bibliography

[AB05]   Kenneth Anderson and David G. Behm. Trunk Muscle Activity Increases With Unstable Squat Movements. *Canadian Journal of Applied Physiology.* 30[1], 2005.

[AHHL07]   RB Abbott, KK Hui, RD Hays, MD Li, T Pan, and T Sarna. A randomized controlled trial of tai chi for tension headaches. *Evidence-Based Complementary and Alternative Medicine.* 4[1], 2007.

[AHKB11]   Mohammad A Alahmadi, Andrew P Hills, Neil A King, and Nuala M Byrne. Exercise intensity influences nonexercise activity thermogenesis in overweight and obese adults. *Medicine and science in sports and exercise.* 43[4], 2011.

[ALRS11]   Enrique G Artero, Duck-chul Lee, Jonatan R Ruiz, Xuemei Sui, Francisco B Ortega, Timothy S Church, Carl J Lavie, Manuel J Castillo, and Steven N Blair. A prospective study of muscular strength and all-cause mortality in men with hypertension. *Journal of the American College of Cardiology.* 57[18], 2011.

[Ang12]   David B. Angus. *The End of Illness.* The Free Press, New York, NY, 2012.

[Ans07]   JR Anshel. Visual ergonomics in the workplace. *Journal of the American Association of Occupational Health Nurses.* 55[10], 2007.

[Ara11]   C Aranow. Vitamin D and the immune system. *Journal of Investigative Medicine.* 59[6], 2011.

[Atr07]   I Atroshi. Carpal tunnel syndrome and keyboard use at work: a population-based study. *Arthritis and rheumatism.* 56[11], 2007.

[BAH08]   JF Babalola, OE Awolola, and TK Hamzat. Reliability Of Kraus-Weber Exercise Test As An Evaluation Tool In Low Back Pain Susceptibility Among Apparently Healthy University Students. *African Journal for Physical, Health Education, Recreation and Dance.* 14[2], 2008.

[BH06]   Steven N Blair and William L Haskell. Objectively measured physical activity and mortality in older adults. *JAMA : the journal of the American Medical Association.* 296[2], 2006.

[BIB97]   W D Bandy, J M Irion, and M Briggler. The effect of time and frequency of static stretching on flexibility of the hamstring muscles. *Physical therapy.* 77[10], 1997.

[BKHJ05] Terra Barnes, Yasuo Kubota, Dan Hu, Dezhe Jin, and Ann Graybiel. Activity of striatal neurons reflects dynamic encoding and recoding of procedural memories. *Nature.* 437, 2005.

[BL04]   Dennis M Bramble and Daniel E Lieberman. Endurance running and the evolution of Homo. *Nature.* 432[7015], 2004.

[BMB10]   Leonard L Berry, Ann M Mirabito, and William B Baun. What's the Hard Return on Employee Wellness Programs?. *Harvard Business Review.* 2010.

[BWSA10] Nicholas A Burd, Daniel W D West, Aaron W Staples, Philip J Atherton, Jeff M Baker, Daniel R Moore, Andrew M Holwerda, Gianni Parise, Michael J Rennie, Steven K Baker, and Stuart M Phillips. Low-load high volume resistance exercise stimulates muscle protein synthesis more than high-load low volume resistance exercise in young men. *PloS one.* 5[8], 2010.

[Bac49]   Carl Philipp Emanuel Bach. *Essay on the True Art of Playing Keyboard Instruments.* Cassell Publishing Company, London, UK, 1949.

[Bla11]   M Blaser. Antibiotic overuse: Stop the killing of beneficial bacteria. *Nature.* 476[7361], 2011.

[Buc02]   David Buchholz MD. *Heal Your Headache: The 1-2-3 Program for Taking Charge of Your Pain.* Workman Publishing Company, New York, NY, 2002.

[Bur09]   Lora Burke. Experiences of Self-Monitoring: Successes and Struggles during Treatment for Weight Loss. *Qualitative Health Research.* 19[6], 2009.

[CB02]   Carl Cotman and Nicole Berchtold. Exercise: a behavioral intervention to enhance brain health and plasticity. *Trends in Neuroscience.* 25[6], 2002.

[CCLC08] Moktar Chtara, Anis Chaouachi, Gregory T Levin, Mustapha Chaouachi, Karim Chamari, Mohamed Amri, and Paul B Laursen. Effect of concurrent endurance and circuit resistance training sequence on muscular strength and power development. *Journal of strength and conditioning research / National Strength & Conditioning Association.* 22[4], 2008.

[CHBE07] Darla Castelli, Charles Hillman, Sarah Buck, and Heather Erwin. Physical Fitness and Academic Achievement in Third- and Fifth-Grade Students. *Journal of Sport and Exercise Psychology.* 29[2], 2007.

[CLFO11]   Ilona Csizmadi, Geraldine Lo Siou, Christine M Friedenreich, Neville Owen, and Paula J Robson. Hours spent and energy expended in physical activity domains: results from the Tomorrow Project cohort in Alberta, Canada. *The international journal of behavioral nutrition and physical activity.* 8, 2011.

[CRPB11]   Christina Chu, Mark Rosenfield, Joan K Portello, Jaclyn A Benzoni, and Juanita D Collier. A comparison of symptoms after viewing text on a computer screen and hardcopy. *Ophthalmic & physiological optics : the journal of the British College of Ophthalmic Opticians (Optometrists).* 31[1], 2011.

[CSMM09]   Virginia R Chomitz, Meghan M Slining, Robert J McGowan, Suzanne E Mitchell, Glen F Dawson, and Karen A Hacker. Is there a relationship between physical fitness and academic achievement? Positive results from public school children in the northeastern United States. *The Journal of school health.* 79[1], 2009.

[Cro04]   Karen Croteau. A Preliminary Study on the Impact of a Pedometer-based Intervention on Daily Steps. *American Journal of Health Promotion.* 18[3], 2004.

[DDCG06]   S Donzelli, E Di Domenica, AM Cova, R Galletti, and N Giunta. Two different techniques in the rehabilitation treatment of low back pain: a randomized controlled trial. *European Journal of Physical and Rehabilitation Medicine.* 42[3], 2006.

[DNLD02]   Martin Descarreaux, Martin C Normand, Louis Laurencelle, and Claude Dugas. Evaluation of a specific home exercise program for low back pain. *Journal of manipulative and physiological therapeutics.* 25[8], 2002.

[DT99]   RJ Dennis and Nicola Torrance. Functional reach improvement in normal older women after Alexander Technique instruction. *The Journals of Gerontology Series A: Biological Sciences and Medical Sciences.* 54[1], 1999.

[DTH11]   David W Dunstan, Alicia A Thorp, and Genevieve N Healy. Prolonged sitting: is it a distinct coronary heart disease risk factor?. *Current opinion in cardiology.* 26[5], 2011.

[DWS91]   P Deurenberg, J A Weststrate, and J C Seidell. Body mass index as a measure of body fatness: age- and sex-specific prediction formulas. *The British journal of nutrition.* 65[2], 1991.

[Duh12]   Charles Duhigg. *The Power of Habit: Why We Do What We Do in Life and Business.* Random House, New York, NY, USA, 2012.

[Dun10]   DW Dunstan. Television Viewing Time and Mortality. *Circulation.* 121, 2010.

[Dur91]   JA Durkan. A new diagnostic test for carpal tunnel syndrome. *The Journal of Bone and Joint Surgery.* 73[4], 1991.

[Duv11]   Jason Duvall. Enhancing the benefits of outdoor walking with cognitive engagement strategies. *Journal of Environmental Psychology.* 31[1], 2011.

[FB09]   Jesse Fox and Jeremy N. Bailenson. Virtual self-modeling: The effects of vicarious reinforcement and identification on exercise behaviors. *Media Psychology.* 12[1], 2009.

[FLSM90]   Janet A. Fuchs, Richard M. Levinson, Ronald R. Stoddard, Maurice E. Mullet, and Diane H. Jones. Health Risk Factors among the Amish: Results of a Survey. *Health, Education & Behavior.* 17[2], 1990.

[FRG00]   L D Fox, W J Rejeski, and L Gauvin. Effects of leadership style and group dynamics on enjoyment of physical activity. *American journal of health promotion.* 14[5], 2000.

[FSM05]   Katsuo Fujiwara, Michie Shigeiwa, and Kaoru Maeda. Relationship between Improvement in Cognitive Function by Balance Board Training and Postural Control Adaptability in the Elderly. *Proceedings of the 8th International Evoked Potentials Symposium.* 1278, 2005.

[Fau02]   Gavin Faunce. Eating Disorders and Attentional Bias: A Review. *Eating Disorders.* 10[2], 2002.

[Fer10]   Timothy Ferriss. *The 4-Hour Body: An Uncommon Guide to Rapid Fat-Loss, Incredible Sex, and Becoming Superhuman.* Crown Archetype, New York, NY, 2010.

[Fla05]   Alice Flaherty. Frontotemporal And Dopaminergic Control Of Idea Generation And Creative Drive. *The Journal of Comparative Neurology.* 493[1], 2005.

[Fuh12]   Joel Fuhrman. *Eat to Live: The Amazing Nutrient-Rich Program for Fast and Sustained Weight Loss, Revised Edition.* Little, Brown and Company, New York, NY, USA, 2012.

[GPS99]   A B Graziano, M Peterson, and G L Shaw. Enhanced learning of proportional math through music training and spatial-temporal training. *Neurological research.* 21[2], 1999.

[GS11]   Lee Goldman MD and Andrew I. Schafer MD. *Goldman's Cecil Medicine.* W.B. Saunders Company, St. Louis, MO, 24th, 2011.

[GSKA98]   Marian Garfinkel, Atul Singhal, Warren Katz, David Allen, Rosemary Reshetar, and Ralph Schumacher. Yoga-based intervention for carpal tunnel syndrome: A randomized trial. *The Journal of the American Medical Association.* 280[18], 1998.

[GSSH00] Traci Galinsky, Naomi Swanson, Steven Sauter, Joseph Hurrell, and Lawrence Schleifer. A field study of supplementary rest breaks for data-entry operators. *Ergonomics*. 43[5], 2000.

[Gil11] Jose-Antonio Gil-Gomez. Effectiveness of a Wii balance board-based system (eBaViR) for balance rehabilitation: a pilot randomized clinical trial in patients with acquired brain injury. *Journal of Neuroengineering and Rehabilitation*. 8, 2011.

[Gil75] John Gill. The use of attractive fixed points in accelerating the convergence of limit periodic continued fractions. *Proceedings of the American Mathematical Society*. 47, 1975.

[Gil77] John Gill. Computational Complexity of Probabilistic Turing Machines. *SIAM Journal on Computing*. 6[4], 1977.

[Gil88] John Gill. Compositions of analytic functions of the form $Fn(z) = Fn-1(fn(z))$, $fn(z) \rightarrow f(z)$. *Journal of Computational and Applied Mathematics*. 23[2], 1988.

[Gri05] James B Grissom. Physical Fitness and Academic Achievement. *Journal of Exercise Physiology*. 8[1], 2005.

[HCMS04] Peter Hoonakker, Passcale Carayon, Alexandre Marian, and Jen Schoepke. Shortage of Skilled Workers and High Turnover in the Information Technology Workforce: What Are the Possibilities for Retention?. *Work with Computing Systems*. 2004.

[HEK08] Charles H Hillman, Kirk I Erickson, and Arthur F Kramer. Be smart, exercise your heart: exercise effects on brain and cognition. *Nature reviews Neuroscience*. 9[1], 2008.

[HJAR05] Alan Hedge, Jason Jagdeo, Anshu Agarwall, and Kate Rockey-Harris. Sitting or Standing for Computer Work — Does a Negative-Tilt Keyboard Tray Make a Difference?. *Proceedings of the Human Factors and Ergonomics Society Annual Meeting*. 49[8], 2005.

[HMZG12] Michael Harrison, Niall Moyna, Theodore Zderic, Donal Gorman, Noel McCaffrey, Brian Carson, and Marc Hamilton. Lipoprotein particle distribution and skeletal muscle lipoprotein lipase acitivty after acute exercise. *Lipids in Health and Disease*. 11, 2012.

[HR03] Alan Hedge and Michelle Ruder. Dynamic Sitting — How Much do We Move When Working at a Computer?. *http://ergo.human.cornell.edu*. 47[6], 2003.

[HSM12] John Hoffman, Judith A. Salerno, and Alexandra Moss. *The Weight of the Nation: Surprising Lessons About Diets, Food, and Fat from the Extraordinary Series from HBO Documentary Films*. St. Martin's Press, New York, NY, 2012.

[Hed11]   Alan Hedge. Alternative Workstations May Be New But Are They Better?. *http://link.springer.com*. 6779, 2011.

[Her04]   Vesa-Pekka Herva. People, Material Culture and Environment in the North. *Proceedings of the 22nd Nordic Archaeological Conference*. 2004.

[HvT05]   JA Hayden, MW van Tulder, and G Tomlinson. Systematic review: strategies for using exercise therapy to improve outcomes in chronic low back pain. *Annals of Internal Medicine*. 142[9], 2005.

[JSSK07]   PJ John, N Sharma, CM Sharma, and A Kankane. Effectiveness of yoga therapy in the treatment of migraine without aura: a randomized controlled trial. *Headache*. 47[5], 2007.

[JWSF08]   Darcy L Johannsen, Gregory J Welk, Rick L Sharp, and Paul J Flakoll. Differences in daily energy expenditure in lean and obese women: the role of posture allocation. *Obesity (Silver Spring, Md)*. 16[1], 2008.

[KBFH02]   WC Knowler, E Barrett-Connor, SE Fowler, RF Hamman, JM Lachin, EA Walker, and DM Nathan. Reduction in the incidence of type 2 diabetes with lifestyle intervention or metformin. *New England Journal of Medicine*. 346[6], 2002.

[KBQ01]   R T Kell, G Bell, and A Quinney. Musculoskeletal fitness, health outcomes and quality of life. *Sports medicine (Auckland, NZ)*. 31[12], 2001.

[KC02]   Peter T Katzmarzyk and Cora L Craig. Musculoskeletal fitness and risk of mortality. *Medicine and science in sports and exercise*. 34[5], 2002.

[KCCB09]   Peter Katzmarzyk, Timothy Church, Cora Craig, and Claude Bouchard. Sitting time and mortality from all causes, cardiovascular disease, and cancer. *Medicine and Science in Sports and Exercise*. 41[5], 2009.

[KDSB10]   S. D. Kulkarni, H. R. Desai, C. S. Sharma, and P. J. Bhatt. Assessment Of Muscular Fitness In School Children Using Kraus-Weber Tests. *National Journal of Integrated Research in Medicine*. 1[4], 2010.

[KKJM84]   Wendy Kim, June Kelsay, Joseph Judd, Mary Marshall, Walter Mertz, and Elizabeth Prather. Evaluation of long-term dietary intakes of adults consuming self-selected diets. *The American Journal of Clinical Nutrition*. 40[1], 1984.

[KL05]   Catherine M Kotz and James A Levine. Role of nonexercise activity thermogenesis (NEAT) in obesity. *Minnesota medicine*. 88[9], 2005.

[KTB08]   Catherine M Kotz, Jennifer A Teske, and Charles J Billington. Neuroregulation of nonexercise activity thermogenesis and obesity resistance. *American journal of physiology Regulatory, integrative and comparative physiology*. 294[3], 2008.

[KTHD88] Abby King, C. Barr Taylor, William Haskell, and Robert Debusk. Strategies for increasing early adherence to and long-term maintenance of home-based exercise training in healthy middle-aged men and women. *The American Journal of Cardiology.* 61[8], 1988.

[KYSB00] H Kaikkonen, M Yrjama, E Siljander, P Byman, and R Laukkanen. The effect of heart rate controlled low resistance circuit weight training and endurance training on maximal aerobic power in sedentary adults. *Scandinavian journal of medicine & science in sports.* 10[4], 2000.

[Kes09] David A. Kessler. *The End of Overeating: Taking Control of the Insatiable American Appetite.* Rodale Books, New York, NY, 2009.

[Key05] LR Keytel. Prediction of energy expenditure from heart rate monitoring during submaximal exercise. *Journal of Sports Sciences.* 23[3], 2005.

[Kin11] Ethan Kind. *An Alexander Technique Approach to Using a Computer.* Amazon Digital Services, Inc., http://amzn.com/, 2011.

[Kra09] John Krakauer. *Eiger Dreams: Ventures Among Men and Mountains.* Lyons Press, Guilford, CT, 2009.

[LKIH10] Q Li, M Kobayashi, H Inagaki, Y Hirata, YJ Li, K Hirata, T Shimizu, H Suzuki, M Katsumata, Y Wakayama, T Kawada, T Ohira, N Matsui, and T Kagawa. A day trip to a forest park increases human natural killer activity and the expression of anti-cancer proteins in male subjects. *Journal of Biological Regulators & Homeostatic Agents.* 24[2], 2010.

[LLTT12] Juyoung Lee, Qing Li, Liisa Tyrväinen, Yuko Tsunetsugu, Bum-Jin Park, Takahide Kagawa, and Yoshifumi Miyazaki. Nature Therapy and Preventive Medicine. *Public Health - Social and Behavioral Health.* 2012.

[LM07] James A Levine and Jennifer M Miller. The energy expenditure of using a "walk-and-work" desk for office workers with obesity. *British journal of sports medicine.* 41[9], 2007.

[LMKI08] Q Li, K Morimoto, M Kobayashi, H Inagaki, M Katsumata, Y Hirata, Y Hirata, K Hirata, H Suzuki, YJ Li, Y Wakayama, T Kawada, BJ Park, T Ohira, N Matsui, T Kagawa, Y Miyazaki, and AM Krensky. Visiting a forest, but not a city, increases human natural killer activity and expression of anti-cancer proteins. *International Journal of Immunopathology and Pharmacology.* 21[1], 2008.

[LNMM06] Q Li, A Nakadai, H Matsushima, Y Miyazaki, AM Krensky, T Kawada, and K Morimoto. Phytoncides (wood essential oils) induce human natural killer cell activity. *Immunopharmacology and Immunotoxicology.* 28[2], 2006.

[LPFB03]   T Lange, B Perras, HL Fehm, and J Born. Sleep enhances the human antibody response to hepatitis A vaccination. *Psychosomatic Medicine.* 65[5], 2003.

[LPLW11]   Edwin Choon Wyn Lim, Ruby Li Choo Poh, Ai Ying Low, and Wai Pong Wong. Effects of Pilates-based exercises on pain and disability in individuals with persistent nonspecific low back pain: a systematic review with meta-analysis. *The Journal of orthopaedic and sports physical therapy.* 41[2], 2011.

[LPTO11]   J Lee, BJ Park, Y Tsunetsugu, T Ohira, T Kagawa, and Y Miyazaki. Effect of forest bathing on physiological and psychological responses in young Japanese male subjects. *Public Health.* 125[2], 2011.

[LRH95]   Rudolph Leibel, Michael Rosenbaum, and Jules Hirsch. Changes in Energy Expenditure Resulting from Altered Body Weight. *The New England Journal of Medicine.* 332[10], 1995.

[Lar05]   Andrew Larner. The Neurology of 'Alice'. *History of Neurology & Neuroscience.* 4[6], 2005.

[Lev02]   James Levine. Non-exercise activity thermogenesis (NEAT). *Best Practice & Research Clinical Endocrinology & Metabolism.* 16[4], 2002.

[Lev07]   J A Levine. Nonexercise activity thermogenesis–liberating the life-force. *Journal of internal medicine.* 262[3], 2007.

[Li10]   Qing Li. Effect of forest bathing trips on human immune function. *Environmental Health and Preventive Medicine.* 15[1], 2010.

[MBHL98]   Karin Mogg, Brendan Bradley, Harpfreet Hyare, and Sui Lee. Selective attention to food-related stimuli in hunger: are attentional biases specific to emotional and psychopathological states, or are they also found in normal drive states?. *Behaviour Research and Therapy.* 36[2], 1998.

[MC58]   Jeremy Morris and Margaret Crawford. Coronary heart disease and physical activity of work. *British Medical Journal.* 2, 1958.

[MDMN02]   JB Mitchell, JP Dugas, BK McFarlin, and MJ Nelson. Effect of exercise, heat stress, and hydration on immune cell number and function. *Medicine & Science in Sports & Exercise.* 34[12], 2002.

[MHAH95]   Antti Malmivaara, Unto Häkkinen, Timo Aro, Maj-Len Heinrichs, Liisa Koskenniemi, Eeva Kuosma, Seppo Lappi, Raili Paloheimo, Carita Servo, Antti Malmivaara, Vesa Vaaranen, and Sven Hernberg. The Treatment of Acute Low Back Pain — Bed Rest, Exercises, or Ordinary Activity?. *The New England Journal of Medicine.* 332[6], 1995.

[MJHS90] MD Mifflin, S Jeor, LA Hill, BJ Scott, SA Daugherty, and YO Koh. A new predictive equation for resting energy expenditure in healthy individuals. *The American Journal of Clinical Nutrition.* 51[2], 1990.

[MK09] Stuart M McGill and Amy Karpowicz. Exercises for spine stabilization: motion/motor patterns, stability progressions, and clinical technique. *Archives of physical medicine and rehabilitation.* 90[1], 2009.

[ML12] Shelly K McCrady-Spitzer and James A Levine. Nonexercise activity thermogenesis: a way forward to treat the worldwide obesity epidemic. *Surgery for obesity and related diseases : official journal of the American Society for Bariatric Surgery.* 8[5], 2012.

[MP04] Paula Moynihan and Poul Erik Petersen. Diet, nutrition and the prevention of dental diseases. *Public Health Nutrition.* 7[1A], 2004.

[MPMB12] Steven C Moore, Alpa V Patel, Charles E Matthews, Amy Berrington de Gonzalez, Yikyung Park, Hormuzd A Katki, Martha S Linet, Elisabete Weiderpass, Kala Visvanathan, Kathy J Helzlsouer, Michael Thun, Susan M Gapstur, Patricia Hartge, and I-Min Lee. Leisure time physical activity of moderate to vigorous intensity and mortality: a large pooled cohort analysis. *PLoS medicine.* 9[11], 2012.

[MR11] K Ashlee McGuire and Robert Ross. Incidental physical activity is positively associated with cardiorespiratory fitness. *Medicine and science in sports and exercise.* 43[11], 2011.

[MT10] Martin A Mainster and Patricia L Turner. Blue-blocking IOLs decrease photoreception without providing significant photoprotection. *Survey of ophthalmology.* 55[3], 2010.

[MTSB04] Monique Muller, Deborah Tsui, Ronda Schnurr, Lori Biddulph-Deisroth, and Julie Hard Hard. Effectiveness of hand therapy interventions in primary management of carpal tunnel syndrome: a systematic review. *Journal of Hand Therapy.* 17[2], 2004.

[Mac12] Ian MacNeill. *The Beginning Runner's Handbook: The Proven 13-Week Run/Walk Program.* Greystone Books, Vancouver, BC, Fourth, 2012.

[Mar12] Norman J. Marcus. *End Back Pain Forever: A Groundbreaking Approach to Eliminate Your Suffering.* Atria Books, New York, NY, 2012.

[McG07] Stuart McGill. *Low Back Disorders.* Human Kinetics, Champaign, Illinois, 2nd, 2007.

[Med09] John Medina. *Brain Rules: 12 Principles for Surviving and Thriving at Work, Home, and School.* Pear Press, Seattle, WA, 2009.

[Mic04]   SL Michlovitz. Conservative interventions for carpal tunnel syndrome. *Journal of Orthopaedic & Sports Physical Therapy.* 34[10], 2004.

[Mil00]   Katharine Milton. Hunter-gatherer diets - a different perspective. *The American Journal of Clinical Nutrition.* 71[3], 2000.

[NGMO07]   K Nemoto, H Gen-no, S Masuki, K Okazaki, and H Nose. Effects of high-intensity interval walking training on physical fitness and blood pressure in middle-aged and older people. *Mayo Clinic Proceedings.* 82[7], 2007.

[NJVW11]   Javaid Nauman, Imre Janszky, Lars Vatten, and Ulrik Wisløff. Temporal Changes in Resting Heart Rate and Deaths From Ischemic Heart Disease. *Journal of the American Medical Association.* 306[23], 2011.

[NTAA07]   Y Netz, R Tomer, S Axelrad, E Argov, and O Inbar. The effect of a single aerobic training session on cognitive flexibility in late middle-aged adults. *International journal of sports medicine.* 28[1], 2007.

[Nö09]   Staffan Nöteberg. *Pomodoro Technique Illustrated: The Easy Way to Do More in Less Time.* The Pragmatic Bookshelf, Raleigh, NC and Dallas, TX, 2009.

[OBB09]   N Owen, A Bauman, and W Brown. Too much sitting: a novel and important predictor of chronic disease risk?. *British Journal of Sports Medicine.* 43, 2009.

[ODSH10]   Gretchen D Oliver, Priscilla M Dwelly, Nicholas D Sarantis, Rachael A Helmer, and Jeffery A Bonacci. Muscle activation of different core exercises. *Journal of strength and conditioning research / National Strength & Conditioning Association.* 24[11], 2010.

[OLGB02]   Ronald J Ozminkowski, Davina Ling, Ron Z Goetzel, Jennifer A Bruno, Kathleen R Rutter, Fikry Isaac, and Sara Wang. Long-term impact of Johnson & Johnson's Health & Wellness Program on health care utilization and expenditures. *Journal of occupational and environmental medicine.* 44[1], 2002.

[OMM08]   D O'Connor, S Marshall, and N Massy-Westropp. Non-surgical treatment (other than steroid injection) for carpal tunnel syndrome. *Cochrane Database of Systematic Reviews.* [4], 2008.

[OSTR12]   Francisco B Ortega, Karri Silventoinen, Per Tynelius, and Finn Rasmussen. Muscular strength in male adolescents and premature death: cohort study of one million participants. *British Medical Journal.* 345, 2012.

[PAF07]   DB Piazzini, I Aprile, and PE Ferrara. A systematic review of conservative treatment of carpal tunnel syndrome. *Clinical Rehabilitation.* 27[4], 2007.

[PDWB08]   Kevin C Parfrey, David Docherty, R Chad Workman, and David G Behm. The effects of different sit- and curl-up positions on activation of abdominal and hip flexor musculature. *Applied physiology, nutrition, and metabolism = Physiologie appliquee, nutrition et metabolisme.* 33[5], 2008.

[PHFT09] Matthew Pontifex, Charles Hillman, Bo Fernhall, Kelli Thompson, and Teresa Valentini. The Effect of Acute Aerobic and Resistance Exercise on Working Memory. *Medicine & Science in Sports Exercise.* 41[4], 2009.

[PKLP12] Nicolaas P Pronk, Abigail S Katz, Marcia Lowry, and Jane Rodmyre Payfer. Reducing occupational sitting time and improving worker health: the Take-a-Stand Project, 2011. *Preventing chronic disease.* 9, 2012.

[PLI07] T Piirainen, K Laitinen, and E Isolauri. Impact of national fortification of fluid milks and margarines with vitamin D on dietary intake and serum 25-hydroxyvitamin D concentration in 4-year-old children. *European Journal of Clinical Nutrition.* 61[1], 2007.

[PMCM04] MD Parra, BE Martínez de Morentin, JM Cobo, A Mateos, and JA Martínez. Daily ingestion of fermented milk containing Lactobacillus casei DN114001 improves innate-defense capacity in healthy middle-aged people. *Journal of Physiology and Biochemistry.* 60[2], 2004.

[PODM12] Ligia M Pereira, Karen Obara, Josilainne M Dias, Maryela O Menacho, Debora A Guariglia, Durcelina Schiavoni, Hugo M Pereira, and Jefferson Rosa Cardoso. Comparing the Pilates method with no exercise or lumbar stabilization for pain and functionality in patients with chronic low back pain: systematic review and meta-analysis. *Clinical rehabilitation.* 26[1], 2012.

[PPBM10] A Paoli, F Pacelli, A M Bargossi, G Marcolin, S Guzzinati, M Neri, A Bianco, and A Palma. Effects of three distinct protocols of fitness training on body composition, strength and blood lactate. *The Journal of sports medicine and physical fitness.* 50[1], 2010.

[PR09] Klaus Podoll and Derek Robinson. *Migraine Art: The Migraine Experience from Within.* North Atlantic Books, Berkeley, CA, 2009.

[PRZL02] Anna Pawlak, Malgorzata Rozanowska, Mariusz Zareba, Laura E Lamb, John D Simon, and Tadeusz Sarna. Action spectra for the photoconsumption of oxygen by human ocular lipofuscin and lipofuscin extracts. *Archives of biochemistry and biophysics.* 403[1], 2002.

[PTKK10] BJ Park, Y Tsunetsugu, T Kasetani, T Kagawa, and Y Miyazaki. The physiological effects of Shinrin-yoku (taking in the forest atmosphere or forest bathing): evidence from field experiments in 24 forests across Japan. *Environmental Health and Preventive Medicine.* 15[1], 2010.

[PZ08]   Oliver R. W. Pergams and Patricia A. Zaradic. Evidence for a fundamental and pervasive shift away from nature-based recreation. *Proceedings of the National Academy of Sciences of the United States of America.* 105[7], 2008.

[Pag12]   Phil Page. Current concepts in muscle stretching for exercise and rehabilitation. *International journal of sports physical therapy.* 7[1], 2012.

[Pea02]   Sharon Pearcey. Food intake and meal patterns of weight-stable and weight-gaining persons. *The American Journal of Clinical Nutrition.* 76[1], 2002.

[Pin05]   Lamia Pinar. Can we use nerve gliding exercises in women with carpal tunnel syndrome?. *Advances in Therapy.* 22[5], 2005.

[Pre06]   S Premoselli. Neutral wrist splinting in carpal tunnel syndrome: a 3- and 6-months clinical and neurophysiologic follow-up evaluation of night-only splint therapy. *European Journal of Physical and Rehabilitation Medicine.* 42[2], 2006.

[RCTH10]   Kimberly Reich, Yi-Wen Chen, Paul Thompson, Eric Hoffman, and Priscilla Clarkson. Forty-eight hours of unloading and 24 h of reloading lead to changes in global gene expression patterns related to ubiquitination and oxidative stress in humans. *Journal of Applied Physiology.* 109[5], 2010.

[RG11]   David A Raichlen and Adam D Gordon. Relationship between exercise capacity and brain size in mammals. *PloS one.* 6[6], 2011.

[RJKB95]   M Rózanowska, J Jarvis-Evans, W Korytowski, ME Boulton, JM Burke, and T Sarna. Blue light-induced reactivity of retinal age pigment. In vitro generation of oxygen-reactive species. *The Journal of Biological Chemistry.* 270[32], 1995.

[RLS06]   R Rydeard, A Leger, and D Smith. Pilates-based therapeutic exercise: effect on subjects with nonspecific chronic low back pain and functional disability: a randomized controlled trial. *The Journal of Orthopaedic and Sports Physical Therapy.* 36[7], 2006.

[RP13]   David A Raichlen and John D Polk. Linking brains and brawn: exercise and the evolution of human neurobiology. *Proceedings Biological sciences / The Royal Society.* 280[1750], 2013.

[RSLK12]   Marc Roig, Kasper Skriver, Jesper Lundbye-Jensen, Bente Kiens, and Jens Bo Nielsen. A single bout of exercise improves motor memory. *PloS one.* 7[9], 2012.

[RSLM08]   Jonatan R Ruiz, Xuemei Sui, Felipe Lobelo, James R Jr Morrow, Allen W Jackson, Michael Sjostrom, and Steven N Blair. Association between muscular strength and mortality in men: prospective cohort study. *British Medical Journal.* 337, 2008.

[RTF91]   Daniel J. Raiten, John M. Talbot, and Kenneth D. Fisher. Executive Summary from the Report: Analysis of Adverse Reactions to Monosodium Glutamate (MSG). *The Journal of Nutrition.* 125[11], 1991.

[Rat08]   John Ratey. *Spark: The Revolutionary New Science of Exercise and the Brain.* Little, Brown and Company, New York, NY, USA, 2008.

[Rey12]   Gretchen Reynolds. *The First 20 Minutes: Surprising Science Reveals How We Can: Exercise Better, Train Smarter, Live Longer.* Hudson Street Press, New York, NY, 2012.

[S E11]   Gene Stone, T. Coli Campbell , and Caldwell B. Esselstyn. *Forks Over Knives: The Plant-Based Way to Health.* The Experiment, New York, NY, 2011.

[SB07]   Benjamin A Sibley and Sian L Beilock. Exercise and working memory: an individual differences investigation. *Journal of sport & exercise psychology.* 29[6], 2007.

[SBWS11]   RH Stiegel, R Bedrosian, C Wang, and S Schwartz. Why men should be included in research on binge eating: results from a comparison of psychosocial impairment in men and women. *International Journal of Eating Disorders.* 45[2], 2011.

[SCEM05]   Karen J Sherman, Daniel C Cherkin, Janet Erro, Diana L Miglioretti, and Richard A Deyo. Comparing yoga, exercise, and a self-care book for chronic low back pain: a randomized, controlled trial. *Annals of internal medicine.* 143[12], 2005.

[SDKB12]   Severine Sabia, Aline Dugravot, Mika Kivimaki, Eric Brunner, Martin J Shipley, and Archana Singh-Manoux. Effect of intensity and type of physical activity on mortality: results from the Whitehall II cohort study. *American journal of public health.* 102[4], 2012.

[SKGR10]   M Schmidt-Kassow, A Kulka, TC Gunter, K Rothermich, and SA Kotz. Exercising during learning improves vocabulary acquisition: behavioral and ERP evidence. *Neuroscience Letters.* 482[2], 2010.

[SRWT95]   Maria Sequeira1, Martin Rickenbach1, Vincent Wietlisbach1, Benoit Tullen1, and Yves Schutz2. Physical Activity Assessment Using a Pedometer and Its Comparison with a Questionnaire in a Large Population Survey. *American Journal of Epidemiology.* 142[9], 1995.

[SSC02]   C Stallibrass, P Sissons, and C Chalmers. Management of chronic pain in primary care. *Clinical Rehabilitation.* 16[7], 2002.

[SSL04]   Ann Scher, Walter Stewart, and Richard Lipton. Headache caused by caffeine withdrawal among moderate coffee drinkers switched from ordinary to decaffeinated coffee: a 12 week double blind trial. *Neurology*. 63[11], 2004.

[SSSS09] C Schoen, A Schulz, J Schweikart, S Schütt, and V von Baehr. Regulatory effects of a fermented food concentrate on immune function parameters in healthy volunteers. *Nutrition*. 25[5], 2009.

[ST11] Blair Smith and Nicola Torrance. Management of chronic pain in primary care. *Current Opinion in Supportive & Palliative Care*. 5[2], 2011.

[STMH11] Jo Salmon, Mark S Tremblay, Simon J Marshall, and Clare Hume. Health risks, correlates, and interventions to reduce sedentary behavior in young people. *American journal of preventive medicine*. 41[2], 2011.

[SWSW01] J Clarke Stevens, John Witt, Benn Smith, and Amy Weaver. The frequency of carpal tunnel syndrome in computer users at a medical facility. *Neurology*. 56[11], 2001.

[Sch12] Susan E.B. Schwartz. *JFK's Secret Doctor: The Remarkable Life of Medical Pioneer and Legendary Rock Climber Hans Kraus*. Skyhorse Publishing, New York, NY, 2012.

[Shi11] Qiyun Shi. Is surgical intervention more effective than non-surgical treatment for carpal tunnel syndrome? A systematic review. *Journal of Orthopaedic Surgery and Research*. 6, 2011.

[Sin98] Simon Singh. *Fermat's Enigma: The Epic Quest to Solve the World's Greatest Mathematical Problem*. Anchor, New York, NY, USA, 1998.

[Sis12] Mark Sisson. *The Primal Blueprint: Reprogram your genes for effortless weight loss, vibrant health, and boundless energy*. Primal Nutrition, Inc., Malibu, CA, Second, 2012.

[TB04] Catrine Tudor-Locke and David Bassett. How Many Steps/Day Are Enough?: Preliminary Pedometer Indices for Public Health. *Sports Medicine*. 34[1], 2004.

[TFO06] Bertrand Tehard, Christine Friedenreich, and Jean-Michel Oppert. Effect of Physical Activity on Women at Increased Risk of Breast Cancer: Results from the E3N Cohort Study. *Cancer Epidemiology, Biomarkers & Prevention*. 15[1], 2006.

[TK93] L Tarasoff and M Kelly. Monosodium L-glutamate: A double-blind study and review. *Food and Chemical Toxicology*. 31[12], 1993.

[TL11] Warren G Thompson and James A Levine. Productivity of transcriptionists using a treadmill desk. *Work*. 40[4], 2011.

[TOND11]   Alicia A Thorp, Neville Owen, Maike Neuhaus, and David W Dunstan. Sedentary behaviors and subsequent health outcomes in adults a systematic review of longitudinal studies, 1996-2011. *American journal of preventive medicine*. 41[2], 2011.

[Tom03]   Phillip D Tomporowski. Effects of acute bouts of exercise on cognition. *Acta psychologica*. 112[3], 2003.

[UK 04]   UK BEAM Trial Team. United Kingdom back pain exercise and manipulation (UK BEAM) randomised trial: cost effectiveness of physical treatments for back pain in primary care. *BMJ (Clinical research ed)*. 329[7479], 2004.

[VVT01]   L Verma, P Venkatesh, and H K Tewari. Phototoxic retinopathy. *Ophthalmology clinics of North America*. 14[4], 2001.

[VWvK11]   LH Vu, DC Whiteman, JC van der Pols, MG Kimlin, and RE Neale. Serum vitamin D levels in office workers in a subtropical climate. *Photochemistry and Photobiology*. 87[3], 2011.

[Vad04]   Vijay Vad. *Back RX: A 15-Minute-a-Day Yoga- and Pilates-Based Program to End Low Back Pain*. Gotham Books, New York, NY, 2004.

[Vyg78]   L S Vygotsky. *Mind in Society: The Development of Higher Psychological Processes*. Harvard University Press, Boston, MA, 1978.

[WBA94]   Robert Werner, C Bir, and TJ Armstrong. Reverse Phalen's maneuver as an aid in diagnosing carpal tunnel syndrome. *Archives of Physical Medicine and Rehabilitation*. 75[7], 1994.

[WBMV07]   Bernward Winter, Caterina Breitenstein, Frank C Mooren, Klaus Voelker, Manfred Fobker, Anja Lechtermann, Karsten Krueger, Albert Fromme, Catharina Korsukewitz, Agnes Floel, and Stefan Knecht. High impact running improves learning. *Neurobiology of learning and memory*. 87[4], 2007.

[WFKM10]   JA Westman, AK Ferketich, RM Kauffman, SN MacEachern, JR Wilkins, PP Wilcox, RT Pilarski, R Nagy, S Lemeshow, A de la Chapelle, and CD Bloomfield. Low cancer incidence rates in Ohio Amish. *Cancer Causes and Control*. 21[1], 2010.

[WGH11]   Fiona Wilson-O'Toole, John Gormley, and Juliette Hussey. *Exercise Therapy in the Management of Musculoskeletal Disorders*. John Wiley & Sons, New York, NY, 2011.

[WHKU10]   Jacob M Wilson, Lyndsey M Hornbuckle, Jeong-Su Kim, Carlos Ugrinowitsch, Sang-Rok Lee, Michael C Zourdos, Brian Sommer, and Lynn B Panton. Effects of static stretching on energy cost and running endurance performance. *Journal of strength and conditioning research / National Strength & Conditioning Association*. 24[9], 2010.

[WK12]   Ludwig Wilhelm and Johannes Kotelmann. *School Hygiene*. Nabu Press, Charleston, SC, 2012.

[WNBL89]   Kipling D Williams, Steve A Nisa, Lawrence D Baca, and Bibb Latane. Social Loafing and Swimming: Effects of Identifiability on Individual and Relay Performance of Intercollegiate Swimmers. *Basic and Applied Social Psychology*. 10[1], 1989.

[Wal05]   John Walker. *The Hacker's Diet*. www.fourmilab.ch, http://www.fourmilab.ch, Fourth, 2005.

[ZEPK12]   Katharina Zinke, Manuela Einert, Lydia Pfennig, and Matthias Kliegel. Plasticity of Executive Control through Task Switching Training in Adolescents. *Frontiers in human neuroscience*. 6, 2012.

[dMd09]   Juliana Limba da Fonseca, Marcio Magini, and Thais Helena de Freitas. Laboratory gait analysis in patients with low back pain before and after a pilates intervention. *Journal of sport rehabilitation*. 18[2], 2009.

[vK90]   Marijke van Dusseldorp and Martijn B Katan. Caffeine as a risk factor for chronic daily headache: A population-based study. *British Medical Journal*. 300, 1990.

[vKM06]   MW van Tulder, B Koes, and A Malmivaara. Outcome of non-invasive treatment modalities on back pain: an evidence-based review. *European Spine Journal*. 15[1], 2006.

Index

The Joy of Math and Programming

Rediscover the joy and fascinating weirdness of pure mathematics, or get your kids started programming in JavaScript.

Mathematics is beautiful—and it can be fun and exciting as well as practical. *Good Math* is your guide to some of the most intriguing topics from two thousand years of mathematics: from Egyptian fractions to Turing machines; from the real meaning of numbers to proof trees, group symmetry, and mechanical computation. If you've ever wondered what lay beyond the proofs you struggled to complete in high school geometry, or what limits the capabilities of the computer on your desk, this is the book for you.

Mark C. Chu-Carroll
(250 pages) ISBN: 9781937785338. $34
http://pragprog.com/book/mcmath

You know what's even better than playing games? Creating your own. Even if you're an absolute beginner, this book will teach you how to make your own online games with interactive examples. You'll learn programming using nothing more than a browser, and see cool, 3D results as you type. You'll learn real-world programming skills in a real programming language: JavaScript, the language of the web. You'll be amazed at what you can do as you build interactive worlds and fun games.

Chris Strom
(250 pages) ISBN: 9781937785444. $36
http://pragprog.com/book/csjava

Easy Mobile Programming

Want to develop a mobile app, but want to do it the easy way? Start here.

Create mobile apps for Android phones and tablets faster and more easily than you ever imagined. Use "Processing," the free, award-winning, graphics-savvy language and development environment, to work with the touchscreens, hardware sensors, cameras, network transceivers, and other devices and software in the latest Android phones and tablets.

Daniel Sauter
(300 pages) ISBN: 9781937785062. $35
http://pragprog.com/book/dsproc

Make beautiful apps with beautiful code: use the elegant and concise Ruby programming language with RubyMotion to write truly native iOS apps with less code while having more fun. You'll learn the essentials of creating great apps, and by the end of this book, you'll have built a fully functional API-driven app. Whether you're a newcomer looking for an alternative to Objective-C or a hardened Rails veteran, RubyMotion allows you to create gorgeous apps with no compromise in performance or developer happiness.

Clay Allsopp
(112 pages) ISBN: 9781937785284. $17
http://pragprog.com/book/carubym

Explore Testing and Cucumber

Explore the uncharted waters of exploratory testing and beef up your automated testing with more Cucumber.

Uncover surprises, risks, and potentially serious bugs with exploratory testing. Rather than designing all tests in advance, explorers design and execute small, rapid experiments, using what they learned from the last little experiment to inform the next. Learn essential skills of a master explorer, including how to analyze software to discover key points of vulnerability, how to design experiments on the fly, how to hone your observation skills, and how to focus your efforts.

Elisabeth Hendrickson
(160 pages) ISBN: 9781937785024. $29
http://pragprog.com/book/ehxta

You can test just about anything with Cucumber. We certainly have, and in *Cucumber Recipes* we'll show you how to apply our hard-won field experience to your own projects. Once you've mastered the basics, this book will show you how to get the most out of Cucumber—from specific situations to advanced test-writing advice. With over forty practical recipes, you'll test desktop, web, mobile, and server applications across a variety of platforms. This book gives you tools that you can use today to automate any system that you encounter, and do it well.

Ian Dees, Matt Wynne, Aslak Hellesoy
(250 pages) ISBN: 9781937785017. $33
http://pragprog.com/book/dhwcr

Tinker, Tailor, Solder, and DIY!

Get into the DIY spirit with Raspberry Pi or Arduino. Who knows what you'll build next...

The Raspberry Pi is a $35, full-blown micro computer that runs Linux. Use its video, audio, network, and digital I/O to create media centers, web servers, interfaces to external hardware—you name it. And this book gives you everything you need to get started.

Maik Schmidt
(120 pages) ISBN: 9781937785048. $17
http://pragprog.com/book/msraspi

Arduino is an open-source platform that makes DIY electronics projects easier than ever. Readers with no electronics experience can create their first gadgets within a few minutes. This book is up-to-date for the new Arduino Uno board, with step-by-step instructions for building a universal remote, a motion-sensing game controller, and many other fun, useful projects.

Maik Schmidt
(296 pages) ISBN: 9781934356661. $35
http://pragprog.com/book/msard

Kick Your Career Up a Notch

Ready to blog or promote yourself for real? Time to refocus your personal priorities? We've got you covered.

Technical Blogging is the first book to specifically teach programmers, technical people, and technically-oriented entrepreneurs how to become successful bloggers. There is no magic to successful blogging; with this book you'll learn the techniques to attract and keep a large audience of loyal, regular readers and leverage this popularity to achieve your goals.

Antonio Cangiano
(304 pages) ISBN: 9781934356883. $33
http://pragprog.com/book/actb

You're already a great coder, but awesome coding chops aren't always enough to get you through your toughest projects. You need these 50+ nuggets of wisdom. Veteran programmers: reinvigorate your passion for developing web applications. New programmers: here's the guidance you need to get started. With this book, you'll think about your job in new and enlightened ways.

Ka Wai Cheung
(250 pages) ISBN: 9781934356791. $29
http://pragprog.com/book/kcdc

The Pragmatic Bookshelf

The Pragmatic Bookshelf features books written by developers for developers. The titles continue the well-known Pragmatic Programmer style and continue to garner awards and rave reviews. As development gets more and more difficult, the Pragmatic Programmers will be there with more titles and products to help you stay on top of your game.

Visit Us Online

This Book's Home Page
http://pragprog.com/book/jkthp
Source code from this book, errata, and other resources. Come give us feedback, too!

Register for Updates
http://pragprog.com/updates
Be notified when updates and new books become available.

Join the Community
http://pragprog.com/community
Read our weblogs, join our online discussions, participate in our mailing list, interact with our wiki, and benefit from the experience of other Pragmatic Programmers.

New and Noteworthy
http://pragprog.com/news
Check out the latest pragmatic developments, new titles and other offerings.

Save on the eBook

Save on the eBook versions of this title. Owning the paper version of this book entitles you to purchase the electronic versions at a terrific discount.

PDFs are great for carrying around on your laptop—they are hyperlinked, have color, and are fully searchable. Most titles are also available for the iPhone and iPod touch, Amazon Kindle, and other popular e-book readers.

Buy now at *http://pragprog.com/coupon*

Contact Us

Online Orders:	*http://pragprog.com/catalog*
Customer Service:	*support@pragprog.com*
International Rights:	*translations@pragprog.com*
Academic Use:	*academic@pragprog.com*
Write for Us:	*http://pragprog.com/write-for-us*
Or Call:	+1 800-699-7764

DA 01/14

CPSIA information can be obtained at www.ICGtesting.com
Printed in the USA
LVOW02s1503030913

350798LV00012B/30/P